Cambridge Opera Handbooks

Leoš Janáček
Káťa Kabanová

Janáček's first version: Act 1 Scene 1, p. 15 (cf. VS 14, fig. 13). Janáček later rewrote this conversation between Kuligin (bass) and Kudrjáš (tenor) for Kudrjáš (tenor) and Glaša (mezzo) (see pp. 54–5) and greatly modified the whole-tone double-dotted theme (Moravian Museum, Music History Division, Brno)

Leoš Janáček
Káťa Kabanová

COMPILED BY
JOHN TYRRELL
Lecturer in music
University of Nottingham

CAMBRIDGE UNIVERSITY PRESS

Cambridge
London   New York   New Rochelle
Melbourne   Sydney

Published by the Press Syndicate of the University of Cambridge
The Pitt Building, Trumpington Street, Cambridge CB2 1RP
32 East 57th Street, New York, NY 10022, USA
296 Beaconsfield Parade, Middle Park, Melbourne 3206, Australia

First published 1982

Printed in Great Britain at the University Press, Cambridge

British Library Cataloguing in Publication Data

Tyrrell, John
Leoš Janáček, Káťa Kabanová – (Cambridge opera handbooks).
1. Janáček, Leoš. Káťa Kabanová
I. Title II. Series
782.1′092′4   ML410.J18

ISBN 0 521 23180 9 hard covers
ISBN 0 521 29853 9 paperback

CAMBRIDGE OPERA HANDBOOKS
General preface

This is a series of studies of individual operas, written for the serious opera-goer or record-collector as well as the student or scholar. Each volume has three main concerns. The first is historical: to describe the genesis of the work, its sources or its relation to literary prototypes, the collaboration between librettist and composer, and the first performance and subsequent stage history. This history is itself a record of changing attitudes towards the work, and an index of general changes of taste. The second is analytical and it is grounded in a very full synopsis which considers the opera as a structure of musical and dramatic effects. In most volumes there is also a musical analysis of a section of the score, showing how the music serves or makes the drama. The analysis, like the history, naturally raises questions of interpretation, and the third concern each volume is to show how critical writing about an opera, like production and performance, can direct or distort appreciation of its structural elements. Some conflict of interpretation is an inevitable part of this account; editors of the handbooks reflect this – by citing classic statements, by commissioning new essays, by taking up their own critical position. A final section gives a select bibliography, a discography and guides to other sources.

In working out plans for these volumes, the Cambridge University Press was responding to an initial stimulus from staff of the English National Opera. Particular thanks are due to Mr Edmund Tracey and Mr Nicholas John for help, advice and suggestions.

Books published

Richard Wagner: *Parsifal* by Lucy Beckett
W. A. Mozart: *Don Giovanni* by Julian Rushton
C. W. von Gluck: *Orfeo* by Patricia Howard
Igor Stravinsky: *The Rake's Progress* by Paul Griffiths

Other volumes in preparation

To Charles Mackerras

Contents

viii   *Contents*

Illustrations

Acknowledgements

My research in Czech libraries has been financed by a Beit Fellowship, by a British Council – Czechoslovak Government reciprocal scholarship, and by the Český Hudební Fond (Czech Music Foundation). I have benefited from the great kindness of Dr Theodora Straková and Dr Jiří Sehnal, past and present directors of the Music History Division of the Moravian Museum, Brno (which houses the Janáček Archive), and of their staffs, who have over many years given me every help and consideration in my work there. In particular Dr Svatava Přibáňová's painstaking assistance and expert knowledge have been invaluable in the preparation of this book. The facsimiles of Janáček's manuscript sketches for *Káťa Kabanová* and of his annotated copy of Ostrovsky's play, and the texts of several unpublished letters, are printed here by kind permission of the director of the Music History Division of the Moravian Museum.

I would like to thank all my Czech friends (notably Dr Miloš Štědroň) who have helped me decipher letters and manuscripts, and who have patiently explained Janáček's idiosyncratic vocabulary to me. I owe a special debt to Dr Alena Němcová, of the Brno section of the Czech Music Information Centre, whose kindness and efficiency are legendary among her many English-speaking friends.

I acknowledge with thanks the permission of Universal Edition, Vienna, to reproduce the music examples, of Dr Jaromír Svoboda, Prague, to reproduce his photograph of the Prague 1964 production (Fig. 6c), of Eric Thorburn, Glasgow, to reproduce his photographs of the Glasgow 1979 production (Figs. 2 and 7), of English National Opera (for Figs. 5c and 8c–d) and of Scottish Opera (for Figs. 2, 7 and 9). I would also like to thank Mrs Zdena Benešová of the Central Archive of the National Theatre, Prague, and the Theatre Institute, Prague, for their invaluable help with picture research.

I am grateful for permission to reprint, or translate, material in

Chapters 7 and 8 to Dr Theodora Straková, Mrs Ilse-Ester Hoffe, Les Editions Rieder, Mr Winton Dean and Bosse-Verlag.

I am indebted to Mr Geoffrey Norris for identifying the Russian text of Kudrjáš's folksong in Act 2, and to several past and present Nottingham students – Miss Rosemary Johnson, Mr Tom Morgan, Mr Mark Audus and Miss Carol Cleal – for their help at various stages. My particular thanks are due to the other contributors to this book and to Mrs Ruth Smith and Mrs Rosemary Dooley of Cambridge University Press, the former for her fastidious and alert editing of the text, the latter for her care in seeing it through the press.

Nottingham   John Tyrrell
July 1981

Note on Names

Ostrovsky's play, on which Janáček based his opera *Káťa Kabanová*, was written in Russian and thus in the Cyrillic script. The names of the characters, when expressed in other languages and scripts, are subject to differing transliteration systems. For instance, the heroine is known as 'Káťa Kabanová' in Czech, 'Katya Kabanova' in English and 'Katja Kabanowa' in German. In his opera Janáček naturally used a Czech transliteration for the names of the characters. Czech employs the roman alphabet but modifies it with a number of diacritical signs (such as appear in the name Janáček). Generally we do not 'transliterate' these into English: there has never been any attempt to promote *Yenoofa* or *The Excursions of Mr Brouchek*. But the Russian origins of *Káťa Kabanová* encouraged Norman Tucker, when he translated it into English for the Sadler's Wells production, to transliterate names directly from the Russian. This dispenses with the need for diacritical signs, but makes these names inconsistent with English usage in Janáček's other operas, and loses the Czech dimension that the work acquired when it was translated into Czech and these Czech words were set to music; Janáček's Káťa is a different character from Ostrovsky's Katya. Except in Chapter 2 (a discussion of Ostrovsky's play) the authentic Czech names have been used throughout this book. For reference the two systems are set out here.

Czech transliteration	English transliteration	Remarks
Savël (Savjol) Prokofjevič Dikoj, a merchant	Savel Prokofevich Dikoy	generally known as Dikoj (dikiy = wild, savage)
Boris Grigorjevič, his nephew	Boris Grigorevich	
Marfa Ignatěvna Kabanová (Kabanicha), a rich merchant's widow	Marfa Ignatevna Kabanova (Kabanikha)	sometimes known by her surname, Kabanová, but more often as Kabanicha, a nickname meaning 'wild sow' and implying fatness, coarseness and aggression
Tichon Ivanyč Kabanov, her son	Tikhon Ivanych Kabanov	generally known as Tichon
Katěrina (Káťa), his wife	Katerina (Katya)	though her full name is occasionally used, she is generally known by the diminutive Káťa
Váňa Kudrjáš, Dikoj's clerk	Vanya Kudryash	Varvara calls him Váňa, but he is generally known as Kudrjáš. Janáček combined his character with that of Kuligin; see below, pp. 42 and 54–5
Varvara	Varvara	Janáček changed her designation as Tichon's sister to that of foster-child in the Kabanov household
Kuligin	Kuligin	in the opera merely a friend of Kudrjáš, see below, pp. 42 and 54–5
Glaša, a servant	Glasha	incorrectly spelt as Gláša in the list of characters in the vocal score
Fekluša	Feklusha	a servant in the opera, a pilgrim in the play; see below, pp. 42–3 and 54

Note on music examples

All instruments are notated at pitch.

Tempos are shown in three different ways:
(1) without brackets: Janáček's marking at that point in the score;
(2) in round brackets: Janáček's marking at an earlier point in the score (round brackets are also used for time signatures of this kind);
(3) in square brackets: editorial.

Square brackets indicate editorial suggestions.

The following list shows the location of the examples:

Abbreviations

FS Full score, Universal Edition 7070 (1922, revised 1971) (cited by page, from revised edition)

VS Vocal score, Universal Edition 7103 (1922 and subsequent reprints) (cited by page)

Translations are by John Tyrrell except where stated otherwise

1   *Introduction*

JOHN TYRRELL

Historical

With *Káťa Kabanová* Janáček began the last, triumphant phase of his career as an opera composer. He was sixty-seven when the work received its première in Brno in 1921, but he was still to compose the other great works of his old age: three more operas, *The Cunning Little Vixen* (1921–3), *The Makropulos Affair* (1923–5) and *From the House of the Dead* (1927–8), as well as some important non-operatic works such as the Sinfonietta, the Glagolitic Mass and several chamber works.

The fecundity of Janáček's last decade is astonishing, but it was preceded by an apprenticeship that was as long and wearying as it was seemingly unsuccessful. Janáček's musical education took him from his birthplace in Hukvaldy, northern Moravia, to Brno and Prague and later to a year of study in Leipzig and Vienna. In 1880, aged twenty-six, he returned to Brno to teach and to activate the musical life of the town, establishing an Organ School (which grew into the Brno Conservatory), founding a music journal, and conducting. He was inspired to compose operas by the opening, in 1884, of the Czech Provisional Theatre, a tiny theatre converted from a former dance-hall and restaurant. His first operas written for it followed traditional Czech nationalist models: a serious opera on Czech mythology (*Šárka*, 1887–8, first performed 1925) after the manner of Smetana's *Libuše*, whose story it continues, and a comic one-act 'village' opera (*The Beginning of a Romance*, 1891, first performed 1894), much in the same vein as Dvořák's early comic operas such as *The Stubborn Lovers*. But it was not until his third opera, *Jenůfa* (1894–1903), that Janáček achieved real distinction. By writing virtually the first serious Czech village opera Janáček broke the Czech nationalist mould. It took him almost ten years to write (he was admittedly working full-time as a teacher and as director of the Organ School), and during this

1

time his style changed from the gauche late Romanticism of *Šárka* and the facile folksong potpourri of *The Beginning of a Romance* to a recognizably personal idiom.

Jenůfa was a success when it was produced in Brno in 1904, but Janáček knew that success in this provincial backwater of the Austro-Hungarian Empire meant little unless the work could then move to the better-equipped and more influential Prague stage. This took twelve years, during which time he almost gave up as a composer. The two operas written during this period, *Fate* (1903–7) and *The Excursions of Mr Brouček* (1908–17), are among Janáček's most interesting, showing another radical change in his approach to opera. They exploit new, bourgeois subject-matter, and experiment with an almost cinematic narrative technique; musically they show signs of Janáček's admiration for fashionable European models like Charpentier and Puccini. *Fate* was first staged as late as 1958, and *Brouček*, with some difficulty, in Prague in 1920.

Meanwhile Janáček's luck had changed. In 1916 the Prague National Theatre mounted *Jenůfa* in a careful, lavish production which took the city by storm and paved the way for the work's adoption by foreign theatres and for its composer's espousal by the Viennese publishing house Universal Edition, which published all Janáček's major works from then on and greatly contributed to the spread of his fame in the German-speaking world.

The success of *Jenůfa* in 1916, Janáček's friendship with Kamila Stösslová from 1917, and the birth of the Czechoslovak Republic in 1918 were all external events which shaped the creative pattern of Janáček's last decade. The fact that now, after almost thirty years of writing operas, his works were at last in demand, with inquiries being made for more, gave him the incentive to finish *Brouček* and the confidence to write a whole series of new works in an Indian summer of intense creativity. His friendship with Kamila Stösslová, the wife of an antique-dealer in the Bohemian town of Písek, has aroused much comment. Kamila was less than half his age – thirty-eight years younger – and both continued in their existing marriages. This did not prevent Janáček from writing Kamila 743 letters, in which he ascribed to her the inspiration for many of his late works. *Káťa* is the chief among these, and it is possible to see in Janáček's choice of heroines for this and the next two operas some reflection of the relationship and his feelings about it: from the gentle, tragic heroine of *Káťa*, whose dilemma in an adulterous triangle is resolved only in her suicide, to the model wife and mother in the *Vixen*, to the 'ice-cold' Emilia Marty in *Makropulos*, who attracts men but no longer loves them. Janáček's comments to Kamila about the nature of his opera and its progress, his repeated attempts to get her to see a performance of it, his hurt at her ingratitude when he sent her a score, and his dedication of the work to her are all documented in Chapter 5.

While Janáček's first five operas all derived from Czech sources and are all set on Czech soil, the last four operas, with the exception of *The Cunning Little Vixen*, reach out to other worlds. There are several reasons for this. Janáček's passionate identification with his land and language resulted in the nationalist inspiration of his earlier operas; he paid his last nationalist debt in his operas in *Mr Brouček's Excursion to the Fifteenth Century* (the Hussite era being a time of great Czech nationalist fervour). But once his country had received its independence in 1918 after the break-up of the Austro-Hungarian Empire and the creation of a new state formed from Bohemia, Moravia (Janáček's home province) and Slovakia, there was no further need for such artistic 'propaganda'; its aims were now achieved. Karel Čapek's play *The Makropulos Affair*, which provided the text for Janáček's penultimate opera, is admittedly set in Prague – but this is almost incidental, considering the many travels of its world-weary heroine. Much of the background is 1920s cosmopolitan (telephones, the theatre backstage, hotel rooms) rather than Czech. Janáček's two other late operas derived from Slavonic, specifically Russian, sources. From his earliest days Janáček had been a passionate Russophile. He gave Russian names to his two children; he learnt Russian, made several visits to Russia (where his brother František had settled), and in 1898 helped form a Russian circle in Brno, serving as its chairman from 1909 until its forced closure during the First World War. A number of his instrumental works were inspired by Russian literature, notably the symphonic poem (1915–18) based on Gogol's *Taras Bulba*, and a piano trio (1908–9) after Tolstoy's short novel *The Kreutzer Sonata*. Janáček later destroyed the trio but allegedly incorporated the material into his First String Quartet. He had already toyed with operas based on two other Tolstoy works, *Anna Karenina* (in 1907) and the posthumous play *The Living Corpse* (in 1916), though neither got further than some initial sketches.

Janáček's attraction to Ostrovsky's play *The Thunderstorm* – which provided the libretto for *Káťa Kabanová* – lay chiefly in the nature of its heroine and Janáček's identification of her with Kamila Stösslová. Shorn of its political implications (discussed by Cynthia

Marsh in her account of the play in Chapter 2), *The Thunderstorm* can be regarded as the story of a young woman, of exceptional goodness of spirit and with a vivid inner life, who is locked in a loveless marriage to a weak husband (Tichon), dominated by his bullying mother (Kabanicha). When Tichon is away on a business trip, Káťa, helped and encouraged by her sister-in-law Varvara, cannot resist the temptation to meet Boris, the one person in the dreary provincial town who has the education and imagination to be able to share her dreams and enthusiasms, and who is in love with her. Their affair is cut short by the return of Tichon, and Káťa, tormented by her conscience and overwrought by a thunderstorm, confesses her adultery publicly. Boris is sent away, and Káťa, after parting with him, throws herself into the River Volga.

We know that Janáček had tried to acquire an edition of Ostrovsky's works in Russian in 1902;[1] this plan failed and no Russian-language copy of *The Thunderstorm* was found in his extensive Russian library.[2] Ostrovsky's plays, however, had been regularly produced in Brno at its Provisional (later National) Theatre, particularly in the period 1898–1903, and *The Thunderstorm* had reached Prague on 10 March 1870, only ten years after Ostrovsky wrote it, in a translation by Emanuel Vávra.[3] But it was not until 1918 that a Czech translation, by Vincenc Červinka, was published. While it is possible that Janáček acquired Červinka's translation as soon as it came out (spring? 1918)[4] and kept the work in mind as a potential opera, it is more likely, despite Jiřikovský's claims (see Chapter 5), that it was at least a year later before he began to think about it seriously, perhaps after the Brno stage production in March 1919. He was busy with two major works, *The Diary of One Who Disappeared* (completed 6 June 1919) and *The Ballad of Blaník* (première 21 March 1920), so there would have been little time to work on *Káťa* much before the autumn of 1919. And it is then that the first evidence of his interest in the play can be found, in his correspondence over the rights (for this and other letters concerning the composition of *Káťa Kabanová* see Chapter 5). The only date in his copy of the play (near the end of Ostrovsky's Act 1) is 1 March 1920, well after he had begun composition. The first version consists of a complete continuous sketch in full score. The first date in it (at the end of Janáček's Act 1) is 1 July 1920. On the basis of other dates in this version and in Janáček's final autograph score it seems that Act 2 was written between 14 September and 15 October, and Act 3 between 28 October and 24 December 1920. For the final version, which is more often than not quite different from the first version, Janáček made use of a few of the original pages, but generally he made a fresh start, writing on the back of the now discarded first version. Oddly, he seems to have revised the work in reverse order; Act 3 in January 1921, Act 2 by 17 February 1921, Act 1 by 27 March and a final revision of Act 1 Scene 1 by 17 April 1921.

These dates are roughly supported by Janáček's correspondence. He wrote to Kamila Stösslová on 9 January 1920 that he had begun composing the opera (having acquired translation rights a week earlier), and on 6 March 1921 that he had finished, though the dates on the score suggest that he continued to work on it well into the next month. By April the news of the opera's completion was public, and Janáček began to receive approaches from the Brno National Theatre, and his publishers. The history of the first performances in Brno and Prague is documented in Chapter 5, the subsequent stage history in Chapter 6.

Janáček's manuscript score was copied out professionally, probably beginning with Act 3 while Janáček continued to revise the earlier acts. Gustav Homola completed his copy on 5 May 1921. As usual Janáček then tinkered with it (as late as 18 August 1921 he wrote to Kamila Stösslová that he had been 'cleaning up' the score). Many of his changes and additions were minor – slight adjustments to voice parts or added doublings in the orchestra. But some, like the violin doublings of the *dolcissimo* oboe tune on VS 76 (last three bars) or the brass added to the five-note accompaniment figure on VS 60 (and the previous bar), substantially altered the character of the music, just as the displacement of Dikoj's 'Zde máte svou Katěrinu' ('Here your Katěrina', VS 164) from a bar earlier affected the vocal balance and dramatic pacing.

Many of the changes to the full score correspond to the last-minute changes to the libretto described in Chapter 3. Janáček's original autograph, for instance, contains the song for Kudrjáš in Act 2 with its original words (one verse only); the subsequent folksong exchange between Varvara and Kudrjáš again has just one verse, and Kudrjáš's words in it peter out into dots (as in Červinka) after 'Tovar nakupuje' ('He buys goods …'). The suggestions of Max Brod, the translator of the libretto into German, were responsible for many of the other substituted words and the addition of extra vocal lines to existing orchestral music. And there are other examples of last-minute superimpositions: several appearances of the 'timpani theme' (Ex. 11) were added later, for instance all those on VS 132, 133 and 136, as were the first three offstage choral interjections which break in on Boris's departure (VS 158–9). In some cases Janáček's alterations to Homola's copy were so radical that pages had to be copied out again (by another copyist, Václav Sedláček) before the score could go to the publishers. Before then, however, a vocal score had to be made. Negotiations with Roman Veselý, who had prepared the vocal score of Janáček's previous opera *Brouček*, broke down in June 1921, and in the end the vocal score was made by one of Janáček's pupils, the conductor Břetislav Bakala. Bakala completed his work by the end of August and the vocal score then went to Max Brod (by 5 September) for his German translation. He sent off Act 1 on 22 October and the remaining two acts by 4 November 1921. It was while he was working on the translation that he suggested the changes detailed in his letters printed in Chapter 3.

The piano score, originally to have been published by Hudební Matice in Prague (the original publisher of *Jenůfa*), was taken on by Universal Edition in Vienna, with Hudební Matice holding the Czech rights. The score was out by February 1922, after the Brno première (23 November 1921) but well before the Prague première (30 November 1922). The full score was also published before the Prague première: Act 1 by 28 August 1922 and Acts 2 and 3 within the next fortnight. Individual orchestral parts were printed by 25 November 1922, so that the Prague National Theatre had to borrow the Brno manuscript parts. Librettos were also issued in 1922: in Czech by the end of March, and in German in July.

In 1927 Janáček extended the interludes in Acts 1 and 2 to facilitate the scene-changes. The history of the composition of these interludes and their subsequent neglect is described by Theodora Straková in Chapter 7.

Style

Where does Janáček's *Káťa Kabanová* belong? It owes little to Czech nineteenth-century models and belongs more, as Winton Dean suggested in his *Listener* article (reprinted in Chapter 8), with works like *Pelléas et Mélisande* and *Boris Godunov*. But such affinities probably reflect shared instincts and casts of mind rather than direct influence. Janáček's interest in Debussy seems to have increased substantially in the 1920s, to judge from the surviving documentary material (programmes of concerts, analyses, scores),[5] and it is unlikely that he knew *Pelléas* before the Prague production in November 1921, a few weeks before the première of *Káťa*. Janáček's connections with Musorgsky are more difficult to assess.[6] His few remarks on him, in lectures and letters, are puzzling and ambiguous. Nothing apart from the piano music survives in his library (a Rimsky version of *Boris*, alleged once to have been there, has disappeared); he saw, and enjoyed, *Boris* on stage for the first time in 1923. But there is clearly much in common between their styles: their treatment of the voice and their respective theories of speech-melody, the repetitive ostinato of their musical continuum, and above all the vigorous life, immediacy and emotional force of their music.

Janáček's placing in fact presents an acute problem for his commentators. He was born in the middle of the nineteenth century, well before the last wave of Romantic composers like Strauss, Mahler and Wolf; and his training and many of his attitudes reflect this. But some of the most potent influences on him were those of opera composers from the first half of the twentieth century (Charpentier, Puccini and Strauss), and his greatest music dates from the end of his life, in the 1920s, when it falls within the context of his younger contemporaries, Stravinsky, Schoenberg, Bartók and Hindemith. *Káťa* itself is almost exactly contemporary with Berg's *Wozzeck*, and in his *Listener* article Winton Dean summarized some of their similarities, emphasizing however that in technique and approach the two composers could not be further apart. As Dean points out, Janáček 'inconveniently proved the continuing vitality of the tonal tradition just when it was to the interest of many to suppose it was exhausted.' But Janáček's attitude to Schoenberg and his school was far from negative;[7] he derived great satisfaction from Schoenberg's presence and congratulations at the Berlin première of *Káťa*. He supported the notorious Prague première of *Wozzeck*; and some details of his final opera *From the House of the Dead* would seem to result from his knowledge of Berg's score.

Though Janáček was undoubtedly eager to keep abreast of contemporary western developments, the cast of his operas was essentially eastern European. The parallels with Puccini and Strauss tend to be of individual details rather than of general character; in their sound Janáček's operas have more in common with those of his east European contemporaries, such as Bartók's *Duke Bluebeard's Castle* (1918) or Szymanowski's *King Roger* (1926), operas which he never knew. Foreign commentators have always remarked on the strong sense of background and locality as one of Janáček's greatest gifts, connected no doubt with his regional roots. Stuckenschmidt (pp. 5–

8) makes the same point when he suggests that it is their country (rather than city) orientation that distinguishes Janáček's operas from those of Puccini and Strauss.

A surprising number of similarities can be found with Tchaikovsky. We know from Janáček's reviews of Brno performances of *Eugene Onegin* and *The Queen of Spades*[8] that he thought highly of these works. Theodora Straková unearthed several Tchaikovskian parallels in her examination of the composition of *Fate*.[9] These could be extended into *Káťa*. The women's voice types show similarities with those in *Onegin* (Káťa/Tatyana the 'serious' soprano; Varvara/Olga the 'frivolous' mezzo) and *The Queen of Spades* (Kabanicha/the Countess). There are also affinities in musical construction. While Janáček's handling of the double love-scene in *Káťa* has superficial similarities with the alternation of the two pairs of lovers in *Onegin*'s first scene, a much more interesting parallel is the Letter Scene in *Onegin* (which Janáček particularly dwelt on in his review). Much of Tchaikovsky's musical material is prepared for in earlier scenes so that it can be 'clinched' in this crucial scene. On a smaller scale Káťa's entrance music is similarly prefigured during Boris's conversation with Kudrjáš so that it can blaze out with a familiar ring when Káťa herself appears. In the same way the changing moods of Káťa's 'monologue' in Act 1 Scene 2, revealing her character over a wide spectrum of emotional situations, may owe something to the way Tchaikovsky handled Tatyana's changing emotions in her Letter Scene.

There is nevertheless an obvious generation-gap between the composers, evident particularly in their handling of lyricism. As Charles Stuart wrote in an early and perceptive defence of the opera (p. 294),

The romantic tints and surgings of Janáček's orchestra sometimes push him willy-nilly towards great lyrical outbursts of precisely the sort he has on principle foresworn. A case in point is the crucial entry of Boris in the last scene. This is attended by a great orchestral stoking-up which in Tchaikovsky, for example, would have denoted a ten- or twenty-page duet for the lovers. Instead of anchoring himself in G flat, Janáček lets the voice parts subside and peter out.

The lyricism is in fact there, but is of quite a different nature from the expansiveness of Strauss or Puccini, as Winton Dean points out: 'Janáček stands in relation to those composers rather as Verdi's "Falstaff" stands to "Rigoletto".'

Káťa represents a considerable change of attitude in Janáček's handling of operatic conventions. The choruses that had figured prominently in every one of his operas up to *Káťa* suddenly vanished. There was no pretext for them, as there had been for instance for the fine Hussite chorales in *Mr Brouček's Excursion to the Fifteenth Century*, and the few lines for chorus in *Káťa*'s storm scene seem ill at ease in this more naturalistic convention. David Pountney reasonably suggests (in Chapter 8) that Janáček treated them realistically as they might have seemed to Káťa – 'disjointed cries penetrating her own confusion'. But in the final scene of *Káťa* Janáček wrote a type of chorus that he was to employ in all his late operas: the offstage 'symbolic' chorus – the 'voices from the forest' in the *Vixen* or the 'voices and shadows' that respond to Marty's dying words in *Makropulos*. Both these were Janáček's own additions to the librettos, and so was the mysterious offstage wordless chorus in *Káťa* which makes concrete the 'singing' that Káťa hears as her death draws near.

Just as the choral element was reduced in *Káťa* to an almost orchestral role, so ensembles, duets and trios, which were few in *Fate* and *Brouček*, are even fewer in *Káťa*. There is a little overlapping of voices at moments of excitement, notably in the storm scene, a few strangely backward-looking bars of 'duet' for Káťa and Tichon as she pleads with him not to leave her (VS 58), and the effective superimposition of offstage and onstage voices in the double love-scene. Apart from this and the symbolic choruses in the last scene almost all the vocal language is limited to solo utterance, either in dialogue form or in monologues, such as the extensive confessional narratives of Káťa and Boris, and Káťa's soliloquies.

Except for the interpolated folksongs, all the words of the opera are in prose, and hence irregular and non-metrical. As recently as *Fate* Janáček had made his librettist write a verse libretto, but by *Káťa* this was no longer necessary: the orchestra carries most of the musical continuity and the text is fitted against this in the realistic manner that Janáček had developed through his preoccupation with 'speech-melody'. For several decades he had taken down in musical notation the speech he heard around him and in particular had tried to determine the effect of emotional and other factors on its patterns. He had drawn attention to this aspect of his work through many newspaper and periodical articles, and he considered the study of 'speech-melodies' an essential training for an opera composer. The effect on his own music was to release his voice parts from their metrical bondage so that they began to approach the rapid and irregular patterns of speech. Voice parts of this kind are especially evident in the more conversational sections of the opera, for instance the opening dialogue for Glaša and Kudrjáš, or most of Kabanicha's part.

Occasionally Janáček restructures the prose text into quasi-verse. Czech stresses the first syllable of words: two-syllable words are naturally trochaic (strong–weak), three-syllable words naturally dactylic (strong–weak–weak), four-syllable words have a subsidiary stress on the third syllable and can thus be scanned as two trochees. The stressing of one-syllable words is subject to certain rules, and to their context. Czech prose is thus usually a mixture of trochees and dactyls; Janáček's quasi-verse restructuring sought to channel it into regular trochaic units, which could then generate, or be fitted to, regular symmetrical tunes, often in duple rhythm. This type of music was used for special emotionally charged occasions and for particular characters.

Káťa's first entry, for instance, in Act 1 Scene 1, is crucial for the audience's initial sympathetic impression of her. Here are the exact words of the Červinka translation, with an approximate scansion:

Pro mě jste vy, maminko, právě tak, jakoby rodnou matkou; co tě napadá, a
Tichon tě také má rád.

You are for me, mother, just like a natural mother; how could you think this? And Tichon loves you too.

If this is compared with the words in Ex. 1 it will be seen that Janáček has made several adjustments to the text. Apart from altering all references to the second person singular ('tě') to the polite plural form ('vás') – which has no metrical effect here – he has omitted the emphatic 'právě tak', substituted a two-syllable 'jako' for 'jakoby' (with a consequent effect on case endings) and rearranged the order of the last four words. There is no essential difference in the meaning; metrically, however, the text is now basically trochaic, and falls into four 'verse' lines:

Pro mne | jste vy, | maminko,
jako | rodná | matka.
Co vás | napadá
a | Tichon | má vás | také | rád![10]

The lines are not of equal length; while the first two are roughly equivalent, each fitting the two-bar phrase structure of the music, the third is short and the fourth long. Nevertheless an impression of

Ex. 1    VS 29–30

symmetry is maintained, chiefly by a further repetition in the orchestra of the two-bar phrase, and by the voice continuing to move in even
quavers and semiquavers.

Káťa's second (and final) entry in this scene (VS 31) is based on the
same orchestral tune as her first, transposed; the first eight bars of the
orchestra are even more regular (four two-bar phrases) and the voice
part even more 'metricalized'. Thus

To říkáš docela zbytečně, maminko ... proč ty mě urážíš?

It's quite unnecessary to say this to me, mother ... why do you insult me?

becomes, after Janáček's adjustments,

To mi | říkat | nemusíte [nemu | síte].
Proč mne | urážíte [urá | žíte]?

Ex. 2   VS 28

Compare these settings with one of Kabanicha's first solos, two pages earlier (Ex. 2). Here is Červinka's Czech translation:

Věřila bych ti, příteli, kdybych vlastníma očima neviděla a na vlastní uši neslyšela ... Dávno už vidím, že ti je žena matky milejší.

I would believe you, my friend, if I hadn't seen with my own eyes and heard with my own ears ... I've seen for some time that your wife is dearer to you than your mother.

By comparison with Ex. 1, Ex. 2 is more faithful to the metre and word order of the original. There is a repeated pattern in the accompaniment, but it consists of a single bar which can be played at will (e.g. in the first two bars); otherwise the accompaniment is minimal – a held note, or a rest. The voice part is written with that mixture of duple and triple subdivisions which Czech composers arrive at when they follow the natural rhythm of the Czech language without super-imposing a metrical pattern on it. Though occasionally the voice part picks up something of the orchestral motif (e.g. the jump of a seventh on 'ti žena') it is less melodic than Káťa's music above, and more inclined instead to recite on single notes. Though the terms are anachronistic in this context Kabanicha's part has the feel of recita-tive, Káťa's of something like aria or arioso.

While Káťa's contributions in the first scene are, with their regular balanced periods, designed to establish her quiet dignity and serenity, other examples can be found where Káťa is in a more excited mood and Červinka's text is adapted to emphasize the lyrical side of her nature. In the next scene, where Káťa is trying to persuade Tichon not to leave, she tries an almost song-like tenderness to influence him as she throws her arms around him. Here is Červinka's original text:

kdybys zůstal doma, anebo mě vzal s sebou, tolik bych tě měla ráda, tak bych tě poláskala miláčka svého.

if you would stay home, or if you would take me with you, how I'd love you, how I'd caress my darling.

In Ex. 3 the orchestra once again has a two-bar theme in 2/4, based on a 'mirror'-rhythm found in Moravian folksong, and apart from the one-bar extension at the end is in regular two-bar periods. It is surprising how few changes Janáček had to make to the text to

accommodate units of varying length to three two-bar phrases. The rhythm of his remaining six syllables being dactylic rather than trochaic, he tried another metrical solution: while the orchestral two-bar pattern is repeated once again the voice sustains a G sharp for two bars and only releases the remaining syllables over a held-chord extension once the orchestral tune has completed its cycle. Nine lyrical bars like this may seem few, but their effect is striking when heard in connection with the same-note recitation over orchestral ostinatos which makes up the next three pages, as Káťa, in a highly dramatic passage, tries to get Tichon to make her swear an oath of fidelity to him.

In addition to this 'metricalizing' of the verbal text, Janáček uses other methods to create a more lyrical vocal line. One way is to lengthen notes, as he does at the end of Ex. 3; this technique can be seen for instance at the climax of Káťa's religious ecstasy in Act 1 Scene 2: when she describes her visions to Varvara (Exx. 4, 5), in the tender phrase 'Varjo! Nemohu spát' ('Varja, I can't sleep', Ex. 6) and – as the climax of this scene – 'a já jdu, a jdu za ním' ('and I follow

[and [I saw angels] sing]

and I weep

him', Ex. 7). There are similar uses of lengthened notes and melisma in Káťa's part in the love-scene with Boris (Act 2 Scene 2) and in her monologue and farewell (Act 3 Scene 2).

Another similar device, which Janáček used in *Jenůfa*, was the actual repetition of verbal lines and phrases, i.e. he not only re-structured prose into metrical units but then repeated them to pro-duce balancing lines to match the repeated periods of his instru-mental music. Many of the repetitions disappeared in Janáček's own revision of the score for its publication in 1908, and more were omitted by Kovařovic when he revised the score for its Prague première in 1916. Many nevertheless remained, and were duly criticized for being out of keeping with an otherwise realistic idiom. Arguments in favour of the repetitions usually depend on the added emphasis they give, but the fact that they largely disappeared from Janáček's music in later operas suggests rather that they were often just a metrical convenience. There are, however, vestiges of them even in *Káťa*. Here are some lines from Červinka's translation which Janáček adapted for use in Act 2 Scene 2.

Boris: . . . jak vás mám rád.
Katěrina: Nedotýkej, nedotýkej se mne! Ach! . . . Jdi ode mne! Jdi pryč, prokletý člověče! Víš-li pak, že toho hříchu neodčiním, *nikdy* neodčiním?

Boris: . . . how I love you.
Katěrina: Don't touch me! Ah . . . leave me, cursed man! Don't you know that I will not wipe out this sin, *never* wipe it out?

The Czech text contains several repeated words ('nedotýkej', 'odčiním'), and it might be supposed that in the interests of shortening the text Janáček would have omitted these in his radical compression of the original. Far from it, as can be seen in Ex. 8, Janáček has made a metrical feature (set sequentially) of 'hříchu neodčiním/nikdy neodčiním', has extended the repeated 'nedotýkej' to include the reflexive ('se') and object ('mne' = me) both times, and has once again placed the repetition in the same part of the bar over a repeated motif to achieve a metrical symmetry. Furthermore he has added a similar metrical repetition of Boris's words 'Jak vás mám rád'. This example contains a rare instance of overlapping duet of the kind mentioned above.

These instances of 'metricalization', of lengthened notes and of metrically repeated phrases have been discussed here as ways of producing a more regular structure than would otherwise available in a work based on a prose text. But their effect on characterization should also be noted. Most such examples of symmetry occur in Káťa's part, while much of Kabanicha's is set in asymmetrical speech-like bursts. These contrasting forms of word-setting constitute one of Janáček's principal musical means for delineating their characters – their 'souls', as he might have put it – and for imposing his own interpretation on Ostrovsky's text. The effect is further heightened when the two styles are directly juxtaposed, as in this initial scene. Much of Janáček's characterization derives from this

simple opposition. In the opening scene, however, there are not just the two characters, but Tichon and Varvara as well. Tichon's lack of independence is stressed by the fact that most of his part is subsumed within Kabanicha's irregular music, often sharing her one-bar motif. On the other hand Varvara's more regular phrases and use of Káťa's two-bar motif (see especially VS 35–6) clearly align her with Káťa.

Tichon's domination by Kabanicha is stressed similarly in the next scene, where Kabanicha insists that her son instruct Káťa how to behave during his absence. As before, the musical substance consists of an opposition: a two-bar theme, again in 2/4 with a mirror-rhythm, contrasted with a one-bar motif associated with Kabanicha. In Ex. 9 Kabanicha gives her instructions to Tichon over repetitions of the one-bar motif; Tichon repeats them to Káťa over the two-bar theme. Two points should be noted: Kabanicha's one-bar motif has a distinct whole-tone colouring which also infects the two-bar theme (at its first appearance, on VS 64, the two-bar theme is in a clear B flat minor); and some of Tichon's entries get out of phase and fall into Kabanicha's sections. The musical symbolism could not be clearer. Furthermore, as Tichon wearily repeats the final instructions, a high radiant version of the two-bar theme is heard (Ex. 33), this time unclouded by whole-tone harmony and given instead in a straightforward A flat minor; this continues in the orchestra, without voices, for another eight bars. Its metrical symmetry, its clear minor harmony and its lyrical nature proclaim this, by association, to be 'Káťa' music despite her silence.

It is clear that Káťa and Kabanicha are distinguished musically not by individual recurring themes so much as by types of music and techniques of word-setting, and of course voice type (Káťa is a soprano, Kabanicha a contralto). The other chief female character, Varvara (mezzo), a less complex figure than Káťa or even Kabanicha, is on the other hand identified mostly by a single recurring theme (Ex. 14) which, as several commentators have pointed out, is closely linked with the folksongs that she and Kudrjáš sing. These repetitive, circular, strophic songs, with their simple alternation of tonic and dominant harmony, are effective musical analogues for the more superficial nature of Janáček's Varvara.

The men are not so clearly differentiated and have little musical life of their own. Tichon, as we have seen, hovers between the worlds of his wife and his mother; Boris for the most part is an extension of Káťa, just as Kudrjáš, with an equal share of folksongs, belongs to Varvara's world. Dikoj, however, emerges with some individuality.

[Tichon: Obey mother.
Kabanicha: Tell her not to be rude...
Tichon: Don't be rude.
Kabanicha: and to honour her mother-in-law like her own mother.
Tichon: Honour mother like your own mother, Káťa.]

He has the only low voice among the men (Boris, Tichon and Kudrjáš are all tenors). Janáček furthermore gives him several grotesque caricature devices in his opening scene to emphasize his irascibility, e.g. the pitchless swoop down on 'Fuj' (VS 17) or his penultimate exclamation 'Aby ses propadl!' ('Just drop dead!') in even notes at cross-rhythm with the orchestra. The whole of this short scene between Dikoj and Boris is set over an energetic dotted ostinato in the orchestra which dissolves into mocking trills as he stumps off. Few of Janáček's other basses are so clearly evil-tempered; the nearest parallel is the sadistic prison commandant in *From the House of the Dead*.

One of Janáček's last-minute additions to the score was the short scene between Dikoj and Kabanicha at the end of Act 2 Scene 1. This has puzzled several commentators; Wörner considered 'inappropriate' its use of material which he associated rather with Káťa and the Volga; Dean found it 'not quite in focus' (see Chapter 8). It is in fact the only scene in the opera where the two principal forces of evil are seen together by themselves, rather than in opposition to the other characters. Some sense of strain is apparent from the opening bars, with Janáček's unaccustomed character-labelling in the dynamic markings of the two phrases used to provide musical material for the scene ('lichotivě' = flatteringly; 'tvrdě' = hard). What are we to make of it? Michael Ewans (pp. 120–1) saw it as farce, as a 'sadomasochistic prelude to love-making' which the music develops with 'malicious wit'. Janáček himself provided a comment on the scene when, several years later, he composed an interlude to follow it and make room for the scene-change. For this he wrote a jaunty little march reminiscent of that in *From the House of the Dead*, Act 2 – hardly surprisingly, since this was what he was writing at the time. It puts a slightly humorous complexion on the old ogres and perhaps weakens the suggestion that some sort of love-making follows the scene.

While Janáček is careful to distribute scenes with Kabanicha (and Dikoj) throughout the opera to emphasize the forces of opposition, Káťa nevertheless has a huge share of the rest. In the scenes of crucial decision – Act 2 Scene 1, where she has to decide whether to take up the chance of seeing Boris, and Act 3 Scene 2, where she commits suicide – she is entirely on her own, and it is no small achievement on Janáček's part, in the long final scene in particular, that he is able to avoid monotony in a work so concentrated on a single character. Even in the extended scene with Varvara (Act 1 Scene 2) Káťa gets very little help from her companion. In this confessional narrative, so typical of Janáček, she describes the serenity and religious feelings of her youth and moves imperceptibly to the disturbing emotions that are now threatening to overwhelm her restricted life. The setting is an impressive exercise in musical transition, effortlessly suggesting not only the changing moods, but also Káťa's near-pathological condition, and the fact that the dividing line between her religious and her sexual ecstasy is a thin one.

Thematic structure

Janáček's use of opposition, rather than thematic differentiation, for characterization sometimes leads to his deploying the same series of notes to evoke musical opposites, by means of contrasts in handling and by his highly resourceful variation technique. Act 2 Scene 1, for instance, is fashioned out of two small themes but, as David Pountney makes clear in his analysis (Chapter 8), they are skilfully varied to suggest a whole gamut of emotions. Both can provide harsh jagged background accompaniments to support Kabanicha's grumblings, but both are equally capable of being softened and regularized into 'Káťa' variants.

The subtlety of Janáček's approach to theme has resulted in a surprisingly wide variety of comments about its nature and use. 'It should be clear', Erik Chisholm wrote in 1971, 'that Janáček employs as highly a complex [sic] system of leitmotif as any composer has attempted since the death of Wagner' (p. 80). Two years earlier Karl-Heinz Wörner applied his theory of 'modular variants' to *Káťa*, producing a table of forty-nine variants which, he suggested Janáček derived from the same cell or 'module' (see Chapter 8). Both approaches seem to me to overstate a particular point of view. While it is true that much of Janáček's melodic material can be seen to be generated from a small number of favourite intervals, seconds and fourths especially, too wide an interpretation of permissible manipulations allows almost anything to creep in. Wörner attempts to regard as a theme what others see simply as an element of style. He fixes a virtually leitmotivic explanation to his 'module' (Káťa = water), and then finds that this 'theme' inconveniently crops up in the Kabanicha–Dikoj scene and moreover, as he admits, in Janáček's other works as well. Chisholm's leitmotivic approach, on the other hand, is able to handle neither the many themes that dominate single scenes or sections of scenes and which never thereafter recur, nor Janáček's variation technique in which one theme may share the same notes as another but is so differentiated in character that no connection is heard between the two. Nevertheless, *Kát'a* does make use of some audibly recurring themes, which are set out in the following section.

Ex. 10   VS 6

Ex. 10. Max Brod (Chapter 8) suggested that this theme was a 'departure motif'. The sleigh bells that accompany it are the bells of the troika waiting to take Tichon off on his fateful journey; after the overture the theme is heard chiefly towards the end of Act 1 as Tichon prepares to leave (VS 55, 62). It also represents, Brod suggested, 'the endless steppe, parting, loneliness', an interpretation Wilfrid Mellers takes up in his analysis (Chapter 4): 'the symmetrically metred reiteration ... suggests the monotony of the Russian steppes and the tepidity of the domestic round'. The French writer Daniel Muller took issue with Brod (see Chapter 8), contending that the flute's rapid arpeggio decoration above the oboe theme alone – presumably with the sleigh bells – represents Tichon's journey. He felt that the theme, with its flattened leading note, carried religious overtones (the same feature presumably led Josef Burjanek (p. 404) to characterize it as 'almost like a folksong'), noting in particular the similarity of the fourth bar (b) to the Dies irae theme. These four notes, moreover, are

Ex. 11   VS 5

the notes of Kabanicha's final words, 'Děkuji vám' ('thank you') and
'za úslužnost' ('for your service'), and Muller, in a striking description of the ensuing orchestral passage based on them, argued that
Janáček was aiming here at a 'satanic effect', to inspire in his audience
a horror of a cruel code of rules. Burjanek added a further argument
for relating the theme to Kabanicha by pointing out that Fekluša's
comment on Kabanicha ('Jací lidé bohabojní', 'what generous
people', VS 25) is made from virtually the same notes.

It is however the first eight notes of the theme (a in Ex. 10) that are
the most important. Detached from the rest, slowed down, and
usually played on trombones and timpani (Ex. 11), they permeate the
whole piece (Muller counted nearly fifty unmodified repetitions). One
third come in the departure scene alone; they are also heard in close
connection with the thunder and lightning of Act 3 Scene 1, and again
at the end of the opera. Muller regarded this as one of the two basic
motifs of the opera, representing the 'old Russia and the iron circle of
tradition'. Other writers from Černušák (at the Brno première)
onwards (see below, p. 99) have seen it as a prophecy of 'fateful
catastrophe', i.e. a 'fate motif', a label Michael Ewans (p. 109) found
'depressingly crude'. The fact that this theme derives from the oboe
tune is a fine example of the difficulties that Janáček's variation
technique can provide for leitmotivists. Both forms have distinct
characters and clear but different associations; yet both are made of
the same notes. Are we to draw any conclusions from this? One thing
we can be sure of is that the repetitions of the timpani theme were
deliberately inserted. There is ample evidence from the sketch
material that many of the fifty recurrences were late appearances in
the score, often superimposed over existing structures, frequently at
rhythmic odds with their surroundings. Even after the vocal score
had been printed Janáček toyed (as can be seen in a vocal score he
marked) with inserting more recurrences.

Ex. 12   VS 27

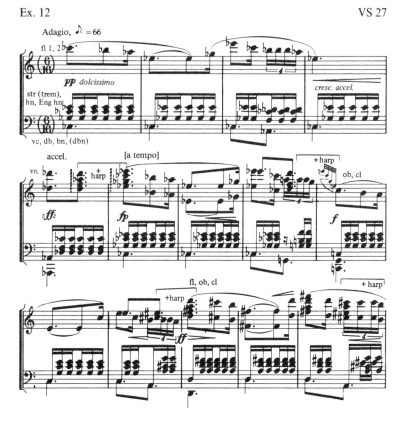

Ex. 12. The short instrumental passage which brings on the Kabanov family is generally agreed to be 'Káťa' music. Though Káťa does not sing at this point its symmetry and clear harmonies are those that we will learn to associate with her within a couple of pages, when she does. I mentioned above that this theme is prefigured in a shadowy whole-tone form when Boris describes to Kudrjáš his love for Káťa, and there is a sense of elation when the tune, suddenly freed from its whole-tone mooring and from Boris's voice, expands into a short intermezzo, growing progressively more confident and radiant as it passes through higher and brighter keys (C flat major, C major, D major). The effect is similar to Butterfly's entrance, when her two-bar theme (Ex. 13) is repeated sequentially a whole tone higher each time. Janáček knew and loved Puccini's *Madama Butterfly*, and it is hard to imagine that this echo (note the similar rhythm and melody of the

Ex. 13

Ex. 14   VS 52

Un poco più mosso (♪ previously = 63)

opening of Ex. 12 at an identical moment in the opera) is coincidental.

Unlike for instance Ex. 16, heard only in Act 1 Scene 2, or Ex. 1, heard only in the overture and Act 1 Scene 1, Ex. 12 does seem to be used throughout the opera. Its first appearance is as an incidental phrase in the overture (VS 10); after the entrance music (prefigured as early as VS 23) there are further appearances: in Act 1 Scene 2 concealed in the bird music (VS 37) and at the height of Káťa's elation (VS 50, beneath 'A já jdu za ním', 'and I follow him'); varied as the second lyrical theme of the prelude to Act 2 Scene 2 (VS 86), developing into the theme of the great outpouring of Káťa's love (VS 99 to the end of the scene – this version is actually hinted at in Act 1 Scene 2, VS 52); and in the final scene set to the words 'Nu, nač mám tu ještě žít?' ('Why do I have to go on living?', VS 147). These are all variants, rather than readily audible recurrences of the same theme, which, Hollander wrote, 'delineate most sensitively and flexibly the various phases of Káťa's destiny' (pp. 140–1).

Ex. 14. Varvara, unlike Káťa, has a single associative theme, which is smuggled in for her very first utterance in Act 1 Scene 1 (VS 30, superimposed over Kabanicha's one-bar motif) and is heard as she leaves with Kudrjáš for Moscow in Act 3 (VS 140–1). At first the theme is heard only in the orchestra (e.g. VS 51–2, 74), but later it passes to the voice part, e.g. in Act 2 Scene 1 at 'aby přišel k vrátkům' ('for him to come to the gate', VS 75) and most obviously in Varvara's folksong 'Za vodou za vodičkou' ('Across the brook, the little brook', VS 93) in Act 2 Scene 2. At the end of this scene the theme provides part of the accompaniment for the final Varvara–Kudrjáš folksong (VS 111). Muller, counting appearances again, reckoned there were fifty, and drew attention in particular to the seductive version in Act 2 Scene 1 (ending in a trill and a flourish, VS 74) as one of the chief arguments with which Varvara tempts Káťa to meet Boris. Like Ex. 11 this theme receives real characterizing force from its orchestration: cross-rhythm chords on four flutes and celesta. The similarity of Ex. 14 to the tune of the Russian folksong which provided the new words of Kudrjáš's ballad in Act 2 Scene 2 (see below, p. 58; same even-quaver rhythm, same tonic–dominant alternation of the harmony) suggests a conscious imitation by Janáček of the Russian model.

Ex. 15   VS 145

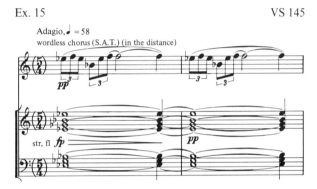

Ex. 15. Though this theme is confined to Act 3, it deserves mention here since it is spread over two scenes and plays a crucial part in the motivic build-up of the final one. It is enunciated climactically (after a series of descending chords, *ritenuto*) in the middle of Káťa's monologue in Act 3 Scene 2 (VS 145), where for the first time the wordless chorus is heard offstage (see Fig. 1). When it is heard again just before Boris finally leaves and the stage is growing dark, the same choral theme has the added instruction 'like the sigh of the Volga'. This has given rise to the theme's frequent description as 'voices of the Volga'. It remains in the musical foreground for another thirty bars until Boris leaves and is heard in a *fortissimo* harmonized version (against Ex. 11) in the final seven bars of the opera. Its significance will be discussed at the end of the chapter; here we should note that, like serveral 'Káťa' themes, its way has been carefully prepared. Wörner traces variants of it (Ex. 37.32–5) from VS 119 onwards in the Act 3 Scene 1 discussion of lightning conductors where, for instance on VS

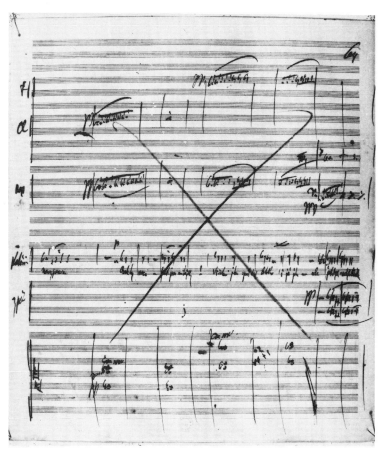

Fig. 1 Janáček's first version: Act 3 Scene 2 (cf. VS 144–5). The Volga theme (Ex. 15) was a stable element from the earliest version. Here, labelled simply 'zpěv' ('song'), it is introduced slightly earlier, at a different pitch and with a different rhythm. The orchestra lacks the thematic construction of VS 144; a version of its ascending theme here was used a later in the final version (cf. VS 148) (Moravian Museum, Music History Division, Brno)

120, it strikingly accompanies Dikoj's words 'Bouře je za trest na nás abychom moc boži pociťovali' ('storms are a punishment on us so we can feel the power of God'); and a slowed-down variant resounds in the final bars of the scene as Káťa rushes out into the storm.

A final point about themes concerns their use in the overture. Many of Janáček's overtures are no more than preludes, setting the scene that follows rather than presenting its principal themes. The overture to *Káťa*, however, replaced an earlier one which Janáček sketched but never finished; its late arrival allowed him to draw, uncharacteristically, on thematic material from the rest of the opera, and use of this material in the overture seems to reflect the opposition of forces on which the action hinges. The opening Adagio, elegiac and beautifully poised as it emerges from the lower strings, is not heard elsewhere in the opera, but its key (B flat minor, cf. Ex. 1) and mood suggest that it is 'Káťa' music. It is interrupted several times by Ex. 11, and the section is brought to an end by a *fortissimo* version of Ex. 11. This is followed at once by its speeded-up variant, Tichon's departure music (Ex. 10). It is twice interrupted by Ex. 11, then by a swirling ostinato derived from Ex. 10c, and finally by a new motif of a minor third (heard first bitingly on two muted trumpets), which leaps irregularly up and down an octave (it will be heard again in the storm scene accompanying the thunder and lightning, VS 132). The tension is increased, and is released only when the music settles down firmly into B flat minor to give an instrumental version of Ex. 1, one of the many 'Káťa' themes. Before a second phrase can follow (the first phrase hangs in the air, helplessly repeating its last few notes) there is another burst of interruptions; the repeated ostinato pattern, which had previously been pushed into the background, is heard on its own; Ex. 11 follows and then Ex. 10b to which, as noted above, is fitted Kabanicha's 'Děkuji vám' ('thank you') at the end of the opera. After an upward surge for the viola d'amore and harp (another recurring element) the second strain of the 'Káťa' theme emerges and is once again drowned by interruptions. The constant tussle between these themes, shifted into different keys (the F sharp minor version, VS 9–10, provides a first glimpse of Ex. 12), makes up the pattern for the rest of the overture. Even when, at the end, the 'Káťa' theme is heard alone in a mournful version on the English horn, it is capped immediately by a *fortissimo* made up of the chief disruptive elements: the ostinato, the leaping thirds, and the timpani theme (Ex. 11).

Criticism and interpretation

In an early review of *Káťa* (see Chapter 5) Vladimír Helfert saw Act 1 as rising to a climax, Act 2 as representing a lyrical contrast and Act 3 as a failure in its inability to cap the Act 1 climax. Other commentators, equally sympathetic to the work, have felt let down by the storm scene in Act 3. 'Physical action', wrote Charles Stuart, 'of which we have samples in the confession and suicide scenes, makes [Janáček] restive. What's the point, he seems to ask impatiently, of all this running about when the only thing that truly matters is what goes on in men's minds and hearts? In *Katya* the physical happenings are confused, untidy, almost ludicrous ... the defects of act three arise because Janáček found the external world and its goings on rather a bore' (p. 294).

Stuart's criticism was directed at the storm scene and, in the final scene, at the music during which Káťa leaps into the Volga and her corpse is hauled out. The latter passage lasts about forty seconds, which, in real-life terms, would be ludicrous timing even if Janáček had not omitted Ostrovsky's explanation of Káťa's death (her head hit an anchor and she was killed instantly). But there is no reason why a 'realistic' time-scale should obtain for this passage (involving physical action) more than for any other part of the opera. There are similar problems of timing with Laca's slashing of Jenůfa's cheek at the end of Act 1 of *Jenůfa*, and Bystrouška's instant pregnancy in Act 2 of the *Vixen*. These manipulations of the time-scale can be criticized only by someone with a most literal view of operatic time. Criticism is more justified in the storm scene. David Pountney (below, p. 197) sees it as 'cinematic' and 'strikingly unreal compared to the following scene'. At a purely practical level it is hard to bring off, since much of the crucial dialogue is obscured by noisy orchestration (to which Janáček added realistic rolls of thunder). The music itself is slightly melodramatic and has less cumulative force than we have come to expect from the composer. The point is made clear by a comparison with the final part of Act 1 Scene 2, whose pattern of events (carefully rearranged by Janáček, see Chapter 3) and musical working out together achieve a shattering climax.

Several elements of this scene have already been mentioned: Káťa's song-like plea to Tichon not to leave (VS 57–8; Ex. 3), followed by her dramatic demand to take an oath (VS 58–62) and its grim sequel, when Kabanicha makes her son extract the oath from Káťa that he

has just refused to accept (VS 63–7; Ex. 9). From VS 53 to the end of the scene the music is shot through with references to Tichon's departure music (Ex. 10) and its ominous eight-note variant on the timpani (Ex. 11). From VS 56 a two-bar orchestral motif (Ex. 16) is heard, whose most significant feature is the semitone clash of its final notes (both F flat) against an E flat pedal. Its significance is suggested by Káťa's words fitted to the tail of its next appearance (VS 59): 'Tišo, stane se bez tebe neštěstí' ('Tichon, something bad will happen without you'), with the voice's F flat now clashing with the orchestral pedal. These strands are gathered together in the final two pages of the act: Kabanicha's whole-tone motif and the contrasting 'Káťa' music (Ex. 9); Ex. 16, with its clashing semitones; and a triple *forte* version of the timpani theme (Ex. 11) which clinches the act. From VS 68, when Kabanicha hustles off her son to the accompaniment of his departure music, there is no let-up in the tension, just a relentless ostinato against which these themes are heard. Janáček wrote no music which has greater menace or which moves more inevitably to its final chord. One of the reasons why his later instructions for Acts 1 and 2 to be played continuously have been generally ignored (see Chapter 7) is that an audience needs some respite after this climax. With Tichon gone, the chief women of the drama are locked in confrontation. The music complements and extends the visual effect, arousing our apprehensions and presaging the tragic outcome.

Tichon's departure is only the culmination of one of Janáček's finest scenes; it is immediately preceded by Káťa's confession to Varvara of her love for Boris. There is an important difference between Káťa's confession to Varvara in Act 1 Scene 2 and her confession in Act 3 Scene 1 to Kabanicha and Tichon of her adultery. In Act 3 we are shown the immediate external circumstances which lead up to the confession; in Act 1 there is no obvious physical cause for the confession. Káťa instead describes her state of mind almost by chance, and Janáček reacts with a masterly manipulation of mood and theme. Russian literature is full of such confessional scenes, and it is clear that Janáček responded to them and seems to have sought out opera subjects which included them. The confessional narrative is of course especially useful for the opera composer in that it allows him, in a realistic convention that permits no soliloquizing arias, space for an extended solo. The confession itself is bound to have emotional depth (otherwise it would not be a confession but merely anecdote), and it is the emotion, rather than the events narrated, that Janáček is exploring. The depth of emotion that led Luka, Skuratov and Šiškov to commit their terrible crimes is depicted musically in *From the House of the Dead*, and has as much power as, or even more than, the actual incidents they describe. And so with Káťa; her confession to Varvara in Act 1 differs from her public confession in Act 3 in that it reveals depths within her that, in the later scene's frantic tumble of events, cannot make themselves known.

Ostensibly Káťa's suicide scene has much in common with the Act 1 Scene 2 confession. It is a lengthy scene for solo voice, with skilfully organized changing moods and motivic development. But whereas the Act 1 confession subtly blends narrative and the revelation of Káťa's state of mind, Káťa's monologue has only a disjointed and illogical 'narrative' (there is, after all, no listener for most of the time) and is given over almost entirely to exploration of her state of mind; were it more flamboyant it would rank as a mad scene. Earlier commentators were dissatisfied with it. Helfert, at the Brno première, felt it was marred by Janáček's concern for realism; Philip Hope-Wallace, at its British première, found it too protracted.[11] But opinion seems now to have changed. Wörner devoted his celebrated analysis 'Katjas Tod' to it, regarding it as one of the finest death-scenes in operatic literature. In its variety of moods it is a scene of great richness and it needs a fine singing actress to do it justice. The music which marks the mute embrace of Káťa and Boris is some of the tenderest and most memorable that Janáček wrote. Charles Stuart found the 'stuttering brassy figure' heard in Boris's farewell against the Volga theme (Ex. 15) 'a masterstroke' which was alone 'sufficient to establish Janáček's technical *bonafides*' (pp. 293–4). And nowhere is Janáček's genius more apparent than in the un-expected calm that reigns during Káťa's last moments, as she con-templates the birds that will fly around her grave and the flowers that will bloom there.

In their different ways the final scenes of each act stand well above the more prosaic and explanatory preceding scenes. Act 1 Scene 1 establishes all the main characters in a series of brief vignettes. Káťa's nature is stamped indelibly on the music of her entrance and her soft-spoken replies to Kabanicha, but the more expansive music of her next scene is needed to establish the range of her personality. While her hesitation over the key (Act 2 Scene 1) is skilfully handled, this brief scene is nevertheless overshadowed by the magnificent double love-scene that has won the admiration of so many commentators. And Act 3 Scene 1, given over mostly to physical action and thus dealing with what Janáček seems least interested in, cannot help but be overtaken by the strengths of the succeeding scene, concentrating almost entirely on Káťa in her final moments.

In all his late operas Janáček made radical changes to the literary texts from which he fashioned his librettos: *From the House of the Dead* was reshaped by his suggestive juxtaposition of materials; in *The Cunning Little Vixen* and *The Makropulos Affair*, both described by their authors as comedies, he made the heroines die. How in this respect does Janáček's *Káťa Kabanová* differ from Ostrovsky's *The Thunderstorm*?

Janáček's changes to the libretto itself are detailed in Chapter 3; the most far-reaching were the elimination of the Russian periphery and most of the social comment. The latter precludes interpretations of the opera as a work principally of social criticism (as the play had been seen by contemporary Russian critics); the former precludes interpretations dependent on specific Russian conditions. The Volga, however, became the focus of many accounts of the opera. Janáček made no change to Ostrovsky's framework, opening with a description of the beauty of the Volga and ending with Káťa's death in it, and he himself encouraged speculation by his enigmatic remarks about *Káťa* in his Autobiography (1924): 'But the masts of the Volga loomed high and the surface of the Volga was as white in the moonlight as Káťa's soul.'[12] Two references to the Volga in the two lines on *Káťa* are striking (as is the fact that Janáček spent many years on another 'river' work, his unfinished tone poem *The Danube*), and Brod seized on this in his analysis: 'the Volga, both in Janáček's libretto and in his music, is the perfect example of an effective – because, at root, inexplicable – symbol'. He suggested that it could represent, in its 'monstrous, ceaselessly flowing masses of water', a symbol of the inexorability with which tsarist Russia 'marched ...

over the corpses of its children'. The Volga triumphs over Káťa just as tsarist orthodoxy trampled over its people (see below, p. 163–4).

This is an illogical interpretation, given Janáček's forthright omission of nearly all other Russian elements (and his failure to introduce much Russian local colour into the music),[13] and later commentators have modified it. Stuckenschmidt (p. 9) saw the river less as a tsarist symbol than as a more widely applicable symbol of the unalterable laws of custom and family. Wörner likewise broadened its symbolic interpretation, taking it as a general image of Nature ('Water as an element, the Volga as an eternal cycle, an event of perpetual grandeur in the lives of those inhabitating its shores', below, p. 175), and argued that this was underpinned by motivic means. Pountney saw the Volga even more broadly as 'the atmospheric basis of the opera … a metaphor for its inner emotional dynamic … a swirling pattern of ebb and flow in the background which instantly creates a sense of emotional stress' (below, p. 188). This too has a musical analogue – the swirl of the ostinato figures that break out in Janáček's music, most remarkably in the overture.

Janáček has left us one intriguing verbal clue, as mentioned above: the instruction attached to Ex. 15 on its second appearance in the final scene, as Boris prepares to go off, that it be sung 'like a sigh of the Volga'. Are we then to take the singing that Káťa hears earlier, and again as Boris's farewells fade and she is left with only one thing to do, as the Volga calling her to her death? And when this theme is heard *fortissimo* in the final bars of the opera should we hear it as the triumph of the river (whatever we think it stands for)? Burjanek saw the combination in the final six bars of the 'Volga theme', the ominous timpani theme and an ostinato made from Kabanicha's 'Děkuji vám' as 'a combination of all the triumphant forces of evil' (p. 407); if this is so it provides a clear-cut commentary on the end of the opera, and on how Janáček regarded it.

While the Volga begins and ends the work, we have also to reckon with another natural element, the 'storm' of Ostrovsky's title. As we know from his letter to Červinka (31 March 1921, see Chapter 5), Janáček changed the title of his opera because there were other competing operatic works with the same title, but also because the storm 'is not the mainspring of the action; it is Kateřina who carries the psychological interest'. Accordingly Janáček omitted Káťa's fear of storms; and although he specifies lightning and thunder, his music for the storm scene has little that could be taken as 'storm music'. There is more to be said in fact for taking the storm as that within

Káťa herself, as the demons who disturb her dreams and are quelled only in her final bars, when she is at peace with herself.

For his title Ostrovsky could have chosen the word 'burya'. Instead he chose the word 'groza' which, as well as 'thunderstorm', can mean 'terror'. The chief source of 'terror' in the play is Kabanicha. In Brod's conception she is the embodiment of Russian autocracy, and he regarded her as 'the true central character of the opera'. It is she who presides over the end of the opera; the violent dance of triumph that the orchestra makes over Káťa's corpse is taken from Kabanicha's music, and this element remains in the texture of the final bars. Stuckenschmidt, on the other hand, saw the end not as a triumph of tsarist orthodoxy, the terror represented by Kabanicha, but as the triumph of Slavonic matriarchy, though this would be more convincing had Kabanicha 'triumphed' at the end over a man rather than over one of her own sex.

These Kabanicha-centred interpretations seem misguided. Janáček retitled the opera *Káťa Kabanová*, not *Marfa Kabanová*, and by restricting Kabanicha's part and retaining so much of Káťa's he tilted the balance even more in Káťa's favour. An important key to Janáček's thinking is provided by his letters to Kamila Stösslová (see Chapter 5). In them he said he was trying to represent someone so gentle and fragile that a puff of wind would carry her off. He found Káťa's vulnerability touching, much in the way that he responded both to Puccini's Butterfly and to Kamila herself:

I have just come from the theatre. They gave *Batrflay* [sic], one of the most beautiful and saddest operas. I had you constantly before my eyes. Batterflay [sic] is also small, with black hair. But you could never be as unhappy as her ... I was moved by the opera. When it was new I would travel to Prague to see it. Even now many places moved me deeply.[14]

The date of this letter to Kamila is 5 December 1919, less than a month before Janáček began composing *Káťa Kabanová*. It is not hard to see the connection he makes between Kamila and Butterfly extending to Káťa as well, especially since it is reinforced by musical similarities such as the one already noted between Káťa's and Butterfly's entrance music (Exx. 12–13).

Janáček's most powerful works seems to have grown from strong autobiographical roots. The first work stamped with his individuality is the cantata *Amarus* (1897) in which he gave expression to the loneliness of his years as a schoolboy in the Augustinian monastery in Brno. Most of his mature operas had similar autobiographical origins; and Káťa's links with Kamila Stösslová are abundantly obvious from his correspondence with her. The view of *Káťa* purely as a portrait of its central character, irrespective of the implications of the storm and the terror, needs no special pleading, and can be based on what is in the musical setting, rather than what is only in the text. It explains, for instance, why Káťa alone is a fully rounded character with no particular 'theme' (such as Varvara has) but instead a distinctive type of music that is instantly recognizable. In contrast all the others are cyphers, or at the most two-dimensional characters, whose actions are predictable, and whose music reveals none of the depths and conflicts that we find in Káťa. The specific Russian circumstances are not significant; despite Janáček's predisposition towards Russian literature, he cut them out. The fact that Ostrovsky's Russia of the 1860s was on the eve of immense social changes mattered not at all to Janáček, since all social concerns are similarly suppressed in the opera. However much Kabanicha may represent autocratic and repressive forces in the play, in the opera she represents nothing more than a forceful and unpleasant mother-in-law jealous of her son's affection (however weak) for wife.

The Volga, alone of the externals of Ostrovsky's play, seems to have impinged on Janáček's view of the opera. While the reference in the Autobiography may reflect nothing more than the Russian nostalgia that predisposed him towards setting the play, the added direction 'like the sigh of the Volga' to the recurring theme Ex. 15 needs to be taken into account in any interpretation of the work, as does the insertion at so many points in Act 1 Scene 2 and Act 3 Scene 1 of the timpani theme (Ex. 11). At its most basic the timpani theme is simply a 'fate' theme; the Volga theme foretells the manner in which that fate is to be accomplished. Fate hammers during Tichon's departure, at Káťa's public confession, and triumphantly at the end of the opera. All through Act 3 the Volga calls to Káťa, offering her the only way out of what has become an impossible situation.

The fact that this interpretation may be called 'depressingly crude' in no way invalidates it. The initial impetus to all Janáček's work was always primitive. The elements that attracted his attention and set his creative powers flowing are obvious and simple. Even at the end of his life, in his final opera, he was drawn by the colouristic possibilities that the prison setting offered his orchestra. The prisoners' chains and the soliders' drums were almost the only survivors, in his final version, of the initial vision caught in his earliest version of *From the House of the Dead*. While the alchemy of the creative process may transform these crude beginnings, and while we are at liberty to make sophisticated interpretations of the score, the basic ingredients of Janáček's inspiration remain clearly discernible.

In this light *Káťa Kabanová* is the tragedy of a young woman whose purity of heart and heightened awareness ill equip her for the dreary provincial life in which she finds herself, and for the limited people who surround her. Her husband's departure at a crucial moment in her life (just after she has confided her love for Boris to the sympathetic Varvara) has fatal consequences. Her husband's absence provides an opportunity for her to see Boris; Varvara's ingenuity and persuasion complete the process. The 'fate' theme heard as Tichon departs warns us of the approaching tragedy, but all we can do is watch helplessly as it unfolds. Varvara and Kudrjáš are equally powerless in Act 3 to prevent Káťa's truthfulness and sense of guilt from making her confess when her husband returns. Once again the 'fate' theme is heard, but in proximity now to a theme which, in the final scene, becomes identified with the waters of the Volga that call Káťa to her death. Boris's brief return to say farewell cannot affect the outcome. He is banished to Siberia and is too weak and ineffectual to take Káťa with him. Even she realizes this. All that is left for her is to throw herself into the Volga. As she does so the music of Tichon's departure is heard for the first time since Act 1. It is wound up into a frenetic dance of triumph as Kabanicha gloats over the catastrophe (it was her decision to send Tichon away); and out of it are fashioned her words of thanks to the bystanders. The final bars of the opera, combining the 'fate' theme, the theme of Kabanicha's triumph (the departure music) and the Volga theme, tell us how Káťa's fateful leap fulfils the prophecies made by the music throughout the opera – notably at the end of Act 1 (Tichon's departure, on his mother's orders), and as far back as the overture, whose quiet opening is disturbed by the first murmerings of the 'fate' theme.

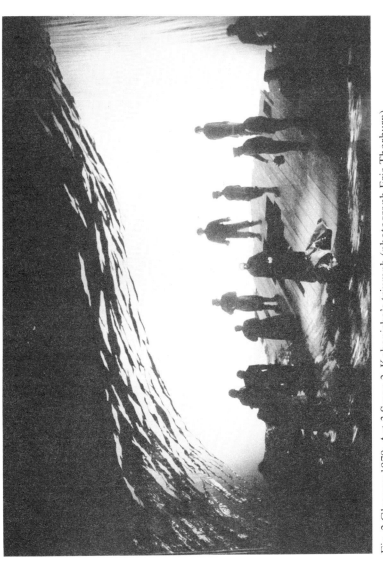

Fig. 2 Glasgow 1979: Act 3 Scene 2. Kabanicha's triumph (photograph Eric Thorburn)

2 Ostrovsky's play 'The Thunderstorm'

CYNTHIA MARSH

In adapting Ostrovsky's play Janáček changed its title, and this suggests the major difference between *The Thunderstorm* and *Káťa Kabanová*: the opera concentrates on the personal tragedy of the heroine at the expense of some of the play's wider issues. The storm of Ostrovsky's title refers both to the central dramatic device of the play and to its social relevance. The storm is not only the trigger to Katerina's[1] public confession of sin but also signals disruption within society itself. The play is as much a vehicle for Ostrovsky's perception of the conflicts and tensions in mid-nineteenth-century Russian society as it is for his mastery of theatrical skills.

Alexander Nikolayevich Ostrovsky (1823–86) wrote forty-eight dramatic works, including comedies, serious plays with contemporary settings, historical dramas and fantasies. He wrote his comedies and serious plays partly to counter the foreign vaudeville and melodrama which dominated the Russian stage in the 1830s and 1840s. *The Thunderstorm* (1859), a serious play, is generally recognized as his masterpiece.

For nearly forty years from 1848 Ostrovsky wrote regularly for the stage. He was the first Russian writer in the nineteenth century to make a successful career exclusively as a dramatist. He set himself to provide the Russian theatre with a home-produced and home-orientated repertoire, and to improve its standards. His sensitivity to the requirements of successful theatrical production encouraged him to adopt the effective aspects of the existing theatrical tradition, despite its general lack of distinction. He recognized the dramatic value of the suspense, tension and emotional appeal typical of popular melodrama, and vaudeville taught him that a prime function of the theatre was to entertain and divert; he frequently made subtle use of interpolated songs and dances to underline his theme.

The Thunderstorm has a melodramatic atmosphere from the very beginning. The first act[2] opens with a description of the Volga, which

38

seems to foreshadow the conclusion of the play when Katerina's corpse is retrieved from the river. Tension is heightened by the prediction of Katerina's doom, uttered by a mad old lady from the local nobility (a sequence omitted in the opera). This tension is further increased in Act 4 when the pilgrim Feklusha's prophecies of catastrophe are echoed in the description of the frescoes in the ruin depicting the flames of hell. The excitement and panic of the storm itself, and Katerina's suicide, give a sensational character to the play. The influence of vaudeville is particularly strong in Act 3 – in the drunken episode between Dikoy and Kabanova, and in the songs and semicomic sequences between Varvara and Kudryash which differentiate their frivolous love from the poignant passion of Boris and Katerina.

Ostrovsky's originality lay in the realism he brought to the Russian theatre. His choice of theme and setting – the life and ways of the bureaucratic and merchant classes among which he had grown up – gave his drama a contemporary, topical appeal. He was not providing a world of make-believe, but transplanting everyday life on to the stage. In those plays with a bureaucratic setting the actors needed no exotic costume, but appeared in the familiar, workaday apparel of the audience. Even more pointedly, in some plays they wore the despised traditional Russian dress of the merchant class, whose lifestyle was largely untouched by the western ways which had influenced the rest of Russia for so long.

In the bureaucratic and merchant classes the family was still the hub of social life, and the plots of Ostrovsky's plays tend to deal with family affairs, centring usually on a pair of young lovers threatened by tragedy. The older generation, the family heads, appear harsh and autocratic, concerned only to preserve their power and family fortunes. Whether intentionally or otherwise, Ostrovsky's work dwells on the grimmer aspects of Russian national life. He emphasizes its tyranny and oppression. He depicts a society motivated by acquisitiveness and by a concern to preserve, at all costs, its rites and customs.

One progressive critic in the 1850s, Nikolay Alexandrovich Dobrolyubov, described Ostrovsky's world as a 'realm of darkness'. It was ruled by tyrants who through their corruption or intimidation of the younger generations prevented any challenge to their own position.[3] However, this was Dobrolyubov's assessment before Ostrovsky wrote *The Thunderstorm*. In 1860 he acknowledged that there was now 'a ray of light in the realm of darkness'.[4] Katerina provides new hope, in that her suicide can be seen as an act of protest against injustice. Dobrolyubov pointed out that *The Thunderstorm* represents a crucial point of development, since it shows resistance to the previously unchallenged tyranny. The extreme nature of Katerina's protest, her suicide, is a reflection of the impasse which tyranny has produced. Other characters join Katerina in rebellion: Varvara, Kudryash, Kuligin and even Tikhon. Dobrolyubov saw *The Thunderstorm*, despite its tragic outcome, as a positive statement that an unhappy era of Russian history was giving way to a future modelled by the vigorous young agents of rebellion, who were capable of the greatest sacrifice. Dobrolyubov belonged to that section of the intelligentsia which promoted radical reform and can be seen as foreshadowing the revolution of 1917. His two articles constitute a searching analysis of Ostrovsky's drama, and set the course for much post-revolutionary criticism.

The lasting success of Ostrovsky's work is not, of course, solely due to Dobrolyubov's approval. The personal tragedy of the heroine, for example, is vividly and convincingly drawn, and the controversy surrounding the themes of the play ensured its success for many generations.

Katerina belongs to a particular class of Russian society which, by the mid-nineteenth century, had a distinctively traditionalist, reactionary and xenophobic character. The merchant class retained an inward-looking, inscrutable attitude inherited from earlier centuries.[5] This had helped to guarantee its survival, and later secured it against the greater social mobility introduced from the time of Peter the Great onward. Katerina's treatment was typical of that endured by young married women in this society – her humiliation by her mother-in-law, the apparent indifference, even cruelty, of her husband, and her incarceration within the family house. As a result Katerina is haunted by images of freedom, and by a desire to escape. Her childhood memories centre on the lack of constraint she then felt: she longs to fly like a bird, and she dreams of the flowers she loved and tended.

From her reminiscences it seems that her upbringing was influenced by two major forces: nature and religion. Both inspired a sense of beauty and ecstasy, and as a result created a highly emotional child. Frequently the two forces combined to overwhelm her sensitive nature: 'I'd go out into the garden early in the morning, just as the sun was rising. I'd fall to my knees and pray and weep, and I wouldn't know what I was praying and weeping about, and there they'd find me' (Act 2 Scene 7).

Petted, dressed like a doll, Katerina took such education as she could from the stories, fantasies and visions of the wandering pilgrims (represented in the play by Feklusha and her extravagant tales of the outside world). She comes to marriage and to life in a strange household unequipped to deal either with the force of her own emotions or with the behaviour of her new family. When she follows her natural inclinations (for she is a child of nature) and transgresses, the religiously moulded part of her character expects and exacts a fitting punishment. Significantly it is a thunderstorm – nature at its most aggressive – which initiates the religiously inspired need for public confession of sin: religion and nature influence her in concert as they did in her childhood. She is unable to moderate her inordinate sensitivity, expressed as fear at this menacing aspect of nature and fear of the consequences of sin. The storm both brings her to confess and begins to unhinge her mind. The brutal treatment she receives at the hands of the Kabanov family, her incarceration, and the denial of her natural passion for Boris produce symptoms of despair and hysteria. Boris completes the process by his inability to offer any support. Suicide becomes the logical answer. The powerful social factors emphasized by Dobrolyubov also contribute to the oppression that Katerina must endure, and hence play their part in her death. She is in conflict as much with herself as with her environment; it is clear that she could not have found a complete solution in challenging the authorities placed over her. Suicide is as much a fulfilment of her need for self-inflicted punishment as it is a reproach to those who abused her.

When Ostrovsky's play of 1859 became Janáček's libretto of 1921 the wider issues of topical relevance to mid-nineteenth-century Russia were avoided principally by the omission or demotion of characters representing them. But the opera preserves the reactionary attitudes, the ingrained antipathy towards the outsider and the brutal treatment of subordinates characteristic of the older generation of Kabanova and Dikoy, which determine Boris's weakness and provide clear grounds for Katerina's unhappiness. These tyrannical attitudes are, as Dobrolyubov suggests, self-regenerating, since they crush the spirit of the rebellious, or corrupt others to behave in similar fashion (like Tikhon), and are rarely challenged on either count. According to Dobrolyubov, challenge by Katerina would have caused her further physical and mental suffering since she is largely incorruptible by the tyrants, while Boris is so intimidated that, far from offering Katerina release, he cannot even offer comfort.

In his adaptation Janáček substantially altered two roles in Ostrovsky's play which gave it particular social relevance. In the libretto Kuligin becomes just a friend of Kudryash, and Feklusha is demoted to a domestic servant. Much of Kuligin's role in the plot is assigned to Kudryash, and his ideas and aspirations are lost. He is the one person in *The Thunderstorm* who has the courage to attack injustice. A self-educated amateur scientist and watchmaker, he has the independence to be able to identify society's faults: the oppressive relationship between wealth and power, the victimization of the peasants, the despotic behaviour of family heads whose power encounters no social limitations, and the poverty and unemployment of urban workers. But he is an idealist, able to identify society's flaws yet incapable of repairing them. He has placed his hopes in the discovery of perpetual motion, which he believes will 'earn him a million' and enable him to undertake his projects for reform. He is one of the dreamers and romantics. As the play opens his ecstasy over the beauty of the landscape and his sense of its effects upon the feelings, and later his references to the poets, suggest his unpractical nature. His social significance, however, is considerable. His language indicates that he is of low social origin, and he identifies himself with Lomonosov, the eighteenth-century scholar and poet of the common people. By the mid-nineteenth century it had become possible for people not of noble origin or wealthy parentage to procure an education and begin to analyse the type of society in which they lived. Kuligin's training as a scientist, however amateur, brings him to understand nature as well as to be affected by it. He welcomes the storm, and his rejection of the superstitious interpretation given by Dikoy is a step towards the welcoming of a storm of change within Russian society. Significantly it is he who attempts to moderate Tikhon's anger at his wife, and he who organizes the recovery of Katerina's body from the Volga, emphasizing that she is a victim of the injustices he has identified in society in the course of the play. Hence Kuligin was regarded by critics like Dobrolyubov as a crucial figure in Ostrovsky's presentation of topical and social issues.

Ostrovsky counterbalances the socially positive role of Kuligin with the socially negative one of Feklusha. She is a colourful representative of the ignorant, superstitious and narrow outlook of a Russia dominated by a folk religion, and of its traditional introspective attitude. She is described as a 'strannitsa', a wanderer, or pilgrim. Such religious devotees were dependent on the charity of orthodox believers. They derived from a sect which broke away from the established church in the eighteenth century to pursue the fight against evil and, in particular, against Antichrist. With no means of sustaining themselves they became wanderers, and by the mid-nineteenth century were a common feature of Russian life, enjoying a position of privilege for their supposed religious insight and as a source of information based on the knowledge and gossip they gathered in their travels. Feklusha and her kind still had the ear of those in power in provincial merchant society, the Dikoys and Kabanovas. The 'wanderers' also exercised a formative influence on the minds of those who, like Katerina, had sufficient intensity of passion to effect change. But their emphasis on superstitution and evil channelled this potential in the wrong direction, and in Katerina it becomes self-destructive.

The claustrophobic way of life of Kalinovo, the imaginary town where the play is set,[6] survives because of its isolation from the principal centres of change. The major point of contact with the outside world seems to be through the 'wanderers'. It was in their interests, of course, to perpetuate the existing structure, since it guaranteed their survival. Hence Feklusha's role is to support the regime of Dikoy and Kabanova. In a purely dramatic sense her predictions of general catastrophe, her insistence that time is coming to an end, help to build up the atmosphere of tension which increasingly affects the actions of the heroine.

Tikhon, too, plays an important role in the social significance of the play. A weak, mother-dominated individual whose treatment of his wife is despicable, Tikhon undergoes the process of corruption described by Dobrolyubov. It seems inevitable that this son will take over the tyrannical role of his mother, yet in the end he rejects her and accuses her of 'murdering' his wife. His recognition that a crime has been committed is an acknowledgement of the corruption of the system that has produced him. Here lie the seeds of hope for social change. However, Katerina's death is the price which has been paid. Ostrovsky does not suggest what should follow, but the responsibility placed on those who remain is not in doubt.

Russia in 1859 was on the eve of a long-awaited and much debated fundamental change in social structure: the emancipation of the serfs came in 1861. The latter part of the 1850s also saw a great debate on the implications of Russia's recent defeat in the Crimean War. The death of Nicholas I in 1855 enabled the issues to be raised publicly; indeed, the initiative came from the new tsar, Alexander II. The relative freedom of discussion of these years opened a period of reform affecting not only the serfs but also the law, administration, local government and military affairs.

Ostrovsky's play reflected the debate in two ways which account for the controversy it aroused. It was widely recognized that the abolition of serfdom would introduce a new era, in which the traditional Russian life-style would be under pressure; and tension between the old and the new is a major theme in the play. There is evident dissatisfaction with the tradition-bound and autocratic ways of the older generation. As well as specific reference to Dikoy's less than human dealings with the peasants, there is Kabanova's pedantic insistence on the preservation of household ritual – the formalities of leave-taking, for example, which demanded that a wife bow low to her husband, and wail after his departure.

The place of women in this changing society was the other issue. Ostrovsky chose an extreme example: a young wife in the merchant class, where it was the custom for a young married woman to be immured in the family house, and where she was expected to be subservient to her mother-in-law. But a new twist was added to the debate: much of the play focuses on Katerina's immorality. Not only does she transgress in taking a lover, she sins unpardonably in taking her own life. Yet her tragedy is so vividly portrayed that she appears to represent the condition of women in general.

Ostrovsky was not alone in treating this topic at this particular time. The 1850s produced a series of striking literary heroines, for example Natalya and Yelena in Turgenev's novels *Rudin* (1855) and *On the Eve* (1859), and Olga in Goncharov's *Oblomov* (1859). The strong heroine is a recurring feature of nineteenth-century Russian literature. Two familiar examples which put Katerina in her true perspective are Tatyana in Pushkin's *Eugene Onegin*, written in the 1820s, and Tolstoy's Anna Karenina, created in the 1870s. All three heroines have a comparable emotional intensity. While she is portrayed as dramatically and vividly as the other two, Katerina has little of Tatyana's or Anna's intelligence, accomplishment or self-knowledge. Yet her situation resembles theirs: like Tatyana she is attracted to an outsider, who (as for Tatyana and Anna) is incapable of meeting the demands that love makes upon him. Both Anna and Katerina experience unbearable feelings of guilt caused by knowledge of their transgression, and find their only escape from an impossible situation in suicide. And Katerina's actions, like both Tatyana's and Anna's, are partly prompted by omens, prophecy and coincidence.

Katerina differs most significantly from Tatyana and Anna in her social origins and in the cause of her death. Both Tatyana and Anna are nobly born, and while both defy society in their own way neither could be described as oppressed. Katerina's lower-class origins help to explain her inordinate fear of the storm, and her urge to public confession. Her action is prompted by a mind under stress, and so is less tragic than Tatyana's decisive denial of her love, or Anna's awareness of her divided soul which can be at peace only in death.

When Katerina is compared with these heroines the extremes in her situation become evident: her remote social position, her exceptionally highly strung nature, her ecstasy and her madness. Hers is a role that many an actress would have delighted in (indeed it was written for one particular actress).[7] It has the sensational and emotional elements of melodrama – in Katerina's reactions to the storm, her humiliated position, her suicide, her madness, the passionate love-interlude and the drama of the key. It may be that as a result Katerina loses some credibility beside her more realistically drawn literary sisters.

The Thunderstorm must also be seen in the context of mid-nineteenth-century Russian theatre. Probably Ostrovsky's greatest achievement lay in giving Russia a national dramatic repertoire. Russian drama had already seen one or two genuinely national works, by Fonvizin in the eighteenth century, by Pushkin and Griboyedov (whose plays remained largely unperformed from the 1820s) and latterly by Gogol. Ostrovsky was a true son of Gogol in that his works dealt with topics of national interest in a thought-provoking way which did not detract from their power to entertain. Ostrovsky went further than Gogol in his devotion to the theatre. He not only wrote plays, but took part in their production, campaigned for a National Theatre, and in the latter part of his life became deeply involved in the administration of the theatres of both capital cities and in the establishment of properly instituted drama schools.

Contending against the foreign influences which had dominated the Russian theatre, Ostrovsky managed to capture quintessential Russian characteristics in his work. He persuaded the Russians to contemplate themselves, however much they despised certain of their national characteristics. The essential Russianness of *The*

Thunderstorm – its setting in a remote town among recognizable provincial types – links it to Ostrovsky's drive for a national repertoire for the Russian theatre. By 1859, however, this aspect of his work was no longer novel: the public had begun to expect it of him. It was the play's inclusion of controversial social and topical themes which gave new life to Russian drama. More specifically, the role of Katerina became the Russian theatre's female equivalent of Hamlet, and many famous actresses were to make their reputations in it. The popularity of the play in Russia has been phenomenal. It was given over 3500 performances between 1875 and 1917. The figure must be even larger for the Soviet period, since in 1937, for example, the play was staged in at least twenty-two theatres in Russia proper.[8]

Music has brought *The Thunderstorm* the international recognition it has never achieved as a play, for in addition to Janáček a number of composers have been inspired by it, as they have been by others of Ostrovsky's dramatic works. Operas based on *The Thunderstorm* have been composed by Asafyev (1940), Dzerzhinsky (1940), Trambitsky (1941), Rocca (1952) and Pushkov (1962).[9] Tchaikovsky composed an overture in 1864 and narrowly missed undertaking the first opera version: this was in fact composed by Vladimir Nikitich Kashperov (1827–94)[10] to a libretto by Ostrovsky himself. The exercise did not succeed, however, and the author preferred to share the writing of the libretto with the composer in subsequent operatic adaptations of his plays.

The libretto of Kashperov's opera of 1867 represents a condensed version of the play. Ostrovsky, like Janáček, omitted the more controversial social issues, and concentrated on the love intrigue and its tragic outcome. He compensated for the resulting impoverishment by adding another dimension to the conflict: Tikhon and Boris meet, and from the beginning Tikhon suspects that Boris loves Katerina. Kuligin and Feklusha are left out, and Kudryash and Varvara do not elope. Attention is concentrated on the resolution of Katerina's personal dilemma. The musical convention of the time required that the original prose of the play be turned into verse. This tends to sound inept not only in literary but also in social terms, since the play's original prose fulfils an important function in suggesting environment and social type. The opera was performed in October 1867. The libretto especially was condemned by the critics, and since then appears to have been quite forgotten.

Ostrovsky remains overshadowed in the West by dramatists such as Chekhov, Gorky and Turgenev. Despite his plays' invaluable contribution to the establishment of the Russian theatre, in which he anticipated some of the elements which were to bring it world recognition in the work of Chekhov and Gorky, they have hardly been appreciated outside Russia. The reason seems to be that the dramatists who have succeeded are recognizably European: their plays deal with the relatively cultured 'Europeanized' sections of Russian society. Ostrovsky made his reputation by writing about essentially Russian folk types whose very national colouring must make them less widely understood. Even Janáček, a fellow Slav and passionate Russophile, omitted from his libretto the essence of those figures who are most limited in an historical sense (Kuligin), or in a national sense (Feklusha). The West would gain from a closer appreciation of Ostrovsky's plays. *The Thunderstorm*, especially, is important for the vivid and sensitive portrayal of its heroine and for its exceptional blend of the elements which make powerful theatre, as well as for its role in the social debate which marked so much of Russian culture in the latter part of the nineteenth century.

3 The libretto

JOHN TYRRELL

As for all his operas based on stage plays, Janáček made his own adaptation of *The Thunderstorm*. By the time of *Káťa* he had acquired considerable experience: the difficulties over finding suitable librettists to adapt Svatopluk Čech's novel *Mr Brouček's Excursion to the Moon* (1908–17) had forced him to fend for himself, and for all his later operas, whether based on plays (*Káťa*, *Makropulos*) or novels (the *Vixen*, *From the House of the Dead*), he wrote his own librettos. He was extraordinarily economical in this. Most of his changes in *Káťa* were cuts (over half the play); where extra lines were needed he would grudgingly invent them only if he was unable to adapt something from another part of the work, sometimes from quite a different context.

Here is Janáček at work in the opening scene (cf. pp. 15–16 of his annotated copy of Červinka's Czech translation of the play, Fig. 3). Left alone after the departure of Kuligin (Kudrjáš in the opera), Boris reflects:

Boris (alone): It's a pity to disillusion a good man like that! He has his dreams and he's happy. Whereas I, it seems, am going to waste my youth in this hole. **I wander around like a dead man** and yet such foolish thoughts still steal into my head. **And now, this as well?** To let myself get involved! I'm a rejected, forgotten man, and yet idiotically I can **still** remember how **to fall in love. And with whom! With a woman** I haven't even managed to speak to. (*Pause.*) And yet whatever I do I can't get her out of my head. **Here she is!** She's coming this way **with her husband, and her mother-in-law with them. Ah, aren't I stupid! Let's have a look at her from behind the corner, and then run off home.** (*He leaves. Kabanicha, Tichon, Katerina and Varvara approach from the opposite side.*)

The words in bold type are the equivalent of those retained in Janáček's final version (cf. VS 25, fig. 29, to VS 27). Some of the contractions alter the sense, and 'zabitý' ('slain', 'killed', 'dead man') became 'omámený' ('stunned'), a change carefully written into Janáček's copy of the play. Janáček retained Kuligin (Kudrjáš in the opera) on stage during this speech, and where Ostrovsky's Boris asks himself, and then answers, the question 'A do koho! Do ženy . . .' ('And with whom? With a woman . . .'), Janáček gave the question to Kudrjáš and the answer to Boris. This change is again registered in Janáček's annotations, though not the later change of 'do ženy' to the stronger 'do vdané' ('with a married woman'). Janáček's next annotation on the page, 'str. 62: Kuligin: Nuž toho musíte nechat! To znamená, že ji chcete zahubit!' ('p. 62: Kuligin: Well, you must leave this! It means you want to destroy her!'), refers to p. 62 of his copy of the play, a conversation between Boris and Kudrjáš while they wait for Káťa and Varvara (before the double love-scene). Janáček took over and modified lines from two speeches of this passage and shortened them still further when he set them. A final addition was Boris's pitchless laughter as he goes off after watching the Kabanovs arrive.

While Janáček's cuts make room for the music, they also produce striking juxtapositions. Once a passage about perpetual motion (Kuligin's *idée fixe*) has been removed, these references to Boris's falling in love come hard on the heels of an earlier discussion of the Kabanov family (that of Boris's beloved). The loaded word 'married' (woman) and the dangers of Boris's position now emerge in the first ten minutes of Janáček's opera, appropriated from Ostrovsky's Act 3. Though Janáček made some small cuts in his copy of the play, most of the detailed adaptation was done as he composed. More common in his annotations was the crossing out of whole sections, e.g. the discussion of perpetual motion on p. 15 of the Červinka translation, though Janáček's crossing out was overhasty here, since he later reprieved Kuligin's initial lines about the Kabanovs. Perhaps the most surprising aspect of his annotations to the play is that they give no hint of his different act structure.

Ostrovsky divided his play into five acts, of which Act 3 alone had two scenes; in addition, each act was further divided into many 'scenes' according to the entrances of individual characters, in the European classical tradition ignored by most English translations of the play but retained in the Czech translation which Janáček used. Janáček cast his opera into his usual three acts, each with one scene-change. Table 1 demonstrates the relationship of the play and the opera. The last three scenes of the opera correspond exactly to Ostrovsky's division. Janáček's biggest structural change was to make an act-end climax out of Tichon's departure – an event which had come in the middle of Ostrovsky's Act 2 – and to add this to the long Káťa–Varvara exchange which had ended Ostrovsky's Act 1.

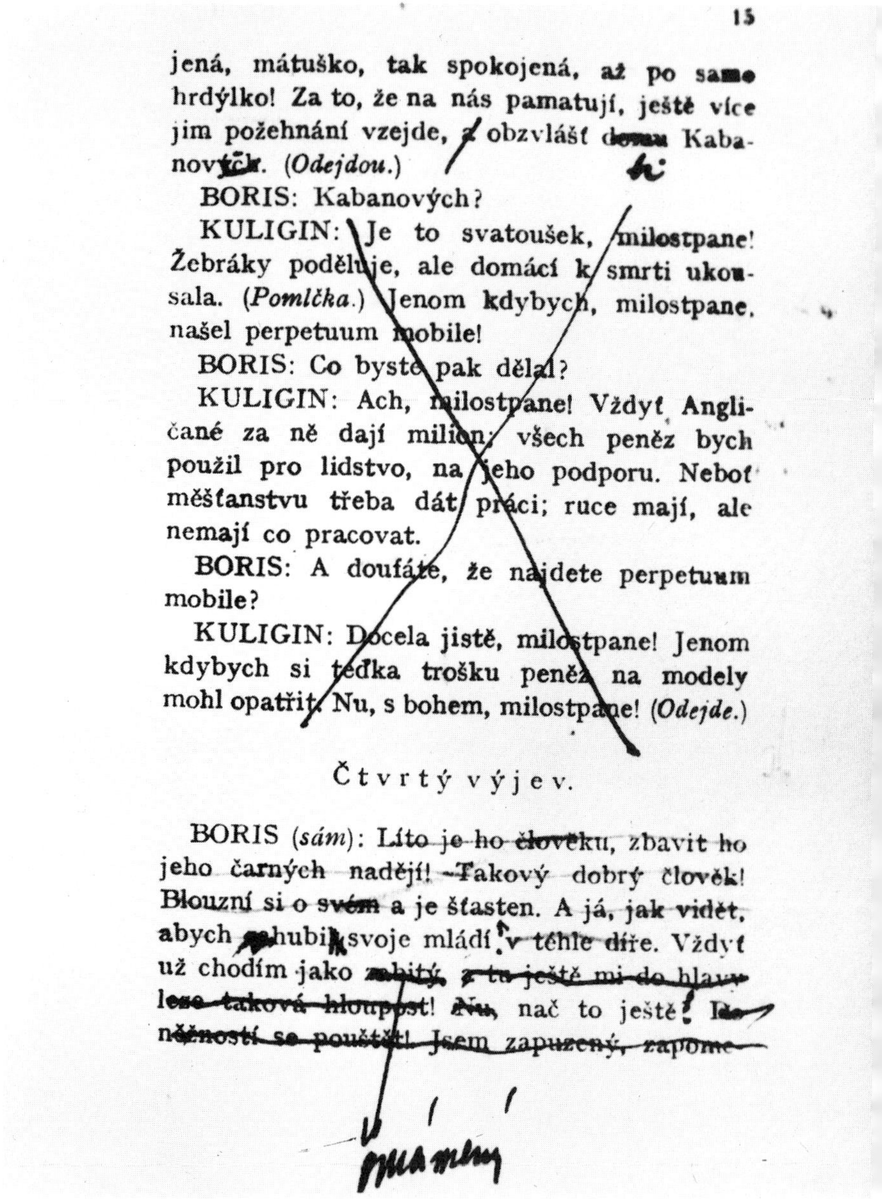

jená, mátuško, tak spokojená, až po samo
hrdýlko! Za to, že na nás pamatují, ještě více
jim požehnání vzejde, z obzvlášť domu Kaba-
nović. (*Odejdou.*)

BORIS: Kabanových?

KULIGIN: Je to svatoušek, milostpane!
Žebráky poděluje, ale domácí k smrti ukou-
sala. (*Pomlčka.*) Jenom kdybych, milostpane.
našel perpetuum mobile!

BORIS: Co byste pak dělal?

KULIGIN: Ach, milostpane! Vždyť Angli-
čané za ně dají milion; všech peněz bych
použil pro lidstvo, na jeho podporu. Neboť
měšťanstvu třeba dát práci; ruce mají, ale
nemají co pracovat.

BORIS: A doufáte, že najdete perpetuum
mobile?

KULIGIN: Docela jistě, milostpane! Jenom
kdybych si teďka trošku peněz na modely
mohl opatřit. Nu, s bohem, milostpane! (*Odejde.*)

Čtvrtý výjev.

BORIS (*sám*): Líto je ho člověku, zbavit ho
jeho čarných nadějí! Takový dobrý člověk!
Blouzní si o svém a je šťasten. A já, jak vidět,
abych zahubil svoje mládí v téhle díře. Vždyť
už chodím jako zabitý, a tu ještě mi do hlavy
lese takováhloupost! Nu, nač to ještě! Ja
něžností se pouštět! Jsem zapuzený, zapome-

Fig. 3 Janáček's annotations to his copy of Červinka's Czech translation
(1918) of Ostrovsky's *The Thunderstorm*, pp. 15–16. Note his excision of
much of p. 15, and his addition on p. 16 of lines for Kuligin (Kudrjáš) from

16

nuty člověk: a teď j~~sem ~~i~~j~~ještě vzpomněl zamilovat ~~se hloupý~~. A do koho! Do ženy, s n~~í, ani pohovořit si nikdy se mi nepodá~~. (*Pomlčka.*) A ~~přece jenom mi nejde z hlavy,~~ ~~a kdybych dělal co chtěl~~. Hle, tady je! Jde s mužem, nu, a tchyně s nimi! Nu, nejsem-li pak hlupák! Podívej se na ni ze za rohu, a běž si domů. (*Odejde. S protější strany vstoupí na scénu*: K a b a n o v á, K a b a n o v, K a- t ě r i n a a V a r v a r a.)

Pátý výjev.

K a b a n o v á, K a b a n o v, K a t ě r i n a, V a r v a r a.

KABANOVÁ: Chceš-li matky poslechnouti, tedy hnedle, jakmile tam půjdeš, udělej tak, jak jsem ti přikázala.

KABANOV: Nu, jak pak bych mohl vás neposlechnouti, maminko!

KABANOVÁ: Však za nynějších dob starší lidé velké vážnosti nepožívají.

VARVARA (*k sobě*): Bodejť, tebe si nebudou vážit!

KABANOV: Doufám, maminko, že jsem bez vasí vůle ani kroku neučinil.

KABANOVÁ: Věřila bych ti, příteli, kdybych vlastníma očima neviděla a na vlastní uši ne- slyšela, jakou teď mají děti úctu k rodičům!

p. 62 of the play to help turn Boris's monologue into a dialogue (see pp. 48–9) (Moravian Museum, Music History Division, Brno)

Together these two half-acts made up Janáček's Act 1 Scene 2. The remaining outer halves of Ostrovsky's Acts 1 and 2 became, respectively, Janáček's Act 1 Scene 1 and (with the addition of Ostrovsky's Act 3 Scene 1) Act 2 Scene 1.

Table 1. *Act divisions in the play and the opera*

Ostrovsky	Janáček
Act 1 (first half)	Act 1 Scene 1
Act 1 (second half) ⎫ Act 2 (first half) ⎬	Act 1 Scene 2
Act 2 (second half) ⎫ Act 3 Scene 1 ⎬	Act 2 Scene 1
Act 3 Scene 2	Act 2 Scene 2
Act 4	Act 3 Scene 1
Act 5	Act 3 Scene 2

The advantage of this arrangement is that each of the three acts of the opera contains one of the three main events: Tichon's departure (Act 1), Káťa's behaviour while he is away (Act 2) and the crisis when he returns (Act 3). Furthermore the second scene in each of Janáček's acts is the sequel to an event in the first scene. In Act 1 Scene 1 Kabanicha orders Tichon to go off on a business trip; we see him leave at the end of Act 1 Scene 2. In Act 2 Scene 1 Varvara gives Káťa the key that secures her assignation in Scene 2. Káťa's confession in Act 3 Scene 1 leads to her suicide in the next scene. The intervals between the acts represent actual passages of time – probably a few hours between Acts 1 and 2, two weeks between Acts 2 and 3. Ostrovsky had ten days between Acts 2 and 3, and 'ten days' remains in the words of Káťa's confession, VS 134–5. Some time also elapses between Ostrovsky's last two acts, i.e. between Káťa's confession and her suicide, but in Janáček's opera these events follow one another without a break, creating problems when Káťa describes to Boris how her family has behaved after her confession (see the exchange between Brod and Janáček on this, below).

Janáček's adaptation was skilful. A master of musical compression, he was fearless in reducing Ostrovsky's play to what he saw as its essentials, freely omitting subsidiary incidents and characters. For all his Russophilism, he ruthlessly expunged most of the distinctively Russian elements of the original (Fekluša was the chief casualty). He also omitted much of the atmospheric and ominous imagery of the original – which music, however, can easily take over. Ostrovsky, for instance, carefully introduced at the end of his Act 1 two omens which upset Káťa and foreshadow her ultimate fate: the appearance of a mad old lady, and the rumbling of thunder. In the family scene after the return from church, Ostrovsky had Tichon and his mother go off together, leaving Káťa and Varvara alone. It is here, in the open, that the story of Káťa's dreams and her excited state of mind emerge. Janáček appropriately transferred this intimate scene indoors (his Act 1 Scene 2), and was thus not able, whether or not he so wished, to incorporate its sequel, the appearance of the old lady, who in the play dramatically prophesies doom for Káťa:

> (*Enter the Lady, with a stick, followed by two footmen in three-cornered hats.*)
> *The Lady:* Well, my pretty ones? What are you doing here? Waiting for young men, for your partners? Are you merry, merry? Enjoying your beauty? Look down there (*she points to the Volga*), that's where beauty leads. Down there, down there, right to the depths! (*Varvara smiles.*) What are you laughing at? You mustn't enjoy yourselves. (*She thumps with her stick.*) You shall all burn in eternal fire. You shall all boil in unquenchable pitch (*going away*). Away down there, that's where beauty leads! (*She leaves.*)

While Janáček found a powerful musical equivalent for the prophecies of doom in the tense orchestral postlude to Act 1 Scene 2, the old lady's brief scene is so well integrated into the verbal imagery of the play that its absence causes problems. In Janáček the descriptions of the frescoes of Gehenna in Act 3 Scene 1 sound curiously out of place; in Ostrovsky they remind the audience of the old lady's prophecies, just as her reference to the Volga prepares the audience for Káťa's suicidal leap into it. Ostrovsky brought back the old lady at the height of the storm scene, again with the thunder, and both have such an effect on Káťa's already troubled state of mind that she blurts out her confession. Janáček confined the thunder (at least in the stage directions) to the storm scene, and omitted the old lady, though clearly with some regrets. In his letter to Červinka (31 March 1921) he wrote, 'I have compressed the mad old lady into the "evil woman" [zlá žena] with a few shouts.' Vogel (p. 269) confessed himself puzzled by this, but the answer can be seen in Janáček's sketches, and even in the first Czech edition of the libretto, where the 'Žena (z lidu)' ('woman from the crowd', see VS 128–9) was changed by Janáček to 'Zlá ženská' (a colloquial form of 'žena'). Janáček took the 'woman from the crowd' from Ostrovsky, but transferred her words (about not being able to escape one's fate) to the choral basses a few bars later, giving her the comment of the 'first man' on Káťa's being 'very frightened'. Even more significant are the interjections for male chorus which follow,

'Vida, krasavice' (VS 129) and 'Ej, krasavice' (VS 130). 'Krasavice' ('a beauty') is undoubtedly a survival of the old lady's second appearance at the height of the storm (which precipitates Káťa's confession). Her speech in Janáček's copy of the play contains two underlinings, both of passages referring to Káťa's beauty ('krása'). The choral interjections in this scene make so little impact that one wonders why Janáček bothered with them, unless it was somehow to compensate for the loss of the old lady.

The minor characters that did not disappear were changed out of all recognition, and the remnants of their parts can be puzzling to those not conversant with Ostrovsky's original. Fekluša, the story-telling pilgrim woman lodged at the Kabanovs', is reduced in the opera to a Kabanov servant, on a level with Glaša. While the enthu-siasm of Fekluša the pilgrim for the hospitality of her hosts is perfectly natural, that of Fekluša the servant, in one of the few lines left her, is distinctly odd. Janáček combined the parts of Kuligin and Kudrjáš (where they actually converse with one another, as in the opening scene, Janáček was obliged to bring in Glaša for the second person). In the play Kuligin is elderly. He is a local inventor, a self-taught watchmaker, interested in perpetual motion, sundials, light-ning conductors (which he tries to get Dikoj interested in) and social justice. His sympathetic nature leads both Boris and Tichon to con-fide in him. To Boris especially he has much to say on the wickedness of the townspeople, declaring that Boris will never get used to their harsh ways. In the last act Tichon comes to him with his troubles after Káťa's confession. It is Kuligin who hauls Káťa out of the Volga and presents her corpse to Tichon. Ostrovsky's Kudrjáš is a smaller figure; a young man, Dikoj's clerk, he is irreverent about his employer and enjoys provoking him. His main function is to provide a like-minded partner for the light-hearted Varvara.

Janáček's amalgamation of Kuligin and Kudrjáš came soon after he had written his first sketch version of the first scene. Here, as in Ostrovsky, it is Kuligin (bass) who describes the beauties of the Volga to the sceptical Kudrjáš (tenor), it is Kuligin who sees a man approaching whom Kudrjáš identifies as Dikoj (see frontispiece) and it is Kuligin who has a heart-to-heart talk with Boris. But when look-ing through his sketch Janáček began to conceive the idea of com-bining the two and many of the 'Kuligin's are crossed through, with 'Kudrjáš' written above, though the part remains in the bass clef.

The chief difficulty in combining Ostrovsky's Kuligin and Kudrjáš is that Kuligin is old, wise and kind, Kudrjáš young and brash. The

Kudrjáš (as the composite part was called) that emerges in the opera has to be young and personable enough to attract Varvara, sympathetic enough for Boris (though not Tichon) to confide in, and with some evidence of scientific interests (Janáček omitted the social ones). At the opening of the play it is Kuligin who admires the beauty of the Volga, and Kudrjáš who is sceptical. Janáček's Kudrjáš has to change sides and admire the Volga, to the scorn of Glaša. The sympathetic interest that Kudrjáš (Kuligin in the play) shows in Boris's predicament in this same opening scene hardly squares with Kudrjáš's somewhat threatening behaviour to Boris, even after Janáček's adjustments, when both find themselves awaiting assignations on the same spot. The earnest explanation of Kudrjáš (Kuligin in the play) to Dikoj about lightning conductors in Act 3 Scene 1 seems out of character with his flippant reply a few bars later to Dikoj's question about whether it has stopped raining. Since Janáček omitted most of the symbolic relevance of Ostrovsky's storm, this passage juxtaposing Dikoj's superstitious interpretation of a storm (God's wrath) and Kuligin/Kudrjáš's more prosaic one (electricity) loses its point, except perhaps as the sole evidence in the opera for Kudrjáš's declared occupation as 'teacher, chemist and engineer'. And even this is something of a muddle on Janáček's part. In the play Kuligin is said by his companion to be a 'chemist', but corrects this to 'an engineer, a self-taught engineer'. Janáček made the correction an addition to the original statement and added 'teacher' for good measure. (Polyakova observes moreover (p. 257 n. 12) that to Russian ears the name Kudrjáš sounds too folksy to be that of a teacher-intellectual.)

At the beginning of his Act 3 Janáček reduced his cast by taking over a conversation between a 'first man', a 'second man' and a 'woman' sheltering from the storm and distributed the parts among Kudrjáš and a male companion (cautious in literary invention, Janáček confusingly called the latter Kuligin). While waiting for the rain to stop they comment on the ruins in which they are sheltering, the knowledgeable 'second man' answering the questions of the less knowledgeable 'first man'. Since Janáček's Kudrjáš has acquired the scientific knowledge of Ostrovsky's Kuligin one would expect him to inherit the lines of the knowledgeable 'second man', but Janáček himself seems to have confused his Kudrjáš here. Apart from these inconsistencies a major difference of the composite Kudrjáš is that he lacks much of Kuligin's naive goodness of heart – one of the few positive elements in the play.

Janáček left the chief characters more intact, though simplified. Boris and Tichon retain their original characters in the opera, and the main difference in Varvara's part is in her description in the list of characters: a foster-child rather than (as in Ostrovsky) Kabanicha's real daughter and thus Tichon's sister. It is hard to find an explanation for this change (carefully marked in Janáček's copy of the play); perhaps he found her character too inconsistent with the rest of the Kabanov family for her to be a true blood-relation. The change moreover sets up a curious parallel with the earlier *Jenůfa* and its central relationship between the Kostelnička and her foster-daughter Jenůfa. Káťa, both through the music Janáček gives her and by his omission of some of her lines, becomes a meeker figure than in Ostrovsky. Janáček's Káťa does not, for instance, utter the words that Ostrovsky gives her in her Act 2 exchange with Varvara: 'Please God, of course it won't come to that, but if I get to hate the place too much no power on earth will stop me. I'll jump out of the window, throw myself into the Volga. If I don't want to live here, I won't, whatever they do to me.'

Kabanicha is likewise simplified in the opera. Janáček retained most of her references to 'good order' which provide the main key to her character. In the play, however, she seems to possess the glimmer of a grim sense of humour that does not survive the union with Janáček's music for her, except perhaps in her scene with Dikoj in Act 2. It is this scene (a late addition to the score) that contains Janáček's greatest liberty with Kabanicha's part (see David Pountney's comments in Chapter 8). In the opera Janáček makes Dikoj fall on his knees in front of Kabanicha. This may be merely to demonstrate how he fell on his knees before the peasant he had wronged in the scene he is describing, but in this context it is ambiguous: 'Vidíš, kam mne až srdce přivádí' ('See how far my heart is leading me'), he says as he kneels. Clearly Ostrovsky did not intend anything compromising here, for Fekluša was originally present for half the scene and it was to have ended with Kabanicha and Dikoj going off for supper, but Janáček brings down the curtain on the couple by themselves, with Dikoj on the floor. Despite Brod's efforts to tone this down (see below, letter of 25 October 1921) it can hardly be argued that Janáček's modifications depart from the spirit of Ostrovsky: a few lines later in the play Glaša comments that 'Dikoj ought to have married Kabanicha'.

One of Janáček's most striking additions was that of Dikoj at the end of the opera. That Janáček had decided on this change at an early date is evident in his copy of the play, where many times Kuligin's name is crossed out and Dikoj's inserted instead. Most forceful of all is Dikoj's appearance with Káťa's corpse. His 'Zde máte svou Katěrinu' ('Here's your Katěrina') is, apart from the first word, identical with Ostrovsky's words for Kuligin, who then continues: 'Do with her what you want. Her body is here, take it; but her soul is yours no longer. It stands before a Judge who will be more just than you.' Janáček's change (turning reproach into sarcasm), together with the omission of Tichon's last anguished cries over Káťa's body (leaving Kabanicha in sole command at the end), is most significant, since it unambiguously allots the final victory to the conservative and repressive forces – Kabanicha and Dikoj.

Janáček showed sound dramatic instincts by depicting on stage some of the incidents Ostrovsky only describes in the play. 'Why do they look at me like that', says Káťa in her anguished monologue in the final scene; Janáček brings on a drunk who looks her over before wandering off the stage (Janáček rather spoilt this later by changing 'divají' ('look') to 'chovají' ('behave'), VS 146). In the play we learn that Káťa has run away when Glaša comes on to tell the news to Tichon (who is pouring out his troubles to the sympathetic Kuligin); in the opera Janáček has both Tichon and Glaša looking for her, Glaša with a lantern and calling her name. In Ostrovsky we hear of Varvara's and Kudrjáš's elopement through Tichon; in Janáček we see them deciding to go. Káťa, hesitating over the key that will let her out to meet Boris, thinks she hears voices, panics and slips the key into her pocket. Janáček makes us hear the voices as well: Kabanicha is talking offstage to Dikoj (Janáček appropriated a few words from their next scene). Most characteristic of all is the offstage wordless chorus that is heard in the play by Káťa alone but in the opera by both Káťa and the audience during Káťa's final scene.

Though he never interfered with the play where the lines fitted his needs, Janáček was not afraid of rearranging sections, often to their advantage. In Ostrovsky, for instance, Káťa's final scene consists of two long monologues framing her farewell to Boris. Her lines about the birds that will fly over her grave and the flowers that will bloom there come at the begining of the second monologue and are some way off from her suicide. Janáček shifts most of the second monologue to precede Boris's appearance, leaving only the touching passage about the birds and the flowers, and it is in this peaceful frame of mind that his Káťa jumps to her death.

Another example of Janáček's skilled judgement, again significantly at the end of an act, is the rearrangement of incidents leading up to Tichon's departure. He cut most of Ostrovsky's opening scene for Glaša and Fekluša (leaving only a couple of lines about Tichon's departure) and all of the next scene between Varvara and Káťa. In Ostrovsky, Kabanicha and Tichon then arrive to join Káťa and Varvara. Kabanicha makes Tichon instruct Káťa how to behave during his absence (notably not to look at other men). Kabanicha leaves the couple to themselves, whereupon Káťa begs Tichon first not to go, then to take her with him, and finally to make her swear a 'terrible oath' not to speak to anyone in his absence. Tichon refuses all these requests. Kabanicha and Varvara rejoin them, there is a brief leave-taking, and Tichon goes off. The act does not end here, however, but continues with the substance of what became Janáček's next scene. Janáček rearranged this material by putting most of the Káťa – Tichon exchange *before* the arrival of Kabanicha. Whereas Káťa's request (in Ostrovsky) for a 'terrible oath' after Kabanicha has extracted a series of humiliating promises seems illogical, in Janáček's version Kabanicha's forcing her son to do what Káťa had previously asked for – and had been refused – comes as a stroke of deadly irony. The subsequent exchange between Káťa and Tichon, when they are left to themselves, is now reduced to the lines 'Are you angry with me?' 'No. Goodbye.', which vividly represent the breakdown of Káťa's marriage.

One small but intriguing change that Janáček made was to the folksong that Kudrjáš sings as he waits for Varvara (Act 2 Scene 2). The opera's song about a young man bringing gifts to an independent-minded young girl (who loves another) replaced Ostrovsky's more grisly song about a Don Cossack who is contemplating killing his wife. She senses his intention, and pleads 'Don't beat me to death in the evening! Let the children get off to sleep first!'. While it has been suggested that this is a folksong Ostrovsky collected, its ominous theme is yet another example of his carefully planned atmospheric imagery. Janáček set it as it stood (see Fig. 4), and copied the text into the libretto he wrote out after completing the score. But in the typescript copy made of the libretto the text of a replacement song was added on a separate sheet, bearing the annotation in Janáček's hand 'Text ruské nár. písně přeložil Bezruč' ('Text of a Russian folksong translated by Bezruč'); and in the Janáček Archive there are indeed several small sheets giving the Russian original ('Vo sadu li, v ogorode devitsa gulyala', from a well-known folksong collection)[1] and a translation both in draft and final version, with Janáček's

Fig. 4 Janáček's first version of the end of Act 2 Scene 1 (cf. VS 87 and VS 80 bars 18–19). Janáček contemplated an alternative ending to Káťa's scene with the key, with Kudrjáš's song heard offstage, from afar ('z dálky') before Káťa's final line 'Jen kdyby už byla noc' ('If only it were night'). Kudrjáš's song is given here in a primitive form (lacking the downward descent in bars 3–4 etc.), and with the original words (see p. 58). Later Janáček extended Act 2 Scene 1 by adding the small scene for Kabanicha and Dikoj and moved Kudrjáš's song to Act 2 Scene 2 (Moravian Museum, Music History Division, Brno)

emendations. The original Russian, and the fair copy of the translation, were written by Olga Vašková, a co-chairman of Janáček's Russian Circle and sister of the celebrated Czech poet Petr Bezruč, whose *Silesian Songs* had a few years earlier provided the words for three of Janáček's most powerful male-voice choruses, *Kantor Halfar*, *Maryčka Magdónova* and *The 70,000*.

The first part of the folksong exchange between Varvara and Kudrjáš ('Za vodou . . .', VS 93–4) comes straight from Ostrovsky, but the second verse,

Varvara: Nech jsem já i děvucha, to z izby temné.
Kudrjáš: To láska zrobila carevnu z tebe.

Varvara: Though I am just a simple girl from a poor dingy home.
Kudrjáš: But love had made a tsar's daughter of you.

comes from the same hand as the draft translation of the poem, in the metre of the preceding verse, noted on the same sheet. Janáček made a couple of small alterations: he split these lines (each repeated) between the couple (which necessitated changing the pronoun at the end) and ignored a further verse that had been provided. The folksongs at the end of the scene (VS 110–12) come from Ostrovsky.

Why did Janáček change the first song, replacing one he had already set? While the replacement song could be said to be more appropriate for Kudrjáš to sing while he waits for the light-hearted, independent Varvara, it is odd to see Janáček going to so much trouble over getting this replacement (which included ensuring that the translator fit his version to Janáček's existing music). The attribution of the translation to Bezruč was suggested as early as 1924 by Max Brod (see p. 207 n. 1), but was challenged by Bezruč himself in a letter to Jan Racek (10 December 1952)[2] flatly denying his involvement. However, Bezruč's memory at the age of eighty-five may not have served him well; Janáček himself ascribed the authorship to him in the typescript libretto, and this is supported by the similarity of his handwriting to that on the sheets, by the involvement of his sister (a convenient go-between), and, as Procházka suggests (p. 10), by the distinctive vocabulary of the verse.

Though he had read through the play and made cuts and annotations in his copy, Janáček did most of the adaptation while he wrote the music. He did not write out a separate libretto before he composed (he wrote one afterwards, for publication purposes) but instead kept his copy of the play in front of him as he worked, writing straight into full score.

As Janáček composed, so he changed the text slightly. Passages might be omitted from one version to the next, or some lines reinstated. But the text did not rest even there. Brod made his German translation in time for it to be printed in the Universal Edition vocal score together with the Czech text. Max Brod (1884–1968) had attracted Janáček's attention through his enthusiastic review of the Prague *Jenůfa*, and the composer had begged him to undertake the German translation of that opera. It was an excellent choice. A German resident of Prague, Brod knew Czech well (Janáček wrote to him in Czech, Brod replied in German); he was a friend of Kafka and a leading German novelist and critic of the time; and he was a perceptive musician and amateur composer of songs and chamber music. A sturdy friendship grew up between the two which, despite Janáček's occasional fiery outbursts, survived till his death. Brod wrote the first full-length biography of Janáček, to celebrate the composer's seventieth birthday in 1924 (the section on *Káťa Kabanová* is reprinted in Chapter 8), and translated all his major operas except *Brouček*. He took infinite pains over his task, sometimes to the extent of rather exceeding his brief. While translating Janáček's next opera, *The Cunning Little Vixen*, he decided that the admittedly loose text needed unifying, and produced what was in effect an adaptation rather than a translation. In *Káťa* we can see the beginnings of this. For example, he made several small changes to help the German audiences who, he assumed, were less familiar with a Russian milieu than the Czechs were. While his first translation, of *Jenůfa*, had been made for an opera already published in Czech and staged in Brno and Prague, in the case of *Káťa* there was still a little time for the thoughtful Brod to change Janáček's mind over details. Since they lived in different towns (Brod in Prague, Janáček in Brno) and managed most of their negotiations by post, their mutual correspondence provides a complete and vivid picture of this stage of the work. Almost all the relevant letters have survived, and are printed below.[3] Two of Janáček's (written between 25 October and 4 November 1921) have disappeared, but since they were clearly reactions to Brod's suggestions in his long letter of 25 October, it is easy to reconstruct them by looking at the score and other material to see whether and how those suggestions were carried out.

Janáček's reactions were always strong and decisive. In Act 1 Scene

1, for instance, he warmly accepted Brod's suggestions of more lines for Boris in his conversation with Kudrjáš, and rejected out of hand any shortening of the scene with Dikoj. Few of Brod's lines were adopted without some modification, though differences between them and the final version of the libretto would have arisen anyway because of the impromptu nature of Janáček's translations into Czech. There was no increase in the length of the opera, since Janáček invariably fitted the new lines over existing orchestral or even vocal lines. In the case of substitute lines suggested by Brod Janáček sometimes added Brod's new lines without deleting the old lines (sung by different characters) which they should have replaced. In this way two of the very few 'duet' passages in the opera (Boris over Fekluša in Act 1 Scene 1, Varvara over Kát'a and Boris in Act 2 Scene 2) were arrived at purely through Janáček's incorporating Brod's suggestions. This is particularly interesting since in his operas Janáček had moved strongly away from a convention that allowed duet texture to one that avoided it, a trend that is evident in his revisions to *Jenůfa* after the Brno première in 1904.

Another point of interest in these last-minute changes lies in Janáček's readiness to substitute new words for old while retaining the existing vocal line, despite the conflict with the implications of his speech-melody theory. Though in this case it could be argued that Janáček would have been inhibited from making extensive changes to the notes because the engraving of the vocal score had already reached an advanced stage, it can also be said that his practice here was quite consistent with many examples in other operas.

Brod to Janáček (*5 October 1921*)

Dear Mr Janáček,

I received your Kát'a K. yesterday and have set to work today. In all possible haste.

I'm puzzled by something on p. 21 [VS 15].[4] It reads:

A syllable is missing at * beneath the fourth C flat. What should I add here?[5]

I'll be leaving for Berlin on 11 October. I'll send whatever I've managed to finish by then directly to Director Hertzka[6] in Vienna. Is this all right with you? I'll be back from Berlin on the 17th (Monday).

Please come and visit me on that day. If possible, between 3 and 4 in the afternoon.

Enclosed: the introductory poem to my *Buch der Liebe* has just appeared in a very good Czech translation: 'Kdybyste znali cit' [If you knew the feeling].

With warmest regards
Your
Brod

5.10.[1921]

Janáček to Brod (6 October 1921)

Dear Friend,

Let's have all your works out in Czech as soon as possible!

The translation is fluent, uncontrived. It reads well, and works well.

Dikoj calls him a 'darmochleba'

Dar - mo - chle - ba!
[idle cadger!]

i.e. he eats bread free, without working, without deserving it.

[...]

On 16 October I'll be in Prague.

On 17 October my first lecture,[7] in the Conservatory hall, has been advertised for 4 p.m. So I won't be able to see you between 3 and 4. Perhaps somewhere that evening.

I hope that we can play K.K. through to Mr Ostrčil![8]

Come back in good health!

Your devoted
Leoš Janáček

NB I'm waiting to hear from Hertzka where you should send the manuscript. Whether directly to the printers, or to him.

Brod to Janáček (20 October 1921)

Dear Mr Janáček,

While translating I noticed the following:

p. 36, vocal score [VS 23]:

z *večerní* bohoslužby [from the evening service]

But the opening of the scene reads 'polední slunce' [midday sun]. Which is correct? Midday or evening?[9]

As soon as I have your reply Act 1, which is practically finished, will go off to Hertzka.

Best greetings
Your
Brod

[postmarked 20.10.1921]

Brod to Janáček (25 October 1921)

Prague, Tuesday [postmarked 25.10.1921]

Honoured master,

Here are my proposed changes:

Act 2 Scene 1

Evil as she is, Kabanicha shouldn't be hypocritical as well. She is *not* so in *Ostrovsky*, and thus remains a bit likeable after all, as a symbol of the old discipline and order *that she has voluntarily subjugated herself to*!

(a) The line 'Půjdu se modlit! Nevyrušujte mne' [I'm going off to pray. Don't disturb me!] is repulsive. I can't recommend strongly enough replacing these words with something else. (They are *not* in Ostrovsky either.)[10] I suggest adding to the words 'bylo by to slušnější' [it's only decent] something like: 'but nowadays there's nothing in the world but nonsense and confusion'. Compare *The Thunderstorm* on this point, p. 50:[11] 'to je ta pomatenost, lid je zmatený' [it's madness; the people are confused]. – p. 44, with Kabanicha's beautiful monologue 'A tohleto taky by chtělo žít po svojí vůli' [And they (young people) would also like to live in just the way they please]. – It's clear from this passage that my view of Kabanicha is correct. – Her morality is *honest* in intent; she is consistent!

(b) Vocal score, p. 15 [VS 78]: 'Vítá Dikoje' [She welcomes Dikoj]. – The word 'ostražitě' [vigilantly] should be cut.[12]

p. 16 [VS 78]. – I consider it very misguided to have Kabanicha lead

Dikoj away and then reappear. The audience will think they've been up to goodness knows what with one another. Besides, this coming and going of the two is completely *unmotivated*. – I suggest *either* leaving both on stage talking quietly to one another while Káťa sings, *or* postponing Dikoj's entrance to p. 20 [VS 80]. Then the line on p. 15 [VS 78] 'Přišel jsi s něčím' [You came for something] would be dropped, and Káťa's line 'Někdo přichází' [Someone's coming] would be a mere figment of her imagination resulting from her state of excitement, which indeed I find much better than the present clumsy motivation.

It's up to you which of these two possibilities I should choose.[13]
(c) At the end of this scene Kabanicha adds the line: 'Nemuč se' [Don't torture yourself] – 'Sit down here, I want to have a sensible talk with you, to comfort you – but don't forget your manners!' The curtain falls *slowly*.[14]
Scene 2
(d)   You were going to send me an addition to the song 'Donský Kozák' [The Don Cossack].[15]
(e) Bottom of p. 37, top of p. 38 [VS 91]: 'Kdo by to mohl být? Zamiloval jste se do někoho' [Who could it be? You've fallen in love with someone]. – This line will simply *not do* now that *Boris* has already confessed *everything* to *Kudrjáš* in Act 1. – I suggest having Kudrjáš say here: 'But I warned you! Are you two really so hopelessly in love?'[16] Then the dialogue can continue. – Next, p. 41 [VS 93]: 'To je tedy Kabanová?' 'Ano' 'Vida, vida' [It's the Kabanová woman then? Yes. Well, well!]. – This is superfluous since they have both known for a long time who's involved. – Here Kudrjáš should say: 'You're forgetting the sort of people you're living among. Boris: Ano [Yes]. [Kudrjáš:] Do be careful!'.[17]
(f) p. 63 [VS 107]. 'Co na tom – ze dvora vedou vrátka, která se zevnitř zavírají. Bude klepat, odejde. Ráno jí řeknu, že jsme tvrdě spaly.' [What of it? The gate from the courtyard locks on the inside. She'll knock, then go away. The next morning I'll tell her we slept heavily.] – Instead of these dull lines I suggest: 'Incidentally, her visitor is still there. Dikoj. Strange, those two old brutes, they quarrel with everyone and only get along with each other.'[18]
Act 3
(g) p. 43 [VS 140–1]. 'Utéci' [Escape] is repeated *four times*. Suggestion: 'Escape!' Varvara: 'But where?' Kudrjáš: 'To Petersburg' Varvara: 'Yes, to a new, merrier life!'.[19]
   p. 63 [VS 154]. 'Strýc mě vyhání' [My uncle is sending me away]. –

From here it should read: 'to a business contact in Jachta, far away near the Chinese border, in Siberia' (Ostrovsky's original p. 88!).[20]

Now, please send me the altered passages as soon as possible with corresponding *music* (*legible*, please) so that I can get on with the translation.

Devotedly yours
Brod

Brod to Janáček (4 November 1921)

Dear Mr Janáček,

I've received your two letters with emendations. – It was quite difficult to alter the folksongs since I had already finished translating them. But it worked out well in the end.

I'd like to mention a technical problem: I couldn't write the new text to Act 2 p. 32 [VS 87–8] into the score, but have simply enclosed it (with translation). Perhaps you should have this and the next page in the vocal score written out again!

As a whole there are still a great many errors in the vocal score. In particular ♭ ♯ ⌐3⌐ ⌐2⌐ and similar signs are very imprecise. For example, on p. 26 there are still many errors, although I myself corrected obvious slips throughout. The last act in particular is swarming with mistakes.

In several passages, as you will note, I have not translated word for word, but have made *slight* alterations to the text with German theatres in mind.

I have high hopes that this work will conquer the German stage. And to this end I have tried to emphasize the Russian setting more clearly, as it is more remote and indistinct to Germans than to Czechs. – Take p. 39 [VS 92], for instance: 'Here in your little town women are kept locked indoors', which I added from Ostrovsky's original since these words clarify the setting![21] – On p. 63 [VS 107] I added a trait to Kabanicha's character that is more interesting than the garden gate story from the preceding scene. I consider this way of characterizing Kabanicha a good one, as it meets the German public's need to understand her psychology more fully.[22]

On pp. 5, 7, 8 [VS 115–17] of the last act I've added a few things to make the Russian setting more precise.[23] I've also taken pains in the German to have the Russian words pronounced with their original syllabic stress (Russian accentuation), while the Czechs use a Czech accentuation. For example, p. 16 [VS 121], German: 'The poet

Der*schá*win' (Czech: '*Děržavín*').[24] – You will note similar changes in many other passages. I hope in this way to have helped your piece along the road to success in Germany.

On 22 October I sent Act 1 to Hertzka. Still no acknowledgement of receipt.

Now I'll send off Acts 2 and 3 with a request to acknowledge receipt.

[...]

> With warmest regards
> Your
> Brod

PS: When is K.K.'s first performance in Brno? As I want to make my arrangements in time please send a precise, definitive date soon! 4.XI.[1921]

Brod to Janáček (*9 December 1921*)

Honoured master,

A few remarks on Act 1 of Kát'a:

(1) I'm *disturbed* about the note in the list of characters 'mezi III. jednání a jeho proměnou uplynou dva dny' [Two days elapse during the scene-change in Act 3]. I think it would be more dramatic if this scene-change were to follow *immediately* after the first part of Act 3, with the time-lapse being no more than a couple of hours.

Should I translate it or leave it out? – naturally I will do just as you see fit.[25]

(2) I also enclose two pages from the vocal score as I think that you ought in fact to have Boris sing another short lyrical passage. An opportunity to do so is provided on *p. 24*, bar 6 (oboe entry). *Boris, at the same time as Fekluša*, could perhaps sing the following lines: 'Hubím svoje mládí! – I'm destroying my youth!' (repeated) 'I'm destroying my youth! Year after year I saw nothing around me but misery – happiness was always far, far away, like a glimmer on the horizon after sunset.'[26]

Fekluša doesn't actually have to sing anything here and would best begin at the top of p. 25: 'Jací lidé bohabojní, štědří, ti Kabanových' [What pious people they are, and generous, these Kabanovs!]. At which Boris starts up from his dream: 'Kabanových!'.

This, too, is merely a suggestion for you to consider; please feel free to reject it if it doesn't suit you. – I know from my *own* experience that an outsider always fancies changes much more readily than the author himself!

(3) On p. 24, penultimate line, I've moved the bass clef [Brod draws a bass clef here] one bar further along. Presumably that's correct?

(4) I would also suggest shortening the Boris–Dikoj scene. – 'Najdeš si práci, jenom chtít' [You would find work if you wanted to], delete to fig. 16, 'Kam se zvrtnu, všude tě potkám' [Wherever I turn I bump into you] etc. – I found this scene weak during the performance; perhaps, though, that was only the fault of the acting.[27]

(5) In the passage 'to také nic není?' [that doesn't amount to anything] (21 bars after fig. 39), why have you written two different pitches, E and G sharp? – For the separate requirements of the German text no deviations from the Czech version are necessary in *pitch*, merely in *rhythm*.[28]

After seeing to these matters I will send off the proofs to Hertzka.

Respectfully yours
Brod

[postmarked 9.12.1921]

Janáček to Brod (*undated, after 9 December 1921*)

Dear Friend,

[1.] In Act 3 Káťa replies to Boris's question: 'And what about your husband?'

Káťa: 'He beats me! Sometimes he's kind!' Is that the sort of man who already knows of Káťa's offence?

If so it would need *at least* those two days to elapse in the Act 3 scene-change.

Had Tichon been like that immediately he returned, not even knowing Káťa's offence, then the two days wouldn't be necessary and it could stand as I wrote it, i.e. Káťa does not return home after the storm; she runs out into the storm; the others look for her.

So put 'after some hours' instead of two days.

2. Now that addition of Boris's. You know, when a ripe apple has fallen from the tree – you wouldn't want it to go on growing?

But it must *sweeten*!

After you pointed it out I had a good idea.

Boris will sing together with Fekluša! From p. 24, bar 6 [. . .][29] The rest is the same. It will be good like that. So now please translate it!

G sharp^2 is tricky for a contralto; so I put E^2 to make it easier.

3. Thanks for the bass clef.

4. It's a shame there isn't *another* exchange between Dikoj and Boris! God forbid that I should shorten it!

Keep well!

Your

Leoš Janáček

NB The Prague National Theatre has accepted *Káťa Kabanová*. Ostrčil, the head, was very taken with it.

Even here it's getting known.

Wish me luck with *Liška Bystrouška*[30] as well!

[...]

NB 3. Please write that change, for Boris, into the libretto!

4 Synopsis: innocence and guilt in 'Káťa Kabanová'

WILFRID MELLERS

As one of the great originals, Janáček is oblivious of time and place. We would not expect him, superficially considered, to be so: for his work derives from a specific locality and agrarian tradition, while at the same time reflecting the nervous stresses under which we, as people of the twentieth century, are obliged to live. Spatially, he would seem to exist in a world that has vanished for ever, temporally in a moment that is still present and unformed. Yet somehow – and this somehow is a shorthand term for the mysterious alchemy of genius – the topical and local elements in Janáček's music interact to become universal. We find his music simply extraordinary, but know too that it is extraordinarily simple; this is why it makes an impact on sophisticated and unsophisticated alike.

Born in mid-nineteenth-century Moravia, Janáček acquired a late Romantic, Germanic technique in order to be able to discard it when his identity was manifest to him. He composed all his characteristic music in the last twenty years of his longish life, and in this music looked not to the 'civilization' of western Europe which Smetana had yearned for, but eastwards, exploiting those elements in Moravian folksong which rely more on additive than on divisive rhythms, and more on subtleties of melodic nuance than on extended harmonic and tonal development. He is a musical 'natural' in that each phrase is a bodily gesture – which of course carries psychological implications. This is evident in all Janáček's music, whether or not it is ostensibly dramatic. Consider a piano work like the Sonata *1.X.1905*. As its movement titles ('Presentiment', 'Death') suggest, it is not 'abstract' music, and it was provoked by a public event – the murder of a student during a political riot. This external occurrence, moreover, mirrors a private event – the death of Janáček's own adolescent daughter, fruit of his marriage to a beautiful child-bride who came to represent everything in bourgeois respectability that his creative imagination rebelled against. Such an equation between public destiny and private experience is crucially relevant to a theatre composer; and the techniques which Janáček explores in this work, though idiomatically effective in terms of the keyboard, are identical with the composer's vocal and instrumental writing in his operas. The piece opens with a broken, wavering cantilena, basically pentatonic, aspiring into progressively wider leaps; both the inflections of speech (which Janáček transcribed into his notebooks) and the gestures of arms and hands are inherent in it. It is shattered by a savagely disruptive descending figure which might be a noise of the external world, of Nature's elemental forces, impervious to human needs and desires; and the structure of the work is a fight between the human and the non-human, the scales being equally weighted. Though the conception is dualistic, like a classical sonata, Janáček's work does not achieve, or even seek, sonata's linear-harmonic resolution. If this in a sense makes him more 'primitive' than a classical composer, his primitivism is his strength, pertinent to us products of a hyper-self-conscious civilization: for although the human song is not resolved, neither is it obliterated; it retains its identity, gaining in pliancy from the assaults it is submitted to.

This takes us to the heart of Janáček's operatic experience, and his first theatrical masterpiece, *Jenůfa* (completed a couple of years before the piano work), which also concerns the relationship between the human and the natural worlds. Humanity just wins through, despite the bestialities of man to man since our post-lapsarian corruption. In a later opera, *The Cunning Little Vixen*, human fallibity matters less, for sin is absolved in Nature's fecundity. *Káťa Kabanová* – the central, most comprehensive and probably the greatest of Janáček's operas – stands between these extremes. Its Russian context enables Janáček to fuse his primitive pagan ritualism with his Christian sense of guilt, thereby creating an art immemorially ancient yet immediately contemporary. Káťa is the feminine principle incarnate: the human creature who would fulfil her nature in loving; and she is destroyed by Society, as personified by her monstrous mother-in-law and by Dikoj, a rich merchant whose material non-values are anti-human. She cannot leave the fustering, festering middle-class world she finds herself in, to embrace her love in 'pagan' intuitiveness; what prevents her is her Christian conscience, which makes her aware of a reality beyond the wanton vacuity of the young lovers, Varvara and Kudrjáš. So Káťa would seem to be related to Janáček's wife both as she might have been and as, transformed by her environment, she was; to the young daughter who died; to

Kamila Stösslová, the woman thirty-eight years Janáček's junior, for whom he nurtured a re-creative (but probably abortive) passion in his sixties and seventies; and even to himself, in so far as his belated surge of eroticism – previously stifled by childhood experience, by his apprentice years at the monastery, and by his weary war with academic and social convention – caused him agonies of guilt. Yet these subjective intensities, firing Janáček's imagination to archetypal expression, are objectified with total lucidity in his art. No opera more strikingly and tersely reveals the identity, essential to an operatic composer, of the private with the public life. Janáček's own story is implicit in *Káťa Kabanová*, which also renders incarnate an eternal human predicament.

Overture

The basic conflict is manifest in the overture, which is centred on a modal-flavoured B flat minor. A timpani rhythm (Ex. 11) suggests a fate oblivious of human aspirations, though they are latent in a chromatic phrase that yearns through, and wriggles around, a diminished third (Ex. 18). The 'fate' motif is metamorphosed into an

Ex. 18   VS 5

apparently jolly tune (Ex. 10) with a sleigh bell accompaniment which represents – though we cannot know this yet – the jingling of horses' harnesses. We can however recognize that the gaiety is hollow, for the symmetrically metred reiteration of the figure suggests the monotony of the Russian steppes and the tepidity of the domestic round to which Káťa is submitted. Eventually it will precipitate catastrophe, since the same figure accompanies the fateful departure of Káťa's husband, and is almost the last sound we hear after her death. Káťa's own theme, as presented in the overture (it recurs to accompany her first utterance in the opera, Ex. 1), is at first innocently pentatonic, delicately flowering in an ambiguous tonality between B flat minor

Ex. 19 VS 11

and its relative D flat major – a key often associated by Janáček with love fulfilled. In a dark D flat *minor* Káťa's spontaneously pentatonic loveliness merges into the broken chromatic motif of her (and everyman's) yearning (Ex. 19). So in instrumental microcosm the overture has presented the story's psychological core.

Act 1 Scene 1

A park on a steep bank of the Volga in the town of Kalinovo in the 1860s. Distant view into the countryside. On the right the Kabanovs' house. Benches on the pathway. Shrubs. Afternoon sun (see Figs. 6a–b, 9).

The first scene carries us into the 'real' world within which the inner drama – Káťa's and Janáček's and ours – will be enacted. It opens, significantly enough, with gossip. Two minor characters, Kudrjáš and Glaša, converse in the afternoon sun on the bank of the Volga. The opera is set in the 1860s but the brief parlando phrases of the two singers sound like heightened everyday speech and therefore set the opera naturalistically in the present, however mundane. Since speech-rhythms and speech-melodies are, with bodily movements, a vital source of Janáček's musical idiom, there is no barrier between the everyday world and the heights and depths of passion which human creatures may hopefully and painfully attain to. There is an anticipatory hint of this even in these perfunctory exchanges; for only after Kudrjáš has referred wonderingly to the beautiful view over the river Volga – by and in which the opera is to end – do the two proceed to chatter about their neighbours.

They spot the merchant Dikoj, arriving in angry petulance with his nephew Boris (Fig. 6c) and grumbling vociferously about his layabout habits. After Glaša and Dikoj have gone we learn from Kudrjáš's conversation with Boris that sordid financial transactions are involved, whereby Boris is in thrall to his rich uncle. Boris also confirms Kudrjáš's suspicion that he has fallen in love: with a married woman, Boris adds – Káťa Kabanová, married to Tichon, who is dominated by his virago of a mother, the widowed Kabanicha. When these three enter, returning from the religious-social propriety of church, with the young foundling Varvara (Kudrjáš's girlfriend), Kabanicha harries her cringing son, simultaneously abusing him for his declining affection for her and for his failure to 'make it' as businessman or husband; her jealousy of her daughter-in-law seems to be well-nigh clinical. Kabanicha's melodic lines move brusquely, with aggressive leaps, though harmonically her music tends to whole-tone instability, for if she is Action, she acts only to a destructive end. The young lovers, Varvara and Kudrjáš, when they meet in Act 2, sing in a simple, folk-like idiom, being will-less and in that sense innocent, vegetative in their sensuality. Yet they too drift into whole-tone harmonies, for although they represent a criticism of the bourgeois world in which Tichon, his mother and, vicariously, Káťa exist, they are too childish to confront Kabanicha's dominating will.

She negatively, they positively, act to no end, and in a sense co-operate in catastrophe, since it is at Varvara's bidding that Káťa yields to the promptings of the flesh, though unable to face their consequences. 'Peasant' passivity and aggressive will-power are not, individually or together, an adequate basis for the flowering of humanity; and the essence of the tragedy lies in the fact that it is Káťa alone, in this pettily degenerating world, who rises to 'the pain of consciousness'; and is destroyed precisely because she has the capacity to be human – to feel and think, to know and love. Even in this first scene, the purpose of which is to convey information and to depict the tedium of a money-grubbing society, the growth of love, which is human reality, is marvellously revealed in the gradual metamorphoses of Káťa's motifs. Though the phrases of her entrance music remain brief and basically pentatonic, their tonal meanderings (rather than modulations) become increasingly wayward, suggesting a straining at the leash, until melodic contours proliferate in a declining lyrical phrase, which aspires through a sixth in C flat major; droops to C major; and wonderingly expands in D (Ex. 12).

Such lyricism is abruptly banished by the snarling, angular-lined Kabanicha, who accuses Káťa of talking soppily and out of turn. After she has stumped off, Varvara blames Tichon for his timid inability to defend Káťa from his mother's gratuitous insults. He slinks off too – to drown his misery in drink, Varvara suspects. The young girl expresses love and pity for Káťa, in a tender pentatonic phrase once more oscillating between B flat minor and D flat major. The diminished thirds expand savagely to fourths in the orchestral postlude; fade into the D flat melody; but disperse on an ambiguously tritonal chord on B flat (VS 36). The F flat of the tritone provides an enharmonic link to the E-centred music of the next scene, a link destroyed by Janáček when he subsequently extended the music here to allow more time for the scene-change.

Act 1 Scene 2

A room in the Kabanov house. Doors right and middle; an alcove on the left (see Figs. 8*a*, 8*c*).

Káťa and Varvara are sitting sewing while exquisite bird music quivers in thirds on violins and flutes over a pedal E. The 'bird music' is a reference to Káťa's words 'proč lidé nelétají tak jako ptáci nelétají?' ('why don't people fly like birds?'). Communing with herself rather than with Varvara, Káťa regrets her divided nature and confesses to dreams of flying. Her hazy phrases, at first in a mixolydian E major, still over the pedal note, float and flitter as gracefully as birds (Ex. 20; Fig. 8*b*). Addressing Varvara now, she remarks that as a young girl she had been as simply sensuous, yet as pure, as these birds; pleasure in the visible and tactile world was an experience related to, and as exalting as, the love of God (she used to love going to church, she says, where she saw wonderful visions). Then, her flying birds were also angels; now, she seems to have some notion of their sexual implications. Since her marriage her dreams and visions have changed to nightmares and, though the birds are still present, agitatedly chittering in the orchestra, her music is undermined by wholetone ambiguities similar to those that so often accompany Kabanicha's violence and the young lovers' pastoral simplicities in Act 2. The point is profound, for it indicates that Káťa will be destroyed by the very forces to which, in her growth towards consciousness, she seems superior. Trying to be honest with herself rather than with Varvara, she finds that her joy in natural affection conflicts with her Christian conscience and her inbred respect for social convention. Her embryonic love-music in the first scene had told us that she sought love with every fibre of her being; if she cannot after all love Tichon it is because he, obliterated by his mother, has no notion of what either Káťa or love is like. She *can* love Boris, who is capable of response; but since their love must be 'guilty' her pentatonic music, at first veering towards D flat major, is increasingly tortured by

Ex. 20   VS 38

[Káťa: Do you know what I've just thought of?
 Varvara: What?
 Káťa: Why don't people fly?
 Varvara: I don't know what you're talking about.
 Káťa: I mean why don't people fly like birds?]

Ex. 21   VS 49

[[as if the devil were whispering to me] such unclean things]

Ex. 22   VS 52

angular leaps (Ex. 21). When Varvara encourages Káťa to conquer
her shame and at least meet Boris she protests hysterically in enharmonically related triads (Ex. 22).

Almost immediately her husband enters, to say goodbye before
he departs on a long business trip. As the 'fate' motif hammers its

rising fourth in the lower reaches of the orchestra, Káťa tries to hold her own against it by appealing to Tichon either to stay with her or to take her with him (VS 54–5). Her entreaties arch in warmly, even amorously, arpeggiated contours, in or around D flat; his fumbling incomprehension and embarrassment are manifest in spasmodically bleating phrases, riddled with tritones. Later, the climax of the scene radiantly extends Káťa's love-music (Ex. 33): she genuinely wishes it were for Tichon while knowing in her heart that it is for Boris. Even if Tichon had been its goal, however, he could not have been man enough to accept it; when she implores him to demand of her a vow of fidelity (VS 59), he sheepishly splutters that such talk is 'sinful'. Any hope of comprehension is shattered by the appearance of Kabanicha, chivvying Tichon off to the waiting horses (Ex. 10 and VS 62). She bullies her reluctant offspring into demanding promises of good behaviour from his wife during his absence; he stutters them out, the more shamefacedly because he had not been able to accede to Káťa's comparable request. He is his mother's tool and, with no voice of his own, echoes her whole-tone unease (Ex. 9). As she hustles her son out to the horses the hammer motif of fate is heard in the bass against its hysterically accelerated transformation into the sleigh bell theme (VS 68). She forces him to kneel before her, releasing a flood of thematic reminiscence from the scene a few minutes earlier where, through him, she had dictated her terms of good behaviour to Káťa (VS 69, cf. Ex. 9). Under the relentless semitonic clash of Ex. 16 these themes combine in a vivid climax. The key, at Tichon's fateful departure, is Janáček's darkest and deathliest A flat minor.

Act 2 Scene 1

The Kabanov house: a cosy alcove for working in, with doors at the back. Doors right. Late afternoon, the room almost dark.

Káťa and Varvara are again sewing, in the unwelcome company of Kabanicha (see Fig. 7). That the situation repeats itself emphasizes the tedious inevitability of provincial life, the more so because Kabanicha is still grumbling, upbraiding Káťa for not mourning Tichon's departure more ostentatiously. Night-noises in alternate thirds and fourths form a background to Káťa's longing – to which she instinctively capitulates when, Kabanicha having taken herself off, Varvara unfolds her plan for a secret assignation between Káťa and Boris. Though Káťa does not verbally agree to it, she pockets the key to the garden which Varvara offers her, at first pretending to herself that she does so only in consternation at the sound of approaching voices. But she soon admits that she is fully compliant, indeed desperately eager, paradoxically deploring her Varvara-like will-lessness while knowing in her heart that the key to the garden might, were she strong enough, be a key to paradise – a word which, in its derivation from the Old Persian *pairidáeza*, literally means an enclosed park or garden. Ironically, the interrupting voices are those of Kabanicha and Dikoj, who reveal themselves as a pretty pair, not merely because Kabanicha is described in the list of characters as 'a rich merchant's widow'. Dikoj is drunk, fuddled because, having manhandled a peasant debtor, he found himself on his knees begging forgiveness. Masochistically he asks Kabanicha to give him a thorough dressing-down (no one in the town is so expert at that as she) for his idiot vacillation and tipsy, literally weak-kneed generosity. His tattered phrases are as directionless as his inebriation. Grotesquely, the scene ends with Dikoj on his knees to Kabanicha, parodying the scenes wherein she has demanded subservience from the members of her family, and anticipating Káťa's own abysmal obeisance. The episode suggests that a corrupt society is inseparable from a perverted will, though which is chicken and which egg remains an open question. The energy of Kabanicha's music, contrasted with the flabbiness of Dikoj's, would seem to indicate that in Janáček's view evil is a force in itself rather than a product of social contingencies: Kabanicha's black will subdues Dikoj's oafish greed, and he and his kind subdue the community. In any case the moral dubieties in the two halves of this scene – Káťa's capitulation to passion and Dikoj's to miasmic self-indulgence – complement one another ironically. The latter shames a society, the former shames an individual who, but for that society, might have recognized in her shame a gateway to the truth.

There is a further irony in that Kabanicha's final imprecations are in the love-key of D flat, which at the curtain oscillates again between major and minor in enharmonically ambiguous thirds and fourths. These night-noises are now sinister, pierced by a tenebrous trombone; the final triad is a grisly D flat minor, wide-spaced. As in Act 1 Janáček later added an orchestral interlude to cover the scene-change. Here, however, apart from the close, the musical material owes nothing thematically to the previous scene and is instead a spirited if repetitive little march.

Act 2 Scene 2

A steep overgrown bank. Above, the Kabanovs' garden fence and gate. A path leads down the slope. A summer night.

The orchestral introduction encapsulates Káťa's divided state: a

Ex. 23   VS 97

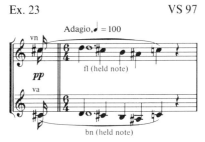

tense six-note fragment, ending in a diminished third (Ex. 23) and
thereby related to the slow introduction to the overture, expresses
Káťa's agonized indecision, but is soon interrupted by lyrical
passages (melodically derived from it, however), first in A flat major,
then G flat, in which her love-song seems resolved. In a sense it is so,
for her choice had been made when she accepted the key to the
garden. This is subtly indicated when her mode of 'consciousness' is
juxtaposed with Kudrjáš's peasant simplicity and unthinking ani-
mality. At the beginning of this next scene he is waiting for his young
love Varvara in the garden on the banks of the Volga. To while away
time he sings to the accompaniment of his guitar a Cossack song
which is metrically simple and non-modulating. Yet the facts that the
words play somewhat cynically with the theme of love and money,
and that the key is a blackly modal minor of the love-key D flat, hint
that humanity cannot, if it is to evade disaster, remain for ever as
unconscious as the birds. The self-rotating tune, like a stylus stuck in
a record groove, irritatingly denies growth; and it is interesting that as
Boris joins Kudrjáš, somewhat tremulously waiting for *his* love, the
thinly scored, tentative music gradually incorporates those uneasy
diminished thirds. When Varvara joins them peasant innocence
momentarily comes into its own again. Her tenderly symmetrical
fourth- and fifth-founded theme significantly remains constant
throughout, unlike the motifs of Káťa and Boris. It is positive in its
own way, exquisitely scored in peasant-band sonorities (Ex. 14), and
to its strains the young people go off to make love in the summer
night. But of course such child-like bliss would not be enough for
Káťa, who has arrived, late and trembling, for her assignation. Both
lovers are at first stricken with silence; when they can utter it is not in
the care-free, care-less pentatonicism of Varvara and Kudrjáš. Their
love-song grows, in tentative timidity, from a metamorphosis of
those diminished thirds.

They attain, however, an ecstasy proportionate to their pain: for although Káťa is at first horrified by Boris's 'sinful' approach, she ultimately admits to a condition of will-lessness which in her case may flower into transcendant exaltation. Melodies are pentatonically spontaneous yet are spaciously open rather than, like Varvara's pentatonics, self-enclosed. Tonal transitions, rather than modulations, are free, blithely initiated by the themes' leaping sixths and sevenths; ostinatos stabilize and enrich the texture. Having attained G flat major (VS 101, Maestoso), the music has no need of 'development' but blissfully floats between A flat major and E major – really the flat submediant, F flat, a relationship of sensuous passivity beloved by Schubert. Though this passionate music overrides consciousness, it can do so only because Káťa has 'grown up' – and momentarily enables Boris to grow up with her, for he sings her kind of music, rather than his own. Janáček interlaces this adult-love scene with recollections of the instinctive love-music of Varvara and Kudrjáš, who are fulfilling their simpler passion in another part of the garden. Their lower level of experience seems to prevail, for Káťa, guilt-racked, steals away as the watchman records the advent of a new day. Kudrjáš sings Varvara's childishly sweet symmetrical song in alternation with her as they too leave the garden, though Varvara, unlike Káťa, has no fear of the prying eye of Kabanicha, because she is either sleeping like a log or cavorting with the loutish Dikoj. The epilogue to the act, however, leaves us with the aftermath of Káťa's transcendent passion, for the D flat major of the young lovers' song changes to minor and then swings to E major (again enharmonically identical with F flat). The adult *fortissimo* love-cry subsides; then aspires upwards from the darker reaches of solo bassoon and cello; and finally floats into Káťa's motive of indecision, teetering frailly through its diminished third on high flutes and violins (Ex. 29). No opera has a more poignant curtain to a climactic act.

Act 3 Scene 1

A ruined building with colonnades and vaulted ceilings; around it grass and bushes. Through the arches a view of the Volga and its bank. Towards evening a fortnight later; overcast with rain (see Fig. 5*a*).

The last act begins with a storm which, like most operatic tempests, projects the psychic turmoil the characters are undergoing. Yet in a manner characteristic of Janáček this storm is positive in effect. Since storms are forces of Nature they cannot be, like Kabanicha, humanly malignant: so this storm's figuration is flickeringly pentatonic, vigor-

Fig. 5a Prague 1922: Act 3 Scene 1. The ruins – a solid structure, with pictures of hell (discussed by Kudrjáš and Kuligin at the opening of the scene) painted on the walls

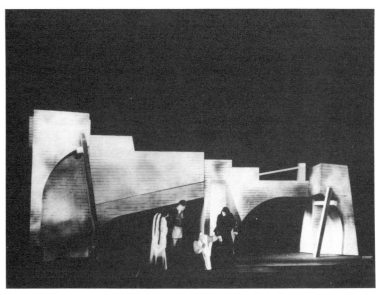

Fig. 5b Prague 1938: Act 3 Scene 1. Káťa's confession is heard in this production by a surprisingly tiny group. Muzika's ruins – a bridge rather than a chapel – are in a fine state of repair; the depiction of hell is sacrificed in the severe stylization, with only crosses to suggest Christian imagery

Fig. 5c London 1973: Act 3 Scene 1. Kátʼa's confession is heard by a large group (cf. Fig. 5b), with Kudrjáš and Varvara to the left, Boris by the back wall, Tichon bending over Kátʼa, and Kabanicha and Dikoj to the right. Back projections (not visible here) were used to suggest the ruins with huge frescoes of hell (photograph Donald Southern)

ous but not in the least scary – and in A flat *major*, again oscillating to E (F flat) major. Kudrjáš, Kuligin and Dikoj meet in a ruined building, presumably once a church, for the walls are decorated with faded murals depicting people falling, or being pitched, into the jaws of hell – which Káťa, who has just entered the gates of heaven, now thinks she is destined for. Kudrjáš, being young, unselfconscious, unaware of damnation, proffers scientific explanations for thunder and lightning and discusses the utility of lightning conductors, all in rapid, emotionally uninvolved parlando. Dikoj, middle-aged, rich, ignorant, stupid and, like his coeval and co-evil Kabanicha, permanently petulant, is prey to superstitious dread; for, being grossly material, dedicated only to money, food and drink, he of course pays lip-service to 'religious' sanctions that would preserve the status quo. Consistently enough he accuses Kudrjáš – in lines loosely emotive if not exactly involved – of blasphemy.

Momentarily the storm abates, and the stage is left empty. Varvara enters distraught, searching for Boris to tell him that Tichon has returned, Kabanicha is more than a little suspicious, and Káťa near breaking-point. The scene beautifully indicates how with Janáček 'natural' forces and psychological tensions tend to be interrelated if not, since the Fall, identified. During the dialogue between Kudrjáš and Dikoj tempest figures electrically flicker in multiple rhythms – fives against fours against threes – through the scrawny orchestral texture; after Varvara's entry they are metamorphosed into an interior nervous frenzy, intensified when Káťa herself rushes in, followed soon after by Dikoj, Kabanicha and Tichon. Refusing social solidarity (Kudrjáš's crass if well-meant suggestion that she might relieve distress by joining him in a song), refusing too religious consolation (Varvara's unconvinced and unconvincing invitation to participate in prayer), Káťa desperately falls on her knees – emulating timid Tichon and doltish Dikoj – and confesses that she has sinned before God and everyone in breaking her oath, and has spent every night with Boris during her husband's absence (see Figs. 5*b–c*). Her obeisance is a failure of nerve but one for which, given the circumstances, she is blameless; though she alone has the wellspring of life within her, she could not fight alone against social oppression and religious repression too strong for anyone. This is her tragedy; and *Káťa Kabanová* is that comparatively rare phenomenon, a genuinely tragic opera. In this situation, love fulfilled is equivalent to disaster – an irrefutably logical if ultimate irony manifest as the 'fate' motif pounds furiously, timpani growl, quintuplets hammer frenetically against the 6/4 pulse,

Ex. 24

while the still innocently pentatonic storm whirls in a key that is basically love's D flat major, if intermittently minor-tainted (Ex. 24).

Act 3 Scene 2

A lonely spot on the bank of the Volga. Dusk turning to night.

Tichon and Glaša are searching for Káťa with the fitful help of lanterns – now that her light of the body and spirit is well-nigh extinguished. In neutral, drained recitative Tichon says that he does not approve of Kabanicha's brisk injunction that Káťa should be buried alive; he still loves her and wants her back. Varvara and Kudrjáš, flitting along the river bank, tell one another and us that, harried beyond endurance by Kabanicha's persecution of them as well as Káťa, they intend to elope to Moscow. The episode does not offer much hope that the younger generation, having escaped the toils of degenerate social conformity and of the paranoia that creates it, will be able to grow to a Káťa-like consciousness without succumbing to her tragic fate, for their dialogue is fleetingly whispered in music unchanged from its original pristine innocence. When the young lovers have gone Káťa slowly enters, seeking Boris. Her love-theme is chromatically distorted, in heart-rending dialogue with oboe and viola d'amore – an instrument dear to Janáček, and closely associated with Káťa as with Kamila Stösslová (see Chapter 7). The diminished third wriggles potently in the tail-piece, suggesting a sob, a catch in

[I have thrown away my honour]

the throat, a wringing of hands: as always with Janáček, psychic tension finds corporeal outlet (Ex. 25).

Her lone monologue is disturbed phantasmagorically by Kuligin singing from across the river; by a passing drunk who lasciviously glowers at her; and by the mysterious night-noises of a wordless chorus which may be the voice of conscience or 'voices of the Volga' – in a pentatonic E flat minor lacerated by Káťa's phrygian F flats (Ex. 15). The figuration of the lurching 6/4 rhythm vacillates hypnotically, then gathers substance as Boris, hearing her cry, rushes to meet her. This second and final embrace becomes uninhibited, surging in phrases that, though nobly lyrical, consistently derive from speech-inflection and from bodily gesture. The protracted obsession with E flat minor is broken; pulsating triplets carry the lovers enharmonically through several keys, and the arrival at G flat conveys a sense of consummation. Káťa and Boris sing, as at the height of their previous love-scene, in octave unison (Ex. 26).

The liberation, and also the ambiguity, of tonality is evident in the odd notation of the orchestral postlude to that magnificent peroration. The double face of freedom is inherent in the equivocations: for Káťa release is bliss, yet also an abnegation; happy, she is lost. Given the conditions of her temporal world, her natural instinct for love is doomed. The only course for her is a return to Nature, and, in a literal sense, a renewal in the unknowable waters.

She makes this clear to Boris after her transport of passion has subsided. The cruelties of her mother-in-law and of her (now drink-crazed) husband have become in fact the surreal nightmares she had dreamed of. Only when she, and perhaps Boris, have left the world of depraved men and women will the little birds sing again; from the

Ex. 26   VS 151–2

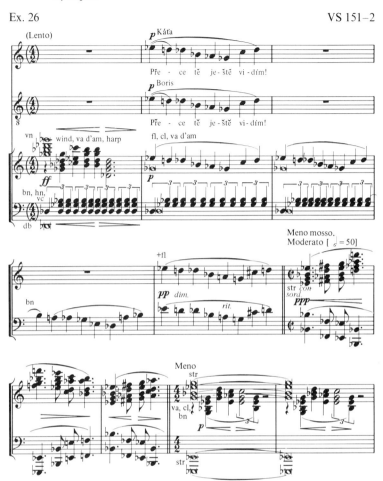

[I see you once again after all]

quintuplets of the tempest itself (VS 136) a bird motif is dreamily refashioned, with the familiar diminished thirds sounding lost, rather than anguished (Ex. 27).

Though the return of the bird motif tells us that Nature is eternal and life survives, the distant voices of the Volga, rocking hypnotically between fourth, fifth and sixth in the darkest A flat minor, sound forlorn, while Káťa's lament droops in whole-tone instability – which itself indicates that Kabanicha will have the last dismal word. Human consiousness is defeated. Káťa throws herself into the river; and

Ex. 27   VS 157

[Wait, wait, what did I want to tell you ... my head is in a whirl...]

Nature welcomes her with an exquisite A flat major twittering of birds! So, dying, Káťa returns to Nature in a key that had been associated with life and love and the oblivious tempest. As the crowd gathers on the river bank, however, human pettiness and depravity once more take over. Tichon belatedly attempts a puny rebellion, accusing his mother of murdering Káťa. Kabanicha, if startled, is hardly alarmed, and promises to sort him out at home. It is Dikoj, money-grubbing merchant of a moribund society, who carries in Káťa's corpse – appropriately enough, since it is his world that has destroyed her. Still more appropriately, it is Kabanicha – the perverted will behind the machinations of society – who pronounces the epilogue, bowing in obscene benediction as she thanks the people for their 'kind services'. Returning to the initial B flat minor, the opera concludes with a frantic jingling of the sleigh bells and an irremediable thumping of fate. The tawdriness of the tinkling harness is perhaps the ultimately ironic point: it may be boredom and triviality that, in such a world, undermine resistance to evil.

Though the opera ends in the stark, dark 'Russian' key of B flat minor and offers no palliatives to despair, its effect is far from depressive. The reason is that we have experienced, through Kát'a's music, what it means, or could mean, to be human. She is not obviously heroic; she is a young girl, more sinned against than sinning, yet so alive in her imaginative being, as made expressive in her music, that she can 'stand for' mankind – especially, of course, for Janáček, and for you and me. In a sense she is the only character in the opera, not merely because her role is extensive, but because the others are foils to her reality: Varvara and Kudrjáš are archetypes of a pre-conscious state, Kabanicha and Dikoj archetypes of (as it were) post-conscious, 'fallen' malignancy and stupidity. Even Boris has no identity apart from that which Kát'a's love lends him. When we first hear of him he is victimized by Dikoj's cupidity; at the end of the opera he does not follow Kát'a to death and Nature but returns, possibly a shade wiser, to the everyday world. Nonetheless, that he responds to her at all, and learns to sing her kind of music, suggests that love, as incarnate in Kát'a, may be a regenerative force and that another world, wherein love is fulfilled and man and Nature are at one in life rather than death, may yet be discovered, or rather created, beyond the horizon. I don't think it is fortuitous – if I may introduce a personal note – that after the grim curtain to the last act I still find echoing in my mind the conclusion to Act 2, that miraculous moment wherein Kát'a's recently consummated love is recalled. Though the last few bars dissipate in alternating major and minor and the quaveringly diminished third, the final orchestral sound is a resonantly spaced E major triad – which in the Baroque period and after was traditionally the key of heaven! The innocence of Act 1's mixolydian birds is now experienced as fulfilled; after the Fall Eden could and may be reborn.

This prompts a reference to Janáček's only ostensibly religious work of his maturity, the Glagolitic Mass, one of his last major compositions. Unlike the opera it is not overtly concerned with sin, conscience and guilt, and is non-mystical, perhaps even non-Christian. An affirmation of God's creativity and of man's potentiality, it evokes a ritual more pantheistic than ecclesiastical, the Gloria ('Slava') being for the most part primitive pattern-making, a ceremonial shout of joy. When in the Credo ('Věruju') man seeks to assert his belief he does so dramatically, in obsessively repeated questioning chords of the thirteenth, trembling on the verge of knowledge. The story of Christ's pilgrimage on earth and his death is told in purely operatic terms, physically realized in aural 'gestures'; and the chorus's yells to God that he should have pity on us are minatory rather than implorative. But if Janáček's 'mankind' is here not shamed, as is Káťa, he/she is certainly in need of compassion; and the 'misereres' of the Agnus Dei ('Agneče Božij') startlingly recall, and in the orchestral postlude directly quote, the end of Act 2 of *Káťa Kabanová*. Weirdly scored bitonal undulations between the major and minor third, expressing precisely the same longing for peace as do Káťa's heaven-aspiring flutes and violins by precisely the same technical means, come to rest on an infinitely remote, infinitely tender A flat major triad – which is brusquely swept aside by the fantastic organ solo, growing cumulatively wilder until it ends, *prestissimo*, in Janáček's deathly black A flat minor. If this is religious experience, so is the conclusion of *Káťa*'s second act. As in the Mass, so in the opera we glimpse a vision and are then remorselessly buffeted back to life's realities, nasty, brutish and short. The reason why *Káťa Kabanová* leaves us exalted is also the reason why Janáček, after the terror of the organ solo, can round off his Mass with a gloriously non-modulating, pentatonically present-celebrating procession, blazing with trumpets and drums, to bring us out of the church into the sun, the rain, the wind and the earth, which is our temporal home. No composer believed more unequivocally in life, however dubious he may have been about man's morality, God's goodness, and the inequities of fate.

5 Composition and the Brno and Prague premières: letters and reviews

COMPILED BY JOHN TYRRELL

From Jiřikovský's Reminiscences of Janáček

Jenůfa with Jeritza [singing the name part] conquered Vienna and the desire grew in Janáček to write a new stage work. He was looking for a subject. He came to me and told me about his plans. I drew his attention to a number of interesting subjects from poems and plays which in my opinion might be suitable, among them Hviezdoslav's poem *The Forester's Wife*, Ogrizović's *Hasanginica* and Ostrovsky's *The Thunderstorm*. Janáček at once acquired the books. After a while he returned. Ostrovsky had caught his imagination. He saw in *The Thunderstorm* a raw earthiness which suited his purposes [. . .] And he had been taken so strongly with the Ostrovsky that he talked about it with complete certainty, although he still had his doubts about a few character traits, and about some situations. He debated these in a highly partial manner, and I felt that in these doubts his process of creation had already begun. He talked about the characters of Ostrovsky's play with such seriousness, and with such interest in their fates, that the apparent faults of these characters were only childish slips in his eyes, slips which had already given rise to the dramatic conflict of Janáček's *Káťa*.

I was delighted that I had drawn Janáček to *The Thunderstorm* and had understood his creative needs. In order to reinforce his decision I had *The Thunderstorm* put on in the theatre on 29 March 1919, produced by Auerswald. The performance, which went very well, completed Janáček's creative preparation, and he began to sketch *Káťa Kabanová*.[1]

Janáček to Procházka[2] (5 November 1919)

I'd like to have the rights to the Czech translation of Ostrovsky's *The Thunderstorm*.

Who represents Mr Vinc. Červinka, the writer and editor at the *Národní listy*? He's said to be in America.[3]

Could you not find out in the Syndicate [of Czech and Slovak Writers] whom he has entrusted his affairs to. He is the translator.

Procházka to Janáček (9 November 1919)

Editor Vincenc Červinka is on the way home now; I've just had a postcard from him. So be patient for a little while. He didn't entrust anyone with his affairs. Červinka wrote to me that he will certainly be home by Christmas.

Červinka to Janáček (31 December 1919)

I am very pleased that you are devoting some attention to Ostrovsky, in my opinion the greatest Russian dramatist.

I give my permission most willingly for the use of my translation of *The Thunderstorm*, and were it to be performed on stage I would ask for a 2% royalty.[4] If with my modest knowledge of Russian conditions and surroundings I can be of any assistance to you do understand that I will always be willingly at your service.

Janáček to Kamila Stösslová[5] (9 January 1920)

I have begun writing a new opera.[6] The chief character in it is a woman, with a gentle nature. She disappears when one merely thinks of her; a breeze would waft her away – let alone the storm which bursts upon her.

Janáček to Červinka[7] (10 January 1920)

Should I need any explanations, naturally I will turn to you. I saw the Volga and its life in Nizhni Novgorod.[8] Even General Inspector Machar[9] rates Ostrovsky's work highly. It contains much that is touching, soft (in the Slav manner); what depth of feeling! If only I can find the right expression, just as deep!

Janáček to Kamila Stösslová (23 February 1920)

I'm working happily and industriously on my new opera.

I tell myself all the time that the main character, a young woman, is of such a soft nature that I'm frightened that if the sun shone fully on her it would melt her, yes even dissolve her.

You know, such a soft, good nature.

Janáček to Kamila Stösslová (17 December 1920)

I was in Prague on Tuesday, but I was hardly there before I came back again. I learnt enough in that space between one and four o'clock.[10]

Perhaps I could again invite you to a new première. You didn't want to go from Písek to Prague; what about Písek to London?

You look on with those black eyes of yours!

It's about my new opera *The Thunderstorm*, but I am going to call it *Katěrina*.

If everything that I have heard about were to come true I would go mad with pleasure, if I were anyone else. I will wait and you must also keep your curiosity on edge.

Janáček to Kamila Stösslová (6 March 1921)

After unusually hard work I have finished my latest opera. I don't know whether to call it *The Thunderstorm* or *Katěrina*. Against *The Thunderstorm* is the argument that another opera of that name already exists; against *Katěrina* that I write nothing but 'female' operas. *Jenůfa – Katěrina*. The best thing, instead of a title, would be to have three asterisks

* *
*

This is the opera which ought to be given in London.

Janáček to Červinka (31 March 1921)

I have finished the opera. The trouble is what to call it. There are already several *Thunderstorms* in music and opera. So that name is not a good idea. Furthermore this natural phenomenon is not the mainspring of the action; it is Katěrina who carries the psychological interest. Director Schmoranz[11] pointed out to me that the title *Katěrina* might be taken to refer to Catherine II ['the Great']. He suggested the name *Káťa*. Both Boris and Tichon call her that. I'd be inclined then to call it this. What do you think about it?

For musical reasons it was of course necessary to shorten much of the 'talking'. Also to concentrate the action on fewer characters. Mr Machar had already drawn my attention to this. Many of the characters were just 'stuck on' to the action. Of course they are merely Russian background figures. 'Kuligin–Kudrjáš' is a single character in my version. I have compressed the mad old lady into the 'evil woman' with a few shouts.

I worked on it eagerly and quickly. The full score is now being copied; Prof. Veselý[12] will make a piano score before the end of the holidays. The head of the opera Mr Ostrčil and the director Schmoranz know about the work. So nothing remains except for people to like it.

Červinka to Janáček (3 April 1921)

I completely agree with you that the name of your new opera composed on Ostrovsky's *The Thunderstorm*, to which I am already keenly looking forward, will have to be differentiated from all earlier *Thunderstorms*. This occurred to me myself some time ago, and your renaming it as *Káťa* would perhaps be the happiest solution. *Káťa Kabanová* might possibly be a little broader. Everyone who had at least a passing acquaintance with Russian plays would then realize at once that it was on a subject taken from Ostrovsky – for it is a famous name in the Russian theatre. Years ago I read in a Russian journal that (on an approximate guess) Ostrovsky's *Thunderstorm* had been played at least three thousand times in European Russia alone! Likewise in literary handbooks, journals, biographical dictionaries of leading Russian actors, the role is usually given as 'Káťa Kabanová' and that of Tichon's mother (also very important) as 'Kabanov's mother, or Kabanicha'.

But otherwise certainly do whatever you think best. The brevity of the title is also important. The subtitle of the opera, the theatre posters and the programmes will definitely mention that the opera is composed after Ostrovsky's tragedy, so the thing will be clear.

The shortening of the action and amalgamating of two characters into one will, in my opinion – though it is not for me to decide – contribute to the compression of the action and the increased force of the tragic climax. I am already such a Russophile and so much in love with the masterpieces of Russian literature, chiefly the earlier ones, that I cannot but greatly welcome your use of Russian material and a plot with such universal human relevance which is nevertheless imprinted with the gloomy fate of feudal Russia.

Nebuška[13] to Janáček (12 April 1921)

We would like news about how far the piano score of *Jekatěrina*[14] has got so that we can arrange to print it in time.
Janáček's draft letter on reverse side:
The full score of *Káťa Kabanová* (the name Jekatěrina would suggest Jek. II [Catherine the Great]) is being copied at present. It will be in the hands of Mr Veselý in the first week in May.

Neumann[15] to Janáček (26 April 1921)

May I ask that we be allowed your opera *Káťa Kabanová* for its first performance.

It is very important to me that the latest work of our leading Moravian composer also be given its première in Moravia.

Janáček to Ostrčil[16] (*2 May 1921*)

News has reached the papers that I have finished *Káťa Kabanová*.

Immediately a letter arrived from Neumann, head of the local National Theatre, asking me to give them this new work for next season.

Today he came to me personally.

I told him that I also want to give *Káťa Kabanová* to the Prague National Theatre.

But after experiences with *Brouček*[17] it isn't all that tempting! To announce a performance four times, and four times not to give it, is evidence of strange goings-on.

I mentioned my work to the director, Schmoranz; but his only reaction was a reminiscence of an excellent stage performance (of Ostrovsky's *The Thunderstorm*).

Ostrčil to Janáček (*5 May 1921*)

Please don't be angry with me about *Brouček*. The last postponement really was because of illness [. . .] What you write of strange goings-on is certainly true. But please don't blame me for it. You know what sort of spirit rules in the theatre as far as modern Czech works are concerned; it has lasted a whole twenty years and won't, unfortunately, change overnight [. . .] As for *Káťa Kabanová* I am happy that you will give it to the Prague National Theatre as well. You mustn't be surprised that Schmoranz was not able to react to your reference to the work other than as a man of the theatre.

As for me, I hadn't, during my stay in Brno, taken the opera to be finished, and thus I didn't ask much about it. I know it is unpleasant for a composer to talk about a work not yet completely finished.

Now of course I take it your opera is completely finished, and so ask you to send us the full score as soon as possible, and possibly the piano score – I believe that Roman Veselý is working on it. You know my attitude to your work and I need not reassure you that it will be an honour and a pleasure for me to study your new composition.

Janáček to Ostrčil (*7 May 1921*)

You were upset by my letter? Don't take it badly. I know that there was illness among the soloists – I only go by the outcome – work put off for so many months. I don't look for the reasons.

Even the remark about *Káťa Kabanová* came into my pen when I compared the flexibility of German advisers and agents with ours.

You can't sell a pig in a poke – and I don't even want to sell it like that.

Janáček to Kamila Stösslová (23 May 1921)

Káťa Kabanová, that latest opera of mine, is going to be given in Brno, and perhaps in Prague. But I don't have much stomach for the Prague theatre [. . .]

What can I say about myself? You know I dream up a world for myself, I bring to life in my compositions a world of my own good people, just as I wish. All invented happiness.

Real happiness shines on you at least sometimes. But on me? When I finish a work – even this dear *Káťa Kabanová* – I'm sad about it. As if I were parting with someone dear to me.

Janáček to Kamila Stösslová (18 August 1921)

I've had work enough. I've been cleaning up the score of *Káťa Kabanová*.

Yesterday the conductors from the theatre were at my house; the work was played, and was liked. I shall see.

Perhaps you would rather be at the première in Brno. It will be here at the beginning of November.

Janáček to Ostrčil (22 August 1921, from Hukvaldy)

Soon I'll bring the score of *Káťa Kabanová*, as soon as they finish writing the piano score in Brno.

Ostrčil to Janáček (27 August 1921)

Thank you so much for your card from Hukvaldy; I look forward greatly to the score of *Káťa Kabanová*.

Janáček to Kamila Stösslová (11 September 1921)

I'll be in Prague on Friday. I'll see what I can do with my *Káťa*.

Ostrčil to Janáček (20 September 1921)

I have looked through both text and score of your new opera *Káťa Kabanová*. Unfortunately I have not received the vocal score from Dr Brod; he says that it's in Vienna with Universal Edition and he will send it to me as soon as they return it. I can't therefore give you my definitive judgement, since I have not been able to study the full score

in detail in such a short time. It is essential that I play through the
piano score for myself in detail, so I ask for your indulgence. Besides I
hope that we shall soon hear the work in Brno. Can the full score stay
here, or do you want it returned for the time being?

Janáček to Kamila Stösslová (*29 October 1921*)

Come to the Brno première; everything promises that it will be
beautiful. And you know, when I became acquainted with you in
Luhačovice during the war and saw for the first time how a woman
can love her husband – I remember your tears – that was the reason
why I turned to *Káťa Kabanová* and composed it.

I invite you, then, now that the work is complete.

Brno National Theatre to Janáček (*12 November 1921*)

At your request we have discussed the set for the second scene of your
new opera with the producer Vladimír Marek and the chief designer
Vladimír Hrska and we were told that there are only twenty seconds
for the scene-change, in which time it is impossible to arrange the
room other than with a so-called backdrop. The same thing happens
in Act 2. Nevertheless we have given new instructions and have had
additional sets painted which in all our opinions should wholly satisfy
you.

As far as the symmetry of the furniture is concerned, against which
you spoke out, Mr Marek will do everything possible given to the
time available. We are convinced that you will be pleased with these
new arrangements.

Max Brod on the première[18]

To assess it correctly you would have to ask Brno theatrical buffs who
could compare it with other Brno successes. The general opinion is
that the success of *Káťa Kabanová* was unprecedented. After only Act
1 the audience was not content merely to recall the performers more
than ten times to the stage. 'Author! Author!' thundered again and
again as the curtains parted. Until Janáček himself appeared with
that touchingly courteous smile of his on his great kind face. When he
bowed it seemed that he murmered some unheard words, for his lips
moved. It was uncommonly moving to see this youthfully vigorous
old man on the stage which still reverberated with the magical sounds
of his passion. This scene repeated itself and intensified after every
act. I have heard that the temperature of theatrical enthusiasm in

Brno is a few degrees lower than in Prague. Well then, on this occasion it was really a Prague temperature in Brno.

Helfert[19] *in* Moravské noviny (*25 November 1921*)

The character of Janáček's music is here basically the same as that of his recent works. Vital, wild, united by a rush of musical ideas, a powerful and unstoppable dynamic current, at the same time almost aphoristic melodic invention, always sharply and suddenly spurting up from a warm source. Musical characterization sharply defined with rough, strong traits. It is instructive how with his music Janáček has been able to master the central dramatic issue. He sets most store by a lively, vital *dynamic* current, which unites this sharp seething and his musical thoughts, as they chase one another. It is with this method in the first act that he has been able to create a musico-dramatic whole of such power that the impression is quite unforgettable. Káťa's ecstasy, her confession to Varvara, it all surges forward inexorably towards her request to be made to take an oath. Into this moment, which itself has so much stirring tragedy, Janáček manages to insert the climax of the act, leaving an impression of a whole created somehow in one breath. After the second act, which with its lyricism demands some respite and calm, the musico-dramatic dynamic rises again in Act 3, towards the catastrophe. What a pity that after that riveting gradation of the first act, this final act does not go higher. I think the main reason is that the wild dynamic of the musico-dramatic current cannot be increased, and not at all that the dramatic situation of Káťa's broken spirit would not allow it. Gradation in this direction would not be possible; but it would be possible another way. That very catastrophe – Káťa's public confession and redemption from her sin by her own death – makes possible a musical development of the cartharsis of Káťa's soul. The music could continue saying what cannot be said in words, expressing that wordless sympathy with an unhappy person dogged by her own enormous love, that sympathy and love for others of which perhaps only a Slavonic soul is capable. But Káťa's catastrophe is solved too much on the surface: Janáček illustrates her last words too much, whereas the specacator, filled with the tragedy of this unhappy being, would prefer to hear the tones of Káťa's soul. Thus it is that, after the first act, this scene carries no climax. It is the result of Janáček's tendency towards realism.

Lyricism is the basis from which the work's other dramatic values grow. Here also one feels most how Janáček moves directly from the heart. And this side of Janáček's music makes up to a large extent what we still lack. It remains almost unprecedented that a composer of Janáček's age still has such great creative powers, so much temperament, explosiveness, and so much ardent passion. Yes, this music is full of ardent passion. Whenever someone sings about love, about desire, the music is almost smothered with the flood of feeling. There is something deeply elemental in these places, and one feels how Janáček has created something *truthful* with his music, always true to himself, uncompromising. You might say that those ardent places are not phrases: such music is written with the heart's blood. And to those pages you can only pay homage. The last meeting of Káťa and Boris before the catastrophe is one of the great lyrical scenes.

In the succession of Janáček's works *Káťa Kabanová* is without doubt the culmination; it shows new sides to the composer. Also the fact that the repetition of words we find in *Jenůfa* has fallen away and that the text is set in its natural expressiveness contributes to the dramatic concision of the work, which belongs to one of the most remarkable of our operatic literature.

The performance[20] of the work was once again a fine achievement by our local theatre. It is not an easy work. Janáček's individual style, his unusual orchestration, abrupt tempos, and the difficulties piled on the human voice, all this sets the operatic team considerable tasks. It overcame them honourably, largely to the credit of the musical director, Mr František Neumann, whose hard work and artistic ability were again displayed to the full. The première, though threatened by the indisposition of two soloists, went smoothly. The title role, entrusted to Mrs Veselá, was admirable and fully committed. Also Mr Zavřel's Boris was excellently sung. Mrs Hladíková found appropriately harsh, hard tones and movements for Kabanicha, though sometimes perhaps she exaggerated, for instance in the scene with Dikoj, or at the end of the opera. Perhaps the production was responsible for this. In the other roles Miss Pustinská acquitted herself well; she made Varvara into a simple girl, peering with curiosity into the world, and was able to support her part with a pleasant voice. Mr Kaulfus, as Dikoj, created one of his most successful roles. The première was a happy event and for our theatre meant a new and well-deserved success, which must certainly give satisfaction and serve as an inspiration to further work for Czech opera at a particularly difficult and unfavourable time.

Černušák[21] *in* Lidové noviny (*25 November 1921*)

Káťa Kabanová is not the bearer of a dramatic idea, forcing the spectator to experience a dramatic conflict within himself, but a poor creature with whom one can only feel deep human sympathy. And this is the key to Janáček's music.

'I am sorry for her', Janáček could have written as a motto for *Káťa Kabanová*, and in fact he says this in the opening mournful bars, in which, for the first time, the ominous motif of fateful catastrophe thunders threateningly.

[...]

Janáček's music is in many places crushingly effective, and yet one feels that the source of this effectiveness is not a cold-blooded search for effect, realized by the perfect mastery of a composer's trade, but the result of an iron will and the burning feeling of a musically self-made man.

[...]

In the episodes, into which everything falls which does not directly concern Káťa, Janáček is a master of detailed genre painting, as for example in the scene between Dikoj and old Kabanicha, which has the striking expressiveness of portraits by Holbein the Elder, or in the delightful scene of Varvara and Kudrjáš, full of light-heartedness and fun. Janáček's return to effective vocal melody is more and more evident in *Káťa*, especially in the lyrical scenes. It is not of course a melody of regular periodic construction, but is still a line of pure music, not growing out of the stylization of spoken speech, which remains the expressive medium of the dramatic portions.

[...]

It is natural that a work with such an effective subject and so accessible in its artistic expression should have a great success, increased further by the firmly rooted respect for Janáček's life's work. An honourable part of this success however belongs to the Brno Theatre. It gave its best forces to the work and raised the level of its musical performance to a point we would like it always to maintain. This applies especially to the excellent performance of the orchestral part, which conceals so many and various difficulties, and the creator of the extensive central title role, Mrs Veselá ... It is evident that this all-round success could be achieved only by the performance of a conductor as aware of the special character of the work, as persevering, experienced and enthusiastic as is the musical director František Neumann.

Janáček to Neumann (*27 November 1921*)

Dear Friend

We come together once again during an artistic event – without comment – just like water and lightning.

The performance of *Káťa Kabanová* was one of these meetings.
It seems that the times of Smetana are being reborn in Brno.
Should I thank you, the orchestra, the singers?
We are certainly glad that we have all grown into our parts, on our own ground.
We can all honour one another, and like each other!
To you and all those involved in the performance of *Káťa Kabanová.*

Devotedly
Leoš Janáček

Ostrčil to Janáček (28 November 1921)

May I congratulate you heartily on the great success of *Káťa Kabanová.* I much regret that I wasn't able to attend the première since I was conducting [Fibich's] *Bride of Messina* that day in Prague. Also the next performances coincide with rehearsals for the concert of the Orchestral Society, but as soon as I have a free evening *I will definitely come.*

Ostrčil to Janáček (5 December 1921)

I'm coming to *Káťa Kabanová* on Thursday.
I'm much looking forward to your new work and to seeing you.

Janáček to Kamila Stösslová (14 December 1921)

I have had a decided success with *Káťa Kabanová.*
Olomouc, Ljubljana and Prague have all taken it.
Reichenberger[22] of the Vienna Staatsoper is coming to have a look at it.
And the *Diary [of One Who Disappeared]* with that gypsy girl is also popular!

Ostrčil to Janáček (24 December 1921)

I have reported to the administration about *Káťa Kabanová* and announced that we will put it on as soon as Universal sends us the material. I also said that they must draw up a contract directly with you. I advise you, dear Master, not to forget on the contract to determine a *deadline for its performance.* In the present circumstances this is very important. Of course don't tell anyone that this advice comes from me.

Janáček to Kamila Stösslová (9 January 1922)

Since the parts for *Káťa Kabanová* are being printed and will not be ready for a while the Prague première won't take place till the autumn.

Kamila Stösslová to Janáček (13 January 1922)

If you want to be nice send me a score of *Káťa Kabanová*. And I would like to ask you to write something in it for me, so that I or my children would have something from you as a keepsake.

Janáček to Kamila Stösslová (10 February 1922)

About now they should finish printing the vocal score of *Káťa Kabanová*. I'll send you a copy; after all I had you much in mind during *Káťa Kabanová*.

Janáček to Kamila Stösslová (25 February 1922)

So here's your *Káťa Kabanová*. During the writing of the opera I needed to know a great measureless love. Tears ran down your cheeks when you remembered your husband in those beautiful days in Luhačovice. It touched me. And it was your image I always placed on *Káťa Kabanová* when I was writing it.

Ostrčil to Janáček (1 March 1922)

Thank you for kindly sending the piano score of *Káťa Kabanová*; may I suggest the following cast.[23] Dikoj – Mr Huml, Boris – Mr Jeník, Kabanicha – Mrs Rejholcová, Tichov [sic] – Mr Wuršer, Kateřina [sic] – Miss Petanová, Kudrjáš – Mr Hruška, Varvara – Miss Šlechtová, Kuligin – Mr Soběský, Gláša [sic], Fekluša – Miss Crhová, Miss Letnianská, Woman – Miss Brodecká.

Kindly tell me if you agree with this, or if your wishes vary in any respect. Apart from this could you let me know if we can buy the piano scores here from Hudební Matice, or whether we must take them with the other material from Universal Edition.

Janáček to Ostrčil (3 March 1922)

I have just one fear about the casting of Kabanicha – as regards her acting.

Good, true-to-life, natural acting has a beneficial effect all around, on the others taking part.

Weak acting, all the worse.

From the acting point of view Mrs Horvátová[24] would be more suitable.

But you know both of them better. Decide for yourself.

As for vocal scores I don't know what contract the Umělecká Beseda has with Universal Edition. It would be safer to ask Universal.

Janáček to Kamila Stösslová (14 March 1922)

Can't you even say thank you for *Káťa*?

Kamila Stösslová to Janáček (16 March 1922)

Yesterday I travelled to Cmund [Gmünd] to meet my husband as he couldn't get home but wanted to have the post, so I went and he left again straight away. While I was sitting in the train I found the card I had sent you when I received *Káťa Kabanová*, so I had left it in a pocket, and I came across it only that evening. So you must please forgive me.

Because really I am so often fed up with the whole world. I was so fed up that I couldn't write to you, or say anything to my husband as my train was going back and if I hadn't caught it I would have had to wait there till late at night.

He will go mad with his business [...]

So forgive my carelessness and accept my thanks today.

I'd like to see it.

Perhaps it is my fate.

Best not to think of anything.

Janáček to Ostrčil (21 September 1922)

Universal Edition tell me that they have sent you the printed score of *Káťa Kabanová*.

The musical director Neumann also said that they sent you the orchestral material.

Can I draw your attention to the fact that the printed score departs in many places from the written score in the Brno production. It is the printed score that is authentic!

I am curious how you will design the work. It's not easy.

In Brno it turned out coarsely and in bad taste, not even in the period 1840–60.[25]

Ostrčil to Janáček (23 September 1922)

It goes without saying that we will do our utmost with the *Káťa* designs in order to satisfy you. If you have any special requirements please let me know.

Janáček to Ostrčil (*26* September 1922)

I think that the parts will soon be ready.

They had my corrections six or seven weeks ago!

Nevertheless it would be good to compare the written Brno parts with the printed score and insert whatever is necessary into the parts. There is something in the trombones and in the second violins (Acts 2 and 3).

Neumann wanted to have it done.

When the soloists know their parts I'd like to hear them at the piano – on account of the tempos. The metronome is like a milestone: it shows distance; we can pass it any way we like.

Ostrčil to Janáček (*17 October 1922*)

Káťa Kabanová is at the stage of ensemble piano rehearsals and orchestral correcting rehearsals. I'm happy to tell you that not only I but the soloists involved are delighted with the work.

[...]

P.S. In addition to Mrs Veselá I have cast Mrs Ungrová as Káťa; the role will suit her excellently both as a singer and as an actress.

Janáček to Ostrčil (*24 October 1922*)

I'm going to be in Prague on Sunday evening, Monday and Tuesday (29, 30, 31 October).

I have a [folk] song [commission] meeting.

On Tuesday I could come to see you at the theatre.

Will you be having a rehearsal of *K.K.*?

Janáček to Ostrčil (*2 November 1922*)

I was pleased with your real understanding of *Káťa Kabanová*.

You yourself found the right, faster tempos for Kudrjáš's songs.

The rest good to the last little point.

From what I heard in the orchestral rehearsals it is necessary to take that passage with the sleigh bells at fig. 3 [Ex. 10] a shade faster. It's a bit difficult for the flute, but it comes off.

Would you be kind enough to have both clarinets write in, the bar before fig. 6 (Act 1) [VS 8] this passage from the violas [see Ex. 28a], thus for B flat clarinet [see Ex. 28b].[26]

I didn't hear this – it is therefore necessary to double it.

Ex. 28a

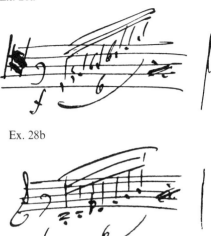

Ex. 28b

I think you will be rehearsing again on Monday and Tuesday; so I'll come and listen.

But I know for sure that the work is safe in your hands.

I'm looking forward to it and am not nervous!

Janáček to Kamila Stösslová (2 November 1922)

Neither sight nor sound of you!

The Prague première of *Káťa Kabanová* will be around 19 November. So in a fortnight!

So get ready to come with your husband.

Kamila Stösslová to Janáček (6 November 1922)

But as for the première, it isn't possible for me to go anywhere. My husband went on his travels for a whole month. I thought that it would be around Christmas, and in that case it would have worked, but now it's impossible for me. We'll leave it until it reaches Plzeň. I don't even have the time to write more.

Janáček to Ostrčil (17 November 1922)

Please tell me in good time when the last rehearsals will be.

I want very much to hear the effect of those harmonics on the second violins (Act 3, full score from p. 78) [VS 107ff].

[On back of envelope:] NB Act 2, not Act 3.

Ostrčil to Janáček (*18 November 1922*)

Allow me to inform you that the last rehearsals for *Káťa Kabanová* are set for Tuesday, Thursday and Friday – 21, 23 and 24 – the première then on Sunday 26 November, so long as we don't have to change these plans since the sets from Vienna[27] are not yet with us. In that case I will let you know of any change.

Ostrčil to Janáček (*20 November 1922*)

I have to tell you that the première of *Káťa Kabanová* must be postponed because the sets have not yet arrived. The Thursday rehearsal this week will thus be cancelled; the next will be on Friday.

Janáček to Kamila Stösslová (*29 November 1922*)

I have my première tomorrow; it will be magnificently staged. – What a pity that you aren't here.

Borecký[28] *in* Národní politika (*2 December 1922*)

If the original text is brief, economical, almost grudging with each word, Janáček made it even shorter; his condensing five acts into three is not in itself decisive, for this still leaves six scenes, but he compresses the dialogue still further. In this way some scenes have come out too short, for example the very first scene (in the park), the third (in the women's workroom), and partly also the fifth scene (the beginning of Act 3 during the storm in the ruins), so that they cannot, especially the first two, engage the attention of the spectator. If long-windedness on stage is a mistake, and all the more so in opera, then rapid scene-changes without appropriate development similarly diminish the effect.

The powerful moments I have tried to point out in my outline of the plot – Káťa's memories of her youth, the scene of her humiliation by Kabanicha, her urgent request to Tichon to make her swear an oath, her confession during the storm, and her decision to quit the world – these are also the powerful moments in Janáček's work and do not lack effect. Janáček has the power of dramatic expression and dramatic concision, a feeling for climax and pacing. He also knows how to depict character through his music. He does this almost always with just a few strokes, but they all come alive here: the harsh, evil Kabanicha, vacillating Tichon, Varvara longing for life, the merry Kudrjáš, the oppressed and provoked Káťa. Only humour is missing; there is not enough of that soft, Russian, gently reproachful humour that Dikoj and Kuligin need, especially Dikoj in the scene where he is drunk.

The abilities to dramatize and characterize are and remain Janáček's chief qualities in his new work. Otherwise his music is considerably impoverished, especially in melodic invention. On the stage there is just speech-song, declamation and recitation without exciting voice parts. In the orchestra just mood painting: a constant ripple of tremolos, those tiny figurations, an accompaniment mostly homophonic, without thematic development. He has not taken over either the type of melody or the psychology of the Wagnerians and post-Wagnerians. It is just impressionism, mood and yet again mood. It is not, however, without effect on the listener, not without suggestive power. His orchestra, for all its simplicity and transparency, sounds effective, full and with clear colours, most clear and full where there are fewer instrumental groups engaged, or just individual instruments. Especially the violins, into whose emotional outbursts there are mixed from time to time, mostly in the love-scene or where there is any mention of love, the silvery tone of the viola d'amore and, once, the dreamy sound of the solo double bass. Rain and storm are beautifully evoked. The offstage choruses in the last act are also evocative. The melodic impoverishment is of course most conspicuous in the summer evening scene with the meeting of the lovers. The composer has made the rustlings of nature speak louder than the beat of the human heart and the seething of human blood. Apart from two Russian folksongs (the only Russian colouring in Janáček's music in the whole piece), love does not sing out in the grip of desire – the lovers remain mute at the highest moments. Of course that also happens in real life in the same way; but opera, the most stylized of the arts, does not suffer mute singers gladly (Rusalka, for example). Janáček's work is very characteristic of its origins. It is possibly an enrichment of our opera. But it takes paths which are individual, viable only for its creator. It cannot stand as a model. It would be a mistake were it to become a school. Czech opera has only one way forward: Smetana.

The opera was quite warmly received at its première,[29] thanks to the excellent performance achieved above all by virtue of its painstaking preparation by the conductor, Otakar Ostrčil. Under his baton the singing was precise, the orchestra light and flexible. The title role was successfully created by Mrs Kamila Ungrová, who managed to deliver expressively the storm of Kátʼa's feelings and conscience, having mastered the technical aspects of role. Mrs Rejholcová as

Kabanicha was brusque, rather too sharp in some places [...] Mr Polák's production and Mr Gottlieb's designs made much of the building up of evocative scenes whose effectiveness was heightened by the new sets, chiefly the broad and distant prospect of the Volga [see Figs. 5*a*, 6*a*, 8*a*].

Vomáčka[30] *in* Lidové noviny (*2 December 1922*)

One could weep with rage when our opera house, as if on purpose, stages the most excellent operatic novelty as miserably as possible, as if it wanted to kill the work. Luckily *Káťa Kabanová* is unkillable! Despite the creased Viennese Danube in the first act, despite those impossible Viennese Empire sets in the central scenes and the un-poetic rock formations from somewhere or other in the *Nutcracker*, Káťa lived her life, deprived of course of the charm and dramatic expression which original sets created with more fantasy and poetry would have given: sets in which the banks of the Volga would have seemed much grander and more captivating, the Kabanov house more oppressive and unbearable, the garden more poetical and the last two scenes, especially the final scene on the bank of the Volga, really tragic. Also they ought to do something about the lighting, which, alas, no one knows how to in the National Theatre. Most recently during *The Flying Dutchman* the shadow of the ghost-ship with mast and rigging fell directly on to the back wall; in *Káťa Kabanová* some artist turned up the light to such intensity that it was disturbing (in Act 2), quite apart from the fact that the choice of colours was distasteful (in the scene at sunset in the house, and in the garden scene).

The singing and acting make a chapter in themselves. In *Káťa Kabanová* it is apparent how little store our artists and producers set by the demands of modern opera. A psychological drama like *Káťa Kabanová* requires more than just being sung and acted after the old models. It is necessary to *think* about the roles, to *create* them. And here our artists have not got even to the beginning of this particular alphabet. The places where emphasis is laid, and on what aspects, can only seem comic to anyone who has got to know *Káťa Kabanová* a little. It was best seen in Marfa Ignatěvna Kabanová [Kabanicha], the evil mother-in-law, who, from the way she ranted, evidently thought she was the centre of the play. In fact she is a sharp energetic person, as mothers-in-law often are, and is just one of the causes of the tragedy. Or why stress the humorous aspects of Váňa Kudrjáš, the teacher, chemist, engineer and progressive free-thinker? He looked like a mad tailor with whom Kabanicha's foster-child would scarcely fall in love or for whose sake she would get herself into danger. The rewarding part of Prokopfjevič [sic] Dikoj was played in a completely un-Russian fashion, especially in his dialogue with Marfa [Kabanicha]. The roles of Boris Grigorjevič and Tichon Kabanov were created neutrally. But the roles of Káťa Kabanová and Varvara remained quite unmastered. They were operatic figures, not dramatic. From her very entrance Káťa showed that she had no idea what to do with the part, consequently the spectator likewise did not know what to make of her. This was true even of the marvellous and important monologue (important for Káťa's characterization) – really a dialogue – in Act 1 Scene 2. Janáček has created here a consummate passage revealing the character of a person – a young woman – with rare skill. The actress able to master this act would have a shattering effect on the hearts of the audience. But Mrs Ungrová let the scene fall apart, scattered into its individual details, and united only by inexpressive acting. At the moment of taking the oath, which is the most dramatic place in the opera, she failed completely; what a shame that for the first time this scene did not have its real effect. With her unnatural acting Varvara weakened the effect of this scene still further. A similar failure in Mrs Ungrová's hands was the scene with the key (the symbol of temptation), a scene where she loses the fight against herself. The scene in the garden lacked the sharpness of passion, the relation of the two pairs of lovers was created quite trivially, as if they were not young, as if they were not in love. What was lacking was that real atmosphere that can be found in the music; the evocative songs offstage had no effect. Similarly the orchestral climax at the end, a sort of apotheosis, was despatched as if it were not the culmination of the scene. Káťa's insecurely created character naturally meant that it could have none of its magnificent effect in the scene of the public confession, and remained uncertain even in the last beautiful farewell with her lover, and in death [. . .]

[A further paragraph from this review is reprinted below, p. 135]

Janáček to Ostrčil (2 December 1922)

On the way back I came across the reviews in *Národní listy*,[31] *Národní politika* and at home *Lidové noviny*.

A fellow could lose his reason at the unpleasant things he reads! What malice!

When this bundle with all its critical understanding is disposed of I will say for my own part that the soloists were inadequate as *actors*, apart from Mr Huml. But that is a result of their training as singers, and of the old school.

This could not be cured at one go during *Káťa Kabanová*.

In this connection you help along Act 2 Scene 1 with a generally slightly faster tempo – especially at the point 'Tak mi srdce přestalo bít' [so my heart stopped beating, VS 78] – faster, and before that fig. 7 the più mosso more lively against that Adagio.

And from fig. 10 a passionate tempo.

Otherwise be true to yourself in everything.

I would be pleased if *Káťa* were to be given everywhere as magnificently as you did it.

Janáček to Kamila Stösslová (14 December 1922)

We have enemies enough in Prague? You must have felt it from *Nár. politika*. On the other hand *Čas*, *Lid. noviny* and all the other papers – even the *Prager Tagblatt*[32] – wrote enthusiastically about *Káťa Kabanová*. There's a war on now over the issue: Smetana or Janáček?[33] I say that no *third* will ever grow from either one or the other.

Each *just for himself*!

[...]

But in Prague it was magnificent. That my success upset some parties is certain. But now people are honest, for instance the composer Jos. Foerster.[34] He sent me a nice note [...]

Janáček to Kamila Stösslová (12 February 1928, on the title page of her vocal score)[35]

Mrs Kamila!

And it was in the summer sun. The slope was warm, the flowers almost fainting bowed towards the earth.

At that time the first thoughts about that unhappy Káťa Kabanová – her great love – went through my head.

She calls to the flowers, she calls to the birds – the flowers to bow to her, the birds to sing to her the last song of love.

'My friend', I said to Professor Knop,[36] 'I know a marvellous lady, miraculously she is in my mind all the time. My Káťa grows in her, in her, Mrs Kamila! The work will be one of my most tender.'

And it happened. I have known no greater love than in her. I dedicate the work to her. Flowers, bow down to her; birds, never cease your song of eternal love.

Dr Leoš Janáček

6 Stage history and reception

General survey
SVATAVA PŘIBÁŇOVÁ

In terms of number of productions *Jenůfa* is Janáček's most popular opera – easily outstripping *Káťa Kabanová*, the *Vixen* and *Makropulos*, which have usually been produced in theatres after Janáček has been introduced through *Jenůfa*. Only in four countries has *Káťa* been performed first: Great Britain (London 1951), Hungary (Budapest 1961), Bulgaria (Plovdiv 1973) and Canada (Toronto 1977), though only in Britain has it become a repertoire work.

From the List of Productions (below, pp. 209–24) it is also clear that outside Czechoslovakia *Káťa* has been most often performed in Germany. The roots of this German interest lie in the recent past: in the patient promotion of the opera by Janáček's translator Max Brod and by his publisher Universal Edition, which from the outset issued the opera in a dual Czech and German version. It is, however, somewhat paradoxical that this Austrian firm, for all its attempts to make Janáček's works better known, has had rather less influence on Viennese opera houses. After the famous Viennese première of *Jenůfa* in 1918 it was revived in Vienna in 1926, but new productions did not follow till much later – in 1948, 1964 and 1978; Viennese productions of the other operas have been confined to *Makropulos* in 1938, the *Vixen* in 1956, *The Excursions of Mr Brouček* in 1971 and *Káťa Kabanová* as late as 1974. *From the House of the Dead* has been heard in Vienna only in concert performance.

Before the Second World War there were more Czechoslovak productions of *Káťa* in Brno than elsewhere: four, as against two each in Prague (apart from the German production there in 1928), Bratislava, Ostrava and Plzeň, and one each in Olomouc and Ústí nad Labem. This was a time when Janáček's operas were just beginning to find an audience; the large number of productions in Brno is a tribute to the attitude of the performers involved as well as to the public which went to them. František Neumann came to Brno as chief conductor in 1919 with the express artistic policy of establishing Janáček's operas there. His successor Milan Sachs continued this tradition in his own way, stressing the *cantabile* aspects of Janáček's music in preference to expressive power and grandeur of Neumann's approach.

During the Second World War *Káťa* was not performed in Czech opera houses since opera with a Russian subject was forbidden during the Occupation. After 1946, however, it once more became part of the repertoire of all major Czechoslovak theatres (Prague, Brno, Bratislava and Ostrava). With varying success it was also produced on the Republic's smaller operatic stages (Plzeň, Ústí nad Labem, Liberec, České Budějovice, Olomouc, Opava and Košice), despite the many demands the score makes on its performers. Ostrava (not far from Janáček's birthplace of Hukvaldy) has a long-standing Janáček tradition established by his biographer Jaroslav Vogel and continued by Rudolf Vašata, Zdeněk Košler (appointed director of the Prague National Theatre in 1980) and Bohumil Gregor. Elsewhere in Moravia *Káťa* was successfully staged in Olomouc, conducted by the composer Iša Krejčí (1948) and after him by Košler (1961), who has conducted all his performances of *Káťa* without score. Post-war productions in Brno have been conducted by Bohumil Liška (1946, 1953), Jaroslav Vogel (1958), František Jílek (1968) and Václav Nosek (1977).

Káťa has always been performed in Brno and Ostrava in accordance with the composer's intentions, and with the orchestration unaltered. But for his performances of *Káťa* at the Prague National Theatre the conductor Václav Talich revised the orchestration. Thus in 1947, when there were two independent opera houses in Prague – the National Theatre and the Grand Opera House of the Fifth of May (the former German Theatre, now the Smetana Theatre), it was possible to hear Talich's version in the National Theatre at the same time as a performance by the conductor and producer Václav Kašlík at the Grand Opera House in which Janáček's original orchestration had been retained.

Talich later had second thoughts about his revisions and arrangements of Janáček's scores. 'We wanted to help him, and he crushed us all', he confessed in a conversation with Jaroslav Vogel. His version of *Káťa* was used for the later Prague productions conducted by

Jaroslav Krombholc (1957, 1964); and it can be heard on what is so far the only complete Czechoslovak recording of the opera. It was not until the 1974 production in Prague that Bohumil Gregor attempted to rid the score of all Talich's changes.

A conservative approach to opera stage sets meant that the first Czech productions of *Káťa* made few innovations, and their attempts at realism tended to hamper the work's dramatic qualities. Muzika's sets for Prague (1938) admittedly presented a unified design but, being typical of their time, they now seem rather sober in relation to Janáček's music (see Figs. 5*b*, 6*b*, 8*b*). In his designs Miloš Tomek (Brno 1953, 1958) had Ostrovsky rather than Janáček in mind, and his set, whose chief aim appeared to be to fill up the stage, had an unduly oppressive effect. The 1977 Brno production, designed by Ladislav Vychodil, was sabotaged by its technical realization: it was too noisy for the work's poetic scenes and for a chamber approach to the opera. Troester's sets for Prague (1947, 1957), Plzeň (1949, 1958) and Brno (1968) were based on a symbolical expression of nature, and, from the technical point of view, on a functional construction which allowed quick scene-changes. Josef Svoboda designed *Káťa* as early as 1947 for the Grand Opera House, but it was not until his later designs for Prague (1964, 1974) that he found ideal solutions which respected the work's musical thought, complementing it sensitively, and admirably releasing stage space. Svoboda's sets are unquestionably among the very best created in Czechoslovakia (see Fig. 6*c*).

In general Czechoslovak productions stress Janáček's conception of *Káťa* rather than Ostrovsky's, and tend to be more lyrical and perhaps also more sober and realistic than productions elsewhere in Europe. As against certain German interpretations characterized by gloomy sets and shock tactics, the Czech emphasis is on the music – in which the composer's feeling for drama is so vividly encapsulated.

The first foreign city to stage *Káťa* was Cologne, in 1922. Otto Klemperer, chief conductor of the theatre since 1917, had successfully introduced Janáček to Cologne audiences with *Jenůfa* in 1918 (shortly after the Viennese première) and wished to add another Janáček opera to the Cologne repertoire. As a former conductor of the German Opera House in Prague (1907–10), Klemperer knew the local artistic conditions intimately and had a high regard for Czech opera; Janáček in particular interested him and he was later to introduce to German audiences such works as the Sinfonietta. He had first thought of staging *Brouček*; in the end, however, he settled

Fig. 6*a* Prague 1922: Act 1 Scene 1. The Kabanov house is on the right. Note the 'Russian' features: the birch tree in the foreground, the cupolas in the distance. The all-important River Volga is restricted to the backdrop

Fig. 6*b* Prague 1938: Act 1 Scene 1. Kudrjáš contemplates the river (again, at the back of the stage). The Kabanov house is still on the right, but now a cubist rather than Russian style predominates

Fig. 6c Prague 1964: Act 1 Scene 1. Dikoj harangues his nephew Boris. As in Svoboda's other designs for this scene, the river and an enormous tree-branch dominate; the house and other clues to localization have disappeared (photograph Dr Jaromír Svoboda)

Fig. 6d Berlin 1972: Act 1 Scene 1. After the Kabanov family return from church Kabanicha sends her son Tichon away on the business journey which precipitates Káťa's catastrophe. The river so much dominates this setting that the characters are confined to a series of narrow gangways (photograph Arwid Lagenpusch)

for the less problematic and more recent *Káťa*, which he brought to Cologne in Max Brod's translation a week after Ostrčil's Prague première and a year after the first performance in Brno.

The Cologne critics were somewhat disconcerted by the opera and criticized its undramatic action, incomprehensible motivation and primitive musical technique. The critic of the *Rheinische Musik- und Theaterzeitung* (16 December 1922), while admiring the folk deriva- tion of Janáček's musical language, found it 'unable to speak to the German heart'. The *Kölnische Volkszeitung* (19 December 1922) expressed surprise that the work was performed at all when so many operas by German composers had not yet been produced in Cologne. The *Kölnische Zeitung* (9 December 1922) hoped that in future Janáček would find more effective texts so that he would not suffer the same fate as Smetana. The *Berliner Börsen-Zeitung* (9 December 1922) alone proclaimed *Káťa Kabanová* a vital and valuable new work for whose performance the Cologne public ought to be grateful to Klemperer. Janáček himself did not see the Cologne *Káťa* and clearly was none too happy with the reviews, especially when he learnt that Klemperer had omitted the scene between Kabanicha and Dikoj (in Act 2 Scene 1). *Káťa* was performed only once in Cologne: more performances were presumably prevented by Klemperer's ill- ness and, soon after, his move from Cologne.

Further performances of *Káťa* in Germany were conducted by Fritz Zweig, a native Moravian from Olomouc, and the opera was staged on 31 May 1926 in Berlin-Charlottenburg in the composer's presence. This time the press reception was favourable and the audi- ences included the conductor Erich Kleiber, Schoenberg, Schrecker and Philipp Jarnach. Janáček himself described the première in his 'Moře – země' ('Sea – land') in the Brno daily *Lidové noviny* (13 June 1926):

Individual performances were absolutely faithful to the score. Every note glowed with joy; each had its space and its time. And it was received in the same spirit in which it was presented. Every little motif of the work was sought out and nurtured so as not to wither but resound and grow joyfully.

Káťa comes down to the fateful meeting. The perceptive conductor in- vested her faltering steps with a hesitant silence in the orchestra and on the stage. The silence thickened, [ripening like] corn into an unusual theme – that of the pause!

And how the storm raged in Act 3 in an orchestra of ninety-five players! Performances like these are dazzling. They open wide the opera's way to the world.

Janáček's article was written to defend Zweig's performances from an attack by Oscar Bie (*Berliner Börsen-Courier*, 1 June 1926) as reported in *Lidové noviny*. But Bie's actual review, which Janáček saw in its original form only after he had published his reply, shows that Bie admired the opera. His objections were that the sets were too robust for the lyrical character of the work and that the Berlin Káťa was too young for her part. He also found Brod's translation incomprehensible in places. *Káťa*'s success in Berlin was so complete that both Berlin opera houses competed for Janáček's latest opera *The Makropulos Affair*; the lack of any performance before the war was due to the unwillingness of singers to take on the title role. Zweig also staged *From the House of the Dead* in Berlin before fleeing Nazi Germany.

After Janáček's death in 1928 only one of the other planned productions of *Káťa* took place in Germany, at the Aachen Stadttheater in 1929. Press reports mention the work's success, but because of poor audiences it was dropped from the repertoire after four performances. Outside Germany and Czechoslovakia *Káťa* was also performed in Yugoslavia (Ljubljana 1934, Zagreb 1936, the latter conducted by Krešimir Baranović).

The outbreak of the Second World War interrupted the process of further familiarization with Janáček's works. Only *Jenůfa*, well established as a repertoire piece, continued to be played in Germany during the war; *Káťa* and Janáček's other operas had to wait until after the war for their discovery by the international public – by now with a certain historical distancing.

Commenting on one of the first post-war productions of *Káťa*, in Dresden in 1949, Ernst Krause wrote (*Sächsische Zeitung*, 16 August 1949) that its music speaks directly to the heart – and thus unwittingly took issue with the Cologne critic of 1922 who had held the opposite view. Káťa was sung in Dresden by Elfride Trötschel, who recorded the Act 1 Scene 2 'monologue', and who created the same role in the 1957 production at the Berlin Städtische Oper. Ernst Krause also wrote about this production (in *Hudební rozhledy*, x (1957), p. 763), noting that in several places Wolf Völker's staging did not match the spiritual tension of the work, but that in comparison with the Prague and Dresden productions the performance was more lyrical. In the same year the producer Carl Riha, in Karl-Marx-Stadt, attempted a more realistic staging, in which Brod's translation was revised against the Czech original with the aim of making it fit the music better (*Sächsisches Tageblatt*, 20 October 1957).

Other productions in Germany followed and it soon became clear that *Káťa* would no longer be rejected on the grounds that it was different from *Jenůfa*. Karl-Heinz Wörner, writing about *Káťa* in

Gelsenkirchen in 1959 (*Hudební rozhledy*, xii (1959), p. 468) stressed that the singers' movements should be in harmony with the style of the opera and that their gestures should not be too obtrusive. Hectic movements by Káťa and desperate running round the stage at the moment of 'the most moving farewell to life that has been written' kill the work. He found the symbolic solution used at the Prague National Theatre more acceptable.

Several important post-war productions of the opera were staged by Joachim Herz. His first was in Leipzig in 1963, where the conductor was the Czech Václav Neumann. For Leipzig and for his important production at the Berlin Komische Oper in 1972 Herz made his own adaptation of Brod's translation. Not all his ideas were accepted without reservation. The critic of *Hudební rozhledy* (xxvi (1974), p. 226), for example, in a detailed analysis of the production, disliked the fact that in Rudolf Heinrich's sets the Kabanov house appeared to be situated in the water (see Fig. 6*d*). In addition to Fekluša Herz also introduced another pilgrim, Avdotya, and in Act 2 he added a superfluous scene with a boy who, during the parting of the lovers, begs a tip from Boris for bringing him his coat. Herz's version of the libretto – with the two pilgrims – was also adopted by the Deutsches Nationaltheater in Weimar in 1973.

Vienna, which had once introduced Janáček's *Jenůfa* to the world, hesitated over the composer's other operas for more than fifty years (*Káťa* had meanwhile been performed elsewhere in Austria – in Linz in 1965, with a Czech conductor, producer and designer, and in Graz in 1966). In Vienna in 1974, however, Herz scored a triumph. Hilde Spiel wrote in *Hudební rozhledy* (xxvii (1974), p. 387) that the première of *Káťa* was the most gripping performance Vienna had seen or heard for a long time. The singers were made to move in a striking manner almost as if in a silent film or a balletic mime: Herz conceived *Káťa* in a highly dramatic though stylized manner and wished it to convey a sense of Greek tragedy. Happily his conception was also based on the fact that Káťa's struggle with her innermost feelings cannot be expressed in words and must be portrayed by the orchestra. Herz's designer was again Rudolf Heinrich, and once again the Volga dominated the whole stage, though there were now no critical reservations about this as there had been in Berlin.

The adaptation of the libretto by Herz (who also mounted a Swedish version in Stockholm in 1976), and the Riha version used in Karl-Marx-Stadt in 1957, were not the only attempts to improve Max Brod's German translation. Reinhold Schubert revised the text for the Mannheim production of 1967, as did Ulrich Brecht for the Nuremberg production of 1977, and Ernst Poettgen for his 1972 production in Stuttgart.

The film director Volker Schlöndorff, in his 1974 production in Frankfurt am Main, translated the action of the opera into a series of poetical tableaux which move towards an abrupt climax. The production was taken on tour to Lisbon (1975) and Edinburgh (1978), where it was received with rather less enthusiasm than in Germany (see below, p. 126). Alan Blyth, in addition to his reservations about the expressionist conception, objected that 'the interludes now included by Mackerras at the Coliseum were not played here, and there were damaging breaks between most scenes' (*Opera*, xxix (1978), festival issue, p. 42). On the other hand the production in Munich by Kurt Horres, conducted by Siegfried Köhler, was played continuously, without intervals, in accordance with Janáček's later wishes (see Chapter 7).

Outside Czechoslovakia, Germany and Austria *Káťa* has been staged several times in Switzerland (Zurich 1948, Basle 1966, Geneva 1975, where it was performed in Czech with the title role sung by Elisabeth Söderström, St Gall 1978 and Berne 1979) and in the Netherlands in 1959 and 1975 (both times with a Czech conductor and producer). Paul Pella's performances in Enschede (1959) differed from those of Krombholc in Amsterdam that year in that he used Janáček's original score and not Talich's arrangement. Although Yugoslavia was one of the first countries to take up the opera, since the war it has seen only three productions: in Belgrade (1956), Ljubljana (1968) and Maribor (1973). The fine Belgrade production conducted by Krešimir Baranović achieved a mere six performances on home soil, but it was taken on tour, and introduced the opera to Italian and French audiences, e.g. in Florence, where its success in 1957 suggested that local productions might follow. To date, however, the only native Italian performances have been a radio studio production (Rome 1965) and a staged version in Trieste (1976). Paris, equally enthusiastic about the Belgrade production in 1959, has staged the work only once, at the Opéra Comique in 1968.

The first Australian production of *Káťa* took place in Sydney in 1980. *Káťa*'s fate in Great Britain, Ireland and the USA is described in the remaining sections of this chapter. *Káťa* has been produced once each in Finland (1959), Belgium (1960), Hungary (1961), Bulgaria (1973), Poland (1978) and Norway (1980); the single production in Buenos Aires (1968) was sung in German by Czech singers. Spain and the Soviet Union know *Káťa* only in performances by touring Czechoslovak companies. *Káťa* has not yet been performed in Japan, which has however seen productions of *Jenůfa* (1976) and *The Cunning Little Vixen* (1977, 1978).

From the List of Productions it can be seen that understanding of *Káťa* has developed slowly. In the 1920s and 1930s it was performed in only three countries, including Czechoslovakia; in the 1940s in four; in the 1950s in eight; and in the 1960s in twelve, not counting foreign tours. The greatest interest in *Káťa*, however, has been shown in recent years: in the decade up to 1980 the opera was performed in sixteen countries, in some of them in several productions. What was once – after Verdi and Wagner, and alongside Puccini and Strauss – difficult to understand, is today more accessible to the listener, and transmitting the Janáček tradition is no longer the exclusive prerogative of Czechoslovak theatres.

'Káťa Kabanová' in the United Kingdom
ADRIENNE SIMPSON

'Katya' had its send-off on 10 April, with Charles Mackerras conducting, and was down for seven further performances which to the time of writing have been ill supported. Whether we shall hear anything more of what is, granted Janáček's technical premises, a near-masterpiece, depends, I suppose, on the missionary zeal of the fervent minority, who hold, rightly I think, that the poetic, innocent, ill-starred Katya is one of the most sensitively realised characters of the lyric stage.

Thus the *Musical Times* critic (xcii (1951), p. 275) greeted the first Janáček opera to be produced in Britain. He was one of the few to display a sympathetic attitude towards the venture. Contemporary ignorance about Janáček was profound. The lack of comprehension can be judged from W. R. Anderson's 'Round about Radio' column (*Musical Times*, xc (1949), p. 56) in which he reports on a Czech broadcast performance: 'Janáček's opera 'Kata Kabanova' is about an ill-treated youth in love with a married woman. Apparently some satire of the merchant class is intended ...' The redoubtable Anderson later wrote (*Musical Times*, xcii (1951), p. 309) that he found Janáček 'a rather simple-minded fanatically industrious old man chained to his theories of peasant speech-melody, and impotent as a writer of large-scale works'. Against a background of stereotyped attitudes or rank ignorance the Sadler's Wells decision to stage *Káťa* in 1951 appears amazingly enterprising.

The instigator was a young Australian conductor, Charles Mackerras. In 1947 he had been studying with Václav Talich in Prague and had heard the opera at the National Theatre. The unique idiom, the power and colour of Janáček's writing, made a profound impression on him. He took vocal scores of Janáček operas back to London and aroused the interest of Norman Tucker, administrator of Sadler's Wells Opera. When a tape-recording of *Káťa* came to hand Mackerras played it to Tucker and the critic Desmond Shawe-Taylor. Their enthusiasm matched his own and the eventual result was the presentation of the work at Sadler's Wells, London, for a season of eight performances commencing on 10 April 1951.

Mackerras conducted, Dennis Arundell was the producer and the sets by John Glass, though full of realistic detail (see Fig. 8*c*), were capable of being completely changed within fifteen seconds. Twenty-six-year-old Amy Shuard played Káťa. She and Marion Studholme (Varvara) probably had the greatest critical success. Kate Jackson provoked mixed reactions as Kabanicha. The male roles were undertaken by Robert Thomas (Kudrjáš), Stanley Clarkson (Dikoj), John Kentish (Tichon) and Rowland Jones (Boris). The English translation by Norman Tucker was so good that it has suffered only minor emendation since.

Harsh words were written about the performance: 'well-intentioned rather than satisfying', declared Philip Hope-Wallace in the *Manchester Guardian* (12 April 1951). An even harsher reception was accorded the opera. The trend of the criticism showed that Janáček's writing was considered inept or tiresome by many of the reviewers. One (*The Stage*, 12 April 1951) described *Káťa* as 'a scholarly score, and no one would dream of doubting its emotional sincerity; but the music is so short-winded and the phrasing so abrupt and broken up that one is never conscious of a continuous flow. It is a kind of perpetual recitative, and one waits in vain for a release into the clear waters of pure song.' Ernest Newman in the *Sunday Times* (15 April 1951) dismissed Janáček as 'rather a scrap-by-scrap composer, finding it difficult to think consecutively for more than two or three numbers at a time'. Some critics felt the story too thin to be acceptable. Others criticized the major share of musical interest allotted to the orchestra as being unfair to the singers and operatically ineffective. Overall reaction was well summarized in the *Glasgow Herald* (11 April 1951): 'The spirit of enterprise that animates Sadler's Wells is, of course, to be fostered by all possible means. It is doubtful, however, whether their latest operatic venture has been worth all the time, energy and youthful talent expended on it.'

Why did *Káťa* fail in 1951? The first performance was certainly ill at ease. Despite thirty orchestral rehearsals singers and players probably found Janáček's unusual idiom as difficult as the critics did. Audiences had not been prepared for the style of writing they were to hear. *Opera* (ii (1951), pp. 227–34) published a preview article by H. H. Stuckenschmidt, but his comparisons with Schubert and Verdi would have misled those unfamiliar with the composer.

Some critics did react favourably to the work, if not the performance. Unfortunately the most enlightened comments came from the already converted. Both Lord Harewood (*Opera*, ii (1951), pp, 368–71) and Desmond Shawe-Taylor (*New Statesman*, 28 April 1951) wrote long and perceptive articles. The finest appreciation was by Charles Stuart in his '*Katya Kabanova* Reconsidered'. Incensed by the 'cold, patronizing or frankly hostile reception' accorded the Wells production, he set out to give an analytic guide to 'a score exceptional alike for its structure and the intensity of its poetry'. He emphasizes the recurring motifs, illustrating the way they are built up into a well-plotted whole, and effectively defends the composer against the critical charges made in various reviews. His justification of Janáček's continuous orchestral commentary, which critics of the day found so puzzling, is masterly. Had Stuart's insights been available before the first night one might, perhaps, have expected a more informed response to the opera. As it was, the critics lacked enthusiasm and the audiences stayed away.

The Sadler's Wells directors needed courage to persist with *Káťa* in 1952. The performances apparently suffered from under-rehearsed orchestral playing but the view of conductor and singers had broadened and carried greater conviction. Slightly more audience enthusiasm was detected. However, 1952 was scarcely more successful in box-office terms than 1951. Better fortune attended the 1954 revival under Rafael Kubelík. Norman Tucker had astutely engaged the Czech conductor to direct four special performances to celebrate the centenary of Janáček's birth. 'This time', wrote Desmond Shawe-Taylor (*New Statesman*, 2 June 1954), 'the response has been enthusiastic from the start. The difference is due in some degree to increased familiarity ... with the strange idiom, but mainly to a performance of such blazing intensity as to dispose of all minor doubts and reservations.'

Greater familiarity – perhaps; better orchestral playing and more publicity beforehand – certainly. But the deficiencies in acting and singing of the 1951 production were still obvious, despite some tightening up by Dennis Arundell. The most telling factor in filling the theatre was the presence of Kubelík. He was internationally famous, Mackerras relatively unknown. In 1954, and at the three subsequent performances in 1955, opera-goers were keen to see in action the music director-elect of Covent Garden. Some critics also subscribed to the fallacy that Czech music is bound to be more authentically performed under Czech direction. Nonetheless, Kubelík's performances marked a step forward. The improved orchestra was vital, with so much of importance occurring there. The impact on musicians was evident. In a poll conducted by the *Music Teacher* (January 1955) three, Edmund Rubbra, Lady Mayer and Julian Herbage, chose it as their outstanding musical experience of the previous year. Two major changes strengthened the cast – Edith Coates as Kabanicha and Owen Brannigan as Dikoj. The *Financial Times* (2 June 1955) extolled 'the sense of dramatic shaping with which the guest conductor Rafael Kubelik invests music and action' and considered that despite imperfections 'it would be worth travelling across Europe to see a Janáček performance as good as this'. Even the popular dailies waxed lyrical. The final accolade came with a direct BBC relay of the opera on 18 April 1955.

The enthusiasm generated in 1954–5 did not last. Audiences in the 1955–6 season plummeted. This was an unfair reflection on Mackerras, again in charge, and Elizabeth Fretwell, who took over as Kát'a when Shuard moved to Covent Garden. The next revival in 1959–60 fared no better. Sweeping cast-changes included Marie Collier as Kát'a. It was generally felt that she pressed her voice too hard. As the *Daily Telegraph* (19 November 1959) put it, she 'succeeded almost too well in suggesting the strong hysterical element in Katya's character'. At least there was a noticeable trend to give Mackerras credit for his handling of the work. Audiences returned when Amy Shuard made a triumphant reappearance in the name part on 10 February 1961. This revival was notable for ninety seconds of 'new' music. Mackerras had discovered two short orchestral interludes, previously thought lost (see Chapter 7). They were of great practical importance in covering the scene-changes in the first two acts and represented a scholarly coup for the Wells company.

By 1960 a recorded version of the opera, emanating from the Prague National Theatre, was available in Britain. It paved the way for that company's visit to the 1964 Edinburgh Festival, where the acclaim which greeted its *Kát'a* can be seen as a turning-point in the acceptance of the opera. Edmund Tracey wrote in *The Observer* (30 August 1964): '*Katya Kabanova* ... never much appealed to me at Sadler's Wells, where it was always done with such a quantity of eye-rolling and hysterical over-emphasis that it emerged as a sort of superior grand guignol.' The Czechs, by contrast, acted with effective restraint: 'Svoboda's simple evocative sets and Hanus Thein's flaw-lessly grouped production were beyond praise. Krombholc con-ducted an orchestral performance of almost unbearable lyric inten-sity; and the entire cast sang and acted with that absolute perfection of ensemble that can be achieved only by an intelligently directed repertory system.'

The Prague performance set a standard for the opera against which other productions have been judged. The strong cast included Viktor Kočí as Boris, Jaroslava Dobrá as Kabanicha and the beautifully voiced Libuše Domanínská as Kát'a. Josef Svoboda's abstract sets, using space and evocative lighting, have influenced all subsequent British designers. The economy of staging and movement was felt by reviewers to make the confrontations of the story more terrible. Thein's view has not found imitators (later British productions have usually been condemned as over-busy). The greatest contrast of all was in the orchestral playing, where long experience told. In retro-spect 1964 certainly appears as a watershed in the history of *Kát'a* performances in the United Kingdom.

The Wexford Festival is a truly Irish occasion. Three unusual operas are presented each year, in their original languages, to an audience crammed into a tiny theatre which poses problems of orchestral balance and stage space. The budget is tight, so up-and-coming or lesser-known artists are used. Wexford's 1972 version of *Kát'a Kabanová* brought together the producer (David Pountney) and designer (Maria Bjørnson) later to be associated with the joint Scottish/Welsh National production and a Kabanicha (Soňa Červená) subsequently heard in the same role in Frankfurt. Two other Czechs in the cast were Ivo Žídek as Boris and Jan Kyzlink as Dikoj. Alexandra Hunt, a young Nebraskan, sang Kát'a. The con-ductor was Albert Rosen. He reduced the orchestral scoring, but it still presented formidable difficulties to the small orchestra. Indeed, passion and commitment, rather than accuracy, characterized the performances. Alexandra Hunt was vocally overstretched as the heroine. With so few native Czech speakers in the cast, the decision to sing in Czech had unhappy results. This flawed but enterprising production was later seen at the 1973 York Festival.

By 1973 Sadler's Wells Opera was installed in its new home at the London Coliseum. Despite the hitherto modest success of the opera a bold decision was made to mount a new production of Káťa. The venture was chiefly interesting for the use of Mackerras's new performing edition (see Chapter 7). The sets and designs by Stefanos Lazaridis broke away from the naturalistic style of 1951 and showed the influence of Svoboda; the producer was John Blatchley. Inevitably critics related the 1973 production to that of 1951. Lorna Haywood's Káťa stood up well to comparison with Shuard's. For Felix Aprahamian in the *Sunday Times* (16 September 1973) it was 'a triumph of characterisation. Not only has she delved behind the notes and presented Katya as the creature of fate that evoked Janacek's love and total sympathy, but she projects her with unfailingly beautiful tone.' Other members of the cast were Sylvia Fisher as Kabanicha, Dennis Wicks as Dikoj and Robert Ferguson and Kenneth Woollam as Tichon and Boris. Paul Crook and Barbara Walker were well received as the younger lovers. One singer remained from the pioneering first performance in 1951 – Sheila Rex as Glaša.

Both singing and orchestral playing were considered better than in 1951. There was praise, too, for David Hersey's lighting and back-projection effects. The sets and the production proved more controversial. Lazaridis had used slatted wood, steeply raked and projecting into the auditorium (see Figs. 5c, 8d), to suggest everything from the Kabanovs' living-room to the banks of the Volga. The British preference for realistic interpretations of Janáček was reflected in the generally hostile reception given to the sets. As to the production, some considered it too bland and static, others liked the many touches of detail. Where it certainly failed was in Káťa's death-scene. 'After such a potent build up', complained the *Daily Mail* (14 September 1973), 'it comes as something of a shock to see the heroine throw herself into the river ... only to bounce gently on a mattress.' Nevertheless, the critics were mostly in agreement on the overall quality of the new Káťa. Andrew Porter in the *Financial Times* (14 September 1979) summarized critical attitudes when describing it as 'one of the greatest achievements of the Sadler's Wells Opera at the Coliseum and ... a measure of the company's new growth in its ampler home'. The new production had its première on 12 September 1973 and there were three more performances in the same month. The last, on 21 September, was broadcast. Audiences were not large, despite the good reviews. There was a full house for the revival on 22 March 1974 which preceded the company's tour of fifteen cities

(*Káťa* was taken to Manchester, Leeds and Newcastle). By now the company had been renamed the English National Opera.

New ground was broken with a first invitation of the ENO to the BBC Promenade Concerts on 8 September 1974. Mackerras regarded the concert format as an opportunity to concentrate on the score rather than the stage drama. Unfortunately the venture was not a musical success, despite some fine singing. The attendance was pitifully small, which may have contributed to the problems of balance remarked upon by most critics. The powerful orchestral writing swamped the singers and the work fell victim to the Albert Hall acoustic and audience indifference. In subsequent seasons at the Coliseum several cast-changes were made. Terry Jenkins and Alan Opie took over the roles of Kudrjáš and Kuligin in 1974–5. In 1977 there was a new Kabanicha (Elizabeth Connell) and a new Káťa in Ava June, whose acting, unhappily, did not stand comparison with her predecessors. During 1976–7 two performances were entrusted to a younger conductor, David Lloyd-Jones. Thus continuity was ensured when Mackerras left the company at the end of 1977. The previous year Mackerras recorded the opera for Decca with an all-Czech cast, apart from Elisabeth Söderström, who was the ideal Káťa. The recording had a considerable impact on the British public and won the 1977 *Gramophone* award.

If the Prague *Káťa* in 1964 marked a turning-point, Frankfurt Opera's visit to the 1978 Edinburgh Festival showed that a British Janáček style had become established. A report by Hildegard Weber of the German première (*Opera*, xxv (1974), p. 429) had indicated that the film producer Volker Schlöndorff's operatic début was unusually interesting. It was described as 'a sensation . . . so self-effacing and so clearly directed towards the service of the music'. British critics disagreed. They objected to the amount read into the characters and the story. The review in the 1978 festival issue of *Opera* (xxix (1978), p. 43) complained that 'Janáček's basically naturalistic opera has been turned into a Germanically expressionist piece with glosses on the story that seemed foreign to both the composer's concept and his music.' These glosses included Dikoj being whipped by Kabanicha and Káťa publicly undressing. The orchestral playing was felt to be understated as compared with the Coliseum version. Among the singers, only Soňa Červená (Kabanicha) and Hildegard Behrens (Káťa) emerged with much credit.

At the time of writing the most recent production has been the third Janáček collaboration between Scottish Opera and Welsh

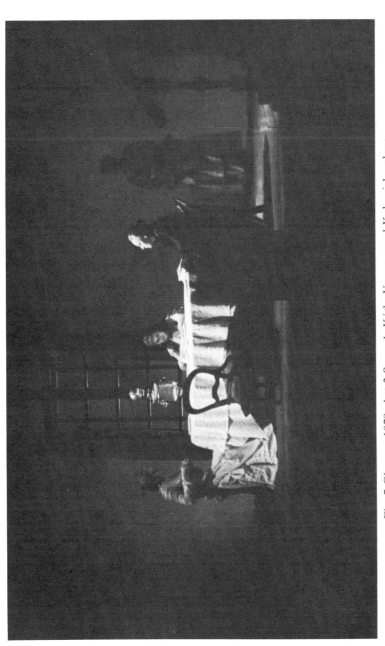

Fig. 7 Glasgow 1979: Act 2 Scene 1. Káťa, Varvara and Kabanicha alone
after Tichon's departure (photograph Donald Southern)

National Opera. Producer (David Pountney), designer (Maria Bjørnson) and conductor (Richard Armstrong) had previously combined for *Jenůfa* and *Makropulos* and could thus demonstrate an integrated approach. The keynote of this production, first performed in Glasgow on 4 April 1979, was its energy. This was reflected in the singing, creating particular problems for Josephine Barstow in the title role. She was praised for her moving characterization but it was generally felt that she placed too much strain on her voice at emotional climaxes. Kerstin Meyer provided a well sung but inconsistently acted Kabanicha. Others in the cast were Allen Cathcart (Boris), William McCue (Dikoj), John Robertson (Tichon), Peter Jeffes (Kudrjáš) and Cynthia Buchan (Varvara). The sombre sets, evoking a claustrophobic atmosphere, were well received. However, many critics felt there was an excess of melodrama and hectic stage business in the production. Others felt the heightening of the drama to be both logical and exciting.

Since 1951 Janáček has been transformed, in British eyes, from a minor eccentric to a major twentieth-century composer. The popularity of his operas at the box office has increased, although more slowly than might have been predicted. Six performances of *Káťa* at the Coliseum in the 1974–5 season attracted audiences averaging only 43% of capacity. There had been a 10% rise by the 1976–7 season. Critics have been converted, audiences educated. *Káťa Kabanová* has achieved a repertoire status undreamt of in 1951. The credit for the current healthy state of Janáček appreciation is undoubtedly due to Charles Mackerras, the late Norman Tucker, and the old Sadler's Wells Company.

'Káťa Kabanová' in the USA
BARBARA HAMPTON RENTON

The history of *Káťa Kabanová* in the USA began in 1957, but little progress was made until the 1970s – fifty years after the opera's creation. Two factors worked against its performance: the circumstances of opera production in the USA, and the general ignorance there of Janáček's music.

Káťa had little chance of appearing in major American opera houses because all of them, dependent on box-office returns for their continuing existence, relied primarily on a safe repertoire of Italian opera. The smaller companies, which ostensibly serve as a training-ground for American singers, tended to concentrate on the same

repertoire, thereby creating a closed system which could be pene-
trated only with great difficulty. Moreover, *Káťa*, which was virtually
unknown, had an even more formidable handicap: Janáček's reputation as an eccentric, highly esoteric composer – a reputation largely
earned from the unsuccessful production of *Jenůfa* at the Metropolitan Opera House in 1924–5.

The long-implanted prejudice and the inertia of the establishment
finally began to yield to the pressure of several forces.One was the
gradual acquaintance with *Káťa Kabanová* made through Artia's
release (1962) of the Supraphon recording. In addition, several conductors and impresarios who had seen Czech productions of *Káťa*
were roused to a state of missionary fervour. And apparently there
was a determined group of Janáček partisans, for, although very little
about him had found its way into popular or scholarly print, critics
often referred to a 'coterie of followers', or the 'much talked about'
Janáček.

Káťa made her official American début on 26 November 1957, on
the stage of a cultural, educational and social centre – Karamu House
in Cleveland, Ohio ('Karamu' is Swahili for 'centre of community').
In its small Arena Theater *Káťa* was produced in English by
Karamu's director-impresario Benno Frank, with costumes and
scenery, and performed to piano accompaniment by a multi-racial
cast of amateurs and professionals. The twenty-five performances
staged in the course of a month received so little notice that the
Karamu Opera Company has not always been credited with the USA
première.

Káťa's second American appearance is thus often cited as the first:
a professional production mounted in 1960 by the Empire State
Music Festival at the urging of Laszlo Halasz, who also conducted.
The festival was held in a tent in Harriman State Park at Bear
Mountain, New York, about forty miles north of New York City.
The proximity of the event, as well as Halasz's reputation, attracted
some attention from the New York music critics, who wrote several
advance articles which revealed little about the opera other than the
plot. The Krombholc recording of *Káťa* had not yet been circulated
and the only available information about Janáček in English was in
Grove's Dictionary (5th edition, 1954) and in Rosa Newmarch's *The
Music of Czechoslovakia* (1942).

At Bear Mountain *Káťa* was performed in Norman Tucker's
English translation, as indeed were all subsequent productions except
one. Amy Shuard, engaged to make her American début as Káťa,

received praise for her performance as well as criticism of her shrill top notes. Although the orchestra was not adequate to the demands of the score, much emotional involvement was evidently generated by the performance. Harold C. Schonberg, the chief music critic of the *New York Times* (4 August 1960), felt that the musical effect was produced by Janáček's 'post-Romantic' writing, but concluded, 'taken as a whole it is essentially a derivative piece of music'. Both Schonberg and Jay S. Harrison (*New York Herald Tribune*, 4 August 1960) observed the functional role of the orchestra, but were unhappy about the lack of soaring vocal lines to convey (as in Puccini) the strong emotions they saw portrayed on the stage. Harrison decided that 'The work is in many ways a gratifying experience, for it demonstrates beyond question that Janacek was a superb craftsman in the orchestral art, so much so that he was able to make an opera out of this craft without much help from the voices.' The performances were scheduled for 30 July and 7 August, but a storm (poetic coincidence) postponed the first performance until 2 August.

Káťa Kabanová first arrived in New York City at the Juilliard School of Music. The Juilliard Opera Theater gave two fully staged performances on 1 and 3 May 1964, using the Empire State Festival's designer, Ming Cho Lee, and its producer, Christopher West. Frederic Waldman, the conductor, noted for his experience with Janáček's music, can be given credit for the germination of the successful production. The performances were by fledgling professionals, many of whom were to become well known. Most noteworthy was Lorna Haywood, who created a sensation as Káťa. Marilyn Zschau (Varvara), who was to go on to other Janáček roles, and Grayson Hirst (Kudrjáš) were also praised.

Public interest ran high, owing to Juilliard's reputation as America's most prestigious conservatory, and to the fact that the Mannes College of Music, another of New York's conservatories, was to stage the première of Janáček's *The Cunning Little Vixen* the following week. The critics were motivated to do some advance work by the new recording of *Káťa* and the recent translation (1962) of Jaroslav Vogel's biography of Janáček. 'Thus there is something to go on', wrote Schonberg (*New York Times*, 26 April 1964); 'we never have had much experience with Janácek in America.' After the performance Schonberg had some reservations, and sceptically referred to the insights claimed by 'those who know the opera in the original Czech' (2 May 1964), but he concluded 'be that as it may, the opera nevertheless makes an impact, and it has moments of piercing sadness and sweetness that are not easily forgotten ... the work is well worth hearing'. Schonberg's reservation was echoed by Martin Bernheimer's review (*Saturday Review*, 16 May 1964): 'In *Katya*'s case, our tardy recognition is partially justified by the language barrier ... Because a translation – no matter how good – can only convey the literal meaning of foreign words, not their sounds or implications, the total impact of *Katya* must remain obscure for non-Czech audiences.' However the New York music critic Alan Rich, one of Janáček's most ardent champions, had no reservations:

It is a work of great beauty. The orchestra creates a web of constant wonderment around the action, breaking upward now and then into a powerful lyric phrase that takes the breath away ... But the rhythmic irregularity, the totally original setting of words, and the murky passion that boils through the score ... are the elements that stamp Janacek as a composer thoroughly on his own, one of the great musical dramatists of our century. (*New York Herald Tribune*, 2 May 1964)

The only professionally staged production of *Káťa* in New York City was that of the Bel Canto Opera Company, which gave three performances with piano accompaniment in the Madison Avenue Baptist Church auditorium on 14, 20 and 21 May 1972. The policy of the company – to give experience to artists and technicians in fully staged productions of operas that could not be heard elsewhere – had gained it a loyal audience of professional musicians and opera-lovers, and Bel Canto's *Káťa* proved to be a critical success in spite of its modest scale. A full version with orchestra under the direction of Leonard Treash took place at the Eastman School of Music in Rochester, New York, on 23 and 24 March 1973. The chief interest of this production is the fact that novice professionals were being trained in Janáček's operas and style, thus increasing the possibility of future performances.

The Kentucky Opera Association in Louisville, Kentucky, one of the more enterprising of the local professional American opera companies, mounted a new production of *Káťa Kabanová* on 16 and 17 January 1976. The KOA's repertoire reflects the artistic taste of its director-conductor Moritz Bomhard, whose affection for Janáček's music can be deduced from William Mootz's description that he 'led passionately', although the orchestra could not manoeuvre its way through Janáček's score unscathed (*Opera News*, 3 April 1976). Mootz also noted that Lorna Haywood, who sang Káťa, brought to the role 'a beauty of sound and dramatic subtlety rarely found in today's lyric theaters'. The opera, however, demonstrated its power to captivate by unexpectedly becoming the high-point of the KOA's season. It was broadcast over radio several times and recorded, thus widening *Káťa*'s American audience by many thousands.

In 1977 *Káťa Kabanová* arrived on the stage of one of America's major houses, the San Francisco Opera Company. Five perform-ances were given on 17, 21, 25, 27 and 30 September, of which the last was simultaneously broadcast. Kurt Herbert Adler, the general direc-tor of the SFO, masterminded this production as he previously had two other Janáček productions, *The Makropulos Affair* (1966, 1976) and *Jenůfa* (1969). His team consisted of international artists with experience of Janáček's works: Günther Schneider-Siemssen (designer), Günther Rennert (producer) and Rafael Kubelík (con-ductor). The sets were a pleasing fusion of literal detail, contem-porary spareness and sepia-toned projections of Russian scenery. Rennert's naturalistic yet stylized direction proved satisfactory; but liberties were taken with Janáček's intentions, particularly in the final scene, in which Kabanicha was made to leave the stage before the final curtain. Changes were also made in Norman Tucker's English translation, and in the music. The opera had only one interval, at the end of Act 2, but the musical climax at the end of Act 1 provoked audience applause despite the attempt at structural elision. Kubelík decided not to include the interludes discovered by Mackerras, claim-ing that they were not 'authentic' – a conclusion based upon his study of microfilms of Janáček's manuscripts (see, however, Chapter 7, 'The interludes') – with the result that the scene-changes took place in awkward silence.

The new recording of *Káťa* with Charles Mackerras and Elisabeth Söderström had been released and warmly praised shortly before the production, so the first-night audience, which included a large number of the nation's music critics, was highly expectant; it was not disappointed. Söderström, singing her first Káťa in English, gave a stunning vocal and theatrical performance. The rest of the cast also received praise: William Lewis, from the Metropolitan Opera (Boris), the American dramatic tenor William Cochran (Tichon), and three singers connected with the New York City Opera: Susan Marsee (Varvara), Beverly Wolff (Kabanicha) and Chester Ludgin (Dikoj). Kubelík's conducting was generally judged to be masterful and authoritative.

The numerous reviews indicate that this *Káťa* was an exceptional production with a tremendous emotional impact, and was considered by many to be a definitive artistic statement. 'What a joy to be enthralled by an opera and production which were thoroughly right', wrote the critic of the *San Francisco Chronicle*, Robert Commanday (19 September 1977). 'Janacek's "Katya Kabanova" was given ... as the composer intended it.' Arthur Bloomfield declared, 'Leos Janacek ... has finally been treated to a genuinely brilliant, totally convincing production' (*San Francisco Examiner*, 19 September 1977). Martin Bernheimer, an earlier sceptic, concluded that 'the result was a revelation' (*Los Angeles Times*, 19 September 1977).

There remained one lingering theory about *Kátʹa* – the belief that it, and all Janáček's operas, could be fully appreciated only when performed in the original Czech. This was put to the test when the Opera Orchestra of New York gave a concert performance of *Kátʹa* in Czech at Carnegie Hall (New York City) on 25 February 1979. Eve Queler, the music director of the Opera Orchestra, who initiated the performance, had obtained Gabriela Beňačková and Naděžda Kniplová from the Prague National Theatre to sing Kátʹa and Kabanicha. The cast also included William Lewis (Boris), the experienced tenor Nicolas di Virgilio (Tichon), a young Ukranian-American singer Natalya Chudy (Varvara) and Boris Martinovich (Dikoj). Although it was not a staged performance, Carnegie Hall was packed for the occasion. Beňačková, making her American début, impressed with her sensitive interpretation and her remarkable voice, but all agreed that the performance was dominated by Kniplová, whose interpretation was familiar from the London recording. In the absence of scene-changes, the Mackerras interludes were omitted. The audience followed the text with a translation by Deryck Viney supplied free of charge; the performance enthralled audience and critics alike. Its powerful impression served to strengthen the demand for a performance of *Kátʹa* by one of New York's major companies.

Kátʹa Kabanová has made slow progress in the USA from obscurity to fame, journeying from community house to tent, church, conservatory and finally major concert halls. This progress shows that repeated acquaintance does make for understanding, and, eventually, enjoyment. Moreover, *Kátʹa*, an example of Janáček's unique musical-theatrical conception, has shown itself to have contemporary relevance. Once held to be a melodramatic tale expounded in a verismo style, it now appears to the audience to have a deeper meaning which stimulates profound inner responses. These have been reflected in the introspective, analytical portions of many of the reviews, whether of the stage productions or of the recordings. The haunting opera, like its heroine, has finally triumphed over the confines of parochialism.

7 Textual problems

The interludes

THEODORA STRAKOVÁ[1]

Among the manuscripts in the Janáček Archive of the Music Department of the Moravian Museum in Brno eight autograph sheets with interludes for *Káťa Kabanová* were recently discovered. They were found (among sketches attached to Janáček's Sinfonietta) and identified by the British conductor Charles Mackerras, an enthusiastic admirer and promoter of Janáček's works, during his first visit to Brno in 1960; he used them in the revival of *Káťa* in London at Sadler's Wells (10 February 1961) and in his appearance as guest conductor at the Brno Opera a month later.[2] The discovery attracted considerable attention among the Czech musical public as well as suprise that Janáček's interludes had been overlooked by Czech musicologists.

The interludes consist of two instrumental insertions: one of forty-three bars to link the two scenes of Act 1; the other of forty-nine bars, including repeats, to link the two scenes of Act 2. They are written on loose blank sheets, 290 × 230 mm, with stave lines hand-drawn by Janáček himself. The first three sheets are numbered in the top left-hand corner and make up the Act 1 interlude. Janáček headed the first sheet 'Klavierauszug, S. 36, 4. Zeile / Zwischen 4.–5. Takt / einsetzen' ('Vocal score p. 36, line 4, insert between bars 4 and 5'), and the third sheet 'Seite 36, 4. Zeile nach / dem letzten Takt / beifügen' (p. 36 line 4, add after the last bar'). The Act 2 interlude is written on the remaining five sheets. Individual sheets are numbered in the top right-hand corner; on the first in the top right-hand corner is a remark in Janáček's hand, 'Seite 85, anstatt Zeile 3, / und Zeile 4, 1. Takt' ('p. 85, instead of line 3, and line 4, bar 1').[3] All these indications refer to the printed piano score, to which Janáček wished the newly composed insertions to be added in a new edition. Some sheets are written

134

on one side only; on the backs of others are sketches in several versions for the second interlude. The autograph score of *Kát'a* does not of course contain the interludes, neither does the printed vocal score (Universal Edition, Vienna, March 1922), nor the full score printed the same year.[4] They can be found, however, copied out exactly and inserted into the original parts made for the Brno première. Interestingly enough they are also written into the new parts which the Janáček Opera House in Brno now uses; they have been crossed out both in the original and in the new parts.[5]

The question arises when and why the interludes came into being and why they have been ignored by performers until now. The solution of these problems is the subject of this section.

Two days before the Prague première of *Kát'a* Janáček, who had been present at rehearsals, wrote from Prague to his wife Zdenka: 'Newspapers are already fighting their way into the theatre [to see] the set; that's the only sort of advertisement they know. But scenes 1 and 2, and scenes 2 and 3 [3 and 4] are broken up! Poor old Bakala with the corrections!'[6] From these comments it is evident that even then, in 1922, Janáček had begun to require individual scenes to follow one another immediately, without a break. We do not know whether he had expressed this wish at the Brno première a year earlier: judging from the newspaper reports it would seem that the scenes were not linked. Neither the authorized copy of the full score, now in the Oesterreichische Nationalbibliothek[5] in Vienna, from which Neumann conducted and which served as copy for the Universal Edition printed score, nor even the first impression of the piano score, has instructions to link the scenes. It is most likely that Janáček arrived at the requirement to link individual scenes at the dress rehearsal in Prague, presumably during discussions with some of the critics; this view is supported in particular by a passage in Boleslav Vomáčka's review in *Lidové noviny* (2 December 1922):

A few more words on the production. It was scarely worth commenting on and it is not possible here to dwell on details. Its chief fault was that it did not cope successfully with the rapid sequence of the acts, which, in the first four scenes, ought to follow in one continuous stream, whereby it would achieve an even greater effect.

Otakar Ostrčil directed *Kát'a* from the printed score; the orchestral parts, however, were presumably borrowed from Brno. I deduce this from the fact that written on the back page of one of the old Brno second violin parts are the dates of all the Prague rehearsals, from 9 October to the première on 30 November 1922; the name of the conductor Otakar Ostrčil is always written against individual dates. That Ostrčil did not link the scenes is shown by the letter which Janáček sent on 19 February 1923 to the director of Universal Edition in Vienna, Julius Hertzka:

The conductor B. Bakala has once again made a thorough check of the full score of *Káťa Kabanová*; he noticed that there are still many printing errors. He will let you know about them; it would be good if these corrections, copied out or in some other way, could be enclosed with each full score.[7] It must also be stated that the two scenes of Acts 1, 2 and 3 should follow one another without a break. In Prague this was ignored; and so the performance fell apart. In Cologne they omitted the first scene of Act 2 (Dikoj–Kabanicha)!

Hertzka, in his reply (22 February 1923), reassured Janáček that an errata slip would be included in all copies of the printed score in accordance with his wishes; theatres wishing to stage the opera would at the same time be told that individual scenes must follow one another without a break. Hertzka expressed surprise at Janáček's information that in the Prague performance the producer overlooked the requirement that the scenes be linked. (Janáček's criticism, however, was unjust, for in 1922 this stipulation had not yet been included with the material.)

The Ostrava production of *Káťa* (première 18 January 1924), after prior consultation with the composer, fully complied with the requirement for linked scenes, to Janáček's great satisfaction (see his letter to Universal Edition, 12 February 1924). But when the Ostrava company wished to perform the work in the nearby town of Opava, Janáček was concerned that it would not be possible to link the scenes on the smaller stage, so this stipulation appeared a number of times in his correspondence with the Opava theatre administration and with Ostrava. From both sides Janáček was assured that the scenes would be linked in Opava as well. The administration wrote to him on 28 January 1924:

Concerning the shortening of the interval between the scenes may we inform you that we have here an excellently trained stage crew so that intervals between acts are usually altogether shorter here than in Ostrava. We hope therefore that in your opera also we can count on the greatest possible speed in the scene-changes, as is your wish. Tomorrow before the performance we will arrange another technical rehearsal so that the scene-changes will go as fast as possible during the evening performance.

The next day (29 January 1924) the Ostrava theatre wrote to Janáček in the same manner:

In reply to your last letter we respectfully inform you that we will arrange the performance of *Káťa Kabanová* according to your wishes, i.e. between scenes 1 and 2, 3 and 4, 5 and 6 there will be no pauses other than those which the music allows. In Opava the stage equipment is such that it is easy to comply with your wishes – which has always been our greatest endeavour.

In 1924 Prague National Opera revived *Káťa Kabanová*. As soon as Janáček heard about this, he wrote to Otakar Ostrčil (4 March 1924):

> I have read the *Káťa Kabanová* is to be given during the international festival celebration at the end of May.
> I earnestly beg you not to let the work be broken up by the scene-changes.
> In Act 1 the living-room need not be so richly furnished.
> Similarly in Act 2 the room could be so simple that in a few seconds it would be cleared away and the sunken path, prepared in advance, would simply appear.
> Similarly the ruins in Act 3 could be simpler so that they could be cleared away quickly and the previously prepared view of the Volga would then just appear.
> In other words the two scenes of Acts 1, 2 and 3 could be stage-set at the same time.
> I don't want magnificent sets.
> Do please comply with my wishes.
> When the music is performed so splendidly by you in Prague, don't let it be broken up by the scene-changes.

That the National Theatre really tried to satisfy Janáček in this respect emerges from remarks in a letter (15 May 1924) to him from the Prague designer J. M. Gottlieb: 'I'm redoing two rooms for *Káťa Kabanová* so that the quick scene-changes can be effected according to your requirements.'

Despite this it seems that neither the Prague performances nor the Brno revival (16 October 1924) was able to cope with the scene-changes entirely to Janáček's satisfaction, so that in view of all these difficulties he eventually decided to extend the orchestral interludes after the first and the third scenes to accommodate the scene-changes. He announced this decision to his friend in Písek, Kamila Stösslová, in a letter dated 24 October 1927:

> I'm now patching up two places in *Káťa Kabanová*; the stage hands cannot set up the stage in time – they need more music.
> I've now done this.

Less than a fortnight later (9 November 1927) Janáček wrote to Universal Edition:

> The music for the scene-changes in Acts 1 and 2 of *Káťa Kabanová* was too short. I have extended the interludes to give more time for setting the stage.

Fig. 8a Prague 1922: Act 1 Scene 2. Interior of the Kabanov house

Fig. 8b Prague 1938: Act 1 Scene 2. Káťa tells Varvara her dreams. Muzika's design is as full of detail as Gottlieb's (Fig. 8a), though now in a contemporary, cubist style

Fig. 8c London 1951: Act 1 Scene 2. Interior of the Kabanov house, with even more realistic detail than in the earlier Prague sets (see facing page). Note the stove (left), the river glimpsed beyond the veranda, the central icon and the samovar on the right (photograph Angus McBean, Harvard Theatre Collection)

Fig. 8d London 1973: Act 1 Scene 2. Kabanicha (centre) orders the family and servants to pray as Tichon (bowing to her) leaves for his journey. Left, Fekluša; centre of group on bench, Varvara; right, Káťa. The setting is limited to basic furniture and there are no details suggesting locality (photograph Donald Southern)

The word 'attacca' is missing before the next scenes.
Because of this the work got broken up into six parts rather than into three acts.
I will send everything to you at the beginning of next week so that the Prague performance can make use of it.

At that time Universal Edition was preparing a new impression of the piano score of *Káťa* and asked Janáček to correct the proofs. He wanted to take advantage of this occasion to insert the extended interludes and the direction 'attacca' at the end of the scenes concerned. On 15 November 1927 he sent the corrected piano score and wrote in a covering letter:

I am returning the piano score of *Káťa Kabanová*, which I have looked through. The interlude music during the scene-changes is slightly extended.
Both the corrections in red and those in pencil are to be observed.[8]

The newly composed insertions were first performed during the production of *Káťa Kabanová* at the German Theatre in Prague, as the extant correspondence shows. On 8 January 1928 the conductor of the German Theatre, Wilhelm Steinberg, approached Janáček with an invitation to the première of *Káťa* on 21 January. At the same time he asked to be sent the insertions for the third scene of the opera:

Mr Max Brod, with whom I have recently had the opportunity to speak in some detail about the work, informed me that at the end of Scene 3 (i.e. before the scene on the footpath) some bars have been composed to extend the conversation between Dikoj and Kabanicha.[9] I would be most obliged if you would have the kindness to provide me with these bars. Moreover I hope it would be your wish that we perform the whole work without cuts.
I would like to stress that I am studying *Káťa Kabanová* now for the second time, since as apprentice conductor in Cologne some years ago I was the only repetiteur for the first German performance and even took the final orchestral rehearsals.

On receipt of this letter Janáček wrote to Universal Edition (twice, in fact, on 12 January 1928 and 16 January 1928) to send the requested insertion for the third scene and, at the same time, the extended interludes.

The performance of *Káťa Kabanová* at the German-Theatre in Prague took place on 21 January 1928 to Janáček's complete satisfaction. Steinberg fully complied with Janáček's wishes, and by using the new interludes he was able to perform the scenes continuously. In addition he surprised Janáček by linking Acts 1 and 2 into a single whole. Janáček told Universal Edition about this in a letter from Hukvaldy (25 January 1928):

Kát'a in Prague under Steinberg was outstanding. Please urge in my name his excellent idea to play the first two acts in one span, wherever *Kát'a* is given. My insertions work marvellously!

The Prague German papers *Prager Tagblatt* and *Prager Presse* both published long articles, enthusiastic not only about the work itself but also about the performance. This increased Janáček's satisfaction still further. We can sense this from his letter to his wife from Hukvaldy (26 January 1928):

The review of *Kát'a* is marvellous. You can't imagine how splendidly they performed it. They compressed everything into two acts. Brno and Prague National Theatre were nothing compared to this. *Kát'a* will now travel the world.

After receiving Janáček's letter of 25 January 1928 in which he once again lavishly praised Steinberg's idea of performing Acts 1 and 2 in one sequence, Universal Edition replied by return of post (28 January 1928):

Thank you very much for your letter. We were delighted to hear about the great success of *Kát'a* in Prague. From your letter we understand that you were pleased with the linking of Acts 1 and 2 without a break, and that you wish that this should be emulated in all future performances. May we inquire whether because of this there are to be any other musical insertions or cuts so that we can then inform the Stadttheater in Duisburg which is to stage the opera next.

From all this it follows that the extended interludes date from the end of 1927 and that they were first used during the production of *Kát'a* by the German Theatre in Prague. When, however, were the interludes written into the Brno parts? Probably in the spring of 1928, when a new production of *Kát'a* was mounted to inaugurate the Exhibition of Contemporary Culture in Brno. Janáček, who had proved to himself during Steinberg's Prague performances the validity and effectiveness of his requirement to link the scenes within each act and was in addition taken with Steinberg's linking of Acts 1 and 2, undoubtedly insisted on this during the Brno production. This assumption becomes a certainty in the light of a postcard from Janáček (18 May 1928) addressed to the Brno conductor František Neumann: 'Don't forget that in *Kát'a Kabanová* Acts 1 and 2 are to be in one continuous sequence!'

The gala performance of *Kát'a Kabanová* to open the Exhibition of Contemporary Culture took place on 26 May 1928. The additions to the interludes inserted in the Brno instrumental parts evidently date from this time. We do not know what material the German Theatre in

Prague used for *Káťa*. It is most likely that it borrowed parts directly from Universal Edition in Vienna. It is impossible to say how the insertions which Universal was to send to theatres were duplicated. We also do not now know whether foreign theatres received these insertions, and whether they used them. There is no trace of them at Universal Edition (much of its material was appropriated by theatres during the war).

It seems that the practice of linking individual scenes in *Káťa*, and consequently the use of the extended interludes, ended with Janáček's death in 1928. A year later Neumann himself died. A new production of *Káťa* took place in Brno only in 1933, under the new chief conductor Milan Sachs, who had initiated the production of *Jenůfa* in Zagreb in 1920. A detailed study of the printed score at the Brno National Theatre revealed many performance markings in thick blue pencil, all in Sachs's hand. The remark 'Čekat' ('wait') written in at the end of Act 1 Scene 1 of *Káťa* is undoubtedly by Sachs. So it was evidently Milan Sachs who discarded the extended interludes, and once again divided up the individual scenes and consequently had the insertions in the parts crossed out. Why this happened and whether conductors after Sachs continued this practice we cannot say today. The Janáček Opera House in Brno does not use the extended interludes. Charles Mackerras performed them again as guest conductor in Brno on 21 March 1961; he brought with him parts of the extended interludes in Acts 1 and 2 which Universal had had duplicated in London and which agreed completely with the insertions in the Brno instrumental parts. The Prague National Theatre does not use the interludes either, although it respects Janáček's wish for the linking of scenes within Acts 1 and 2. This was the version in which *Káťa* was recorded by Supraphon.[10]

Outside Czechoslovakia nothing is known about the extended interludes, which is why individual theatres have had trouble with the requirement to link the scenes. This has led to various solutions to extend the music in order to make the work of the producer and designer easier. Mackerras, when he first conducted *Káťa* in London, 'arranged repeats *ad lib.* in the scene-change music just to be on the safe side, in case anything went wrong'.[11]

It is to Charles Mackerras's credit that he not only identified the insertions but brought them to life. Janáček wrote them after due consideration, wanting to facilitate the quick scene-changes so that the musico-dramatic conception of the work should not suffer. And when he had proved their effectiveness and aptness in performance he insisted unswervingly on his requirement for continuity throughout each act. It was only Janáček's death which led to the lapse of this requirement and it is most certainly proper that the insertions be played once again. It was Janáček's last change to the work, and one which ought to be respected unconditionally.

Orchestration problems and the revised edition
CHARLES MACKERRAS[12]

Janáček created an entirely new style – one might almost say a new musical language – even though he used only normal harmonic means, which he inherited from Debussy's whole-tone harmony, and from Dvořák and the Russians. He also created a completely new style of orchestration: no other composer has ever evoked such a sound from an orchestra. Just as he used ordinary harmonic structures, so he used only normal orchestral instruments, perhaps with the exception of his beloved viola d'amore. But Janáček differed from his contemporaries in that, unlike Strauss, Bruckner and Mahler with their ever-expanding orchestras and rich sonorities, he continually strove to reduce the density of orchestral sound, even when using a gigantic orchestra. Approaching from a point of view very different from that of his contemporaries, he transformed instrumentation.

When Janáček composed *Káťa Kabanová* he had not yet completely abandoned 'conventional' orchestration, and yet, given the time at which it was written, there are interesting new sounds on almost every page. He was becoming less satisfied with what he called the 'varnishing' of orchestration with tone-colour, but he had not yet, when writing operas, adopted the practice of actually drawing his own staves, so as not to be tempted by all those empty lines of printed music paper to over-orchestrate. On the other hand his unconventional attitude to orchestration and to the practical problems of orchestral playing led him into writing almost unplayable passages, some even outside the ranges of the instruments involved. He also appeared to be little concerned about the natural differences in strength between different instruments; for instance, he would entrust a main theme to weaker instruments like the English horn and harp, with a massive penetrating accompaniment of almost the whole orchestra.

Janáček's attitude to the question of orchestration is difficult to define. On the one hand he tailors his music paper skintight to the orchestration, on the other he leaves the conductor free to make fairly substantial retouchings to the score. He wrote to at least two conductors that he would be perfectly agreeable to their filling out the orchestration, should they consider it necessary. He was present at Talich's Prague première of *Taras Bulba*, and appeared fully satisfied, despite much retouching of the score. But he seemed equally satisfied with his pupil Břetislav Bakala's literal performance of the original text.

This is true not only of *Taras Bulba* but also of the operas *The Cunning Little Vixen* and *Káťa Kabanová*. The difference between Talich's version of *Káťa*, which until 1974 was still being played in the Prague National Theatre, and the original version, used both in Czechoslovakia and abroad, is like the difference between the original version of Musorgsky's operas and the reorchestrations by Rimsky-Korsakov and Shostakovich. At the time they were composed, the orchestral colours and exotic sounds that Rimsky-Korsakov introduced and his followers copied were all the rage in Russia, and so Musorgsky's instrumentation seemed by comparison drab and unimaginative. Janáček's case is similar. He was fully capable of using the orchestra, as his *Dances from Lašsko* demonstrate. Here not only the musical content but also the treatment of the various instruments recall Dvořák's *Slavonic Dances*. And we see the advantage of Dvořák's orchestration, but also the disadvantages: the inclination to cover the melodic line with accompaniment, and to write unviolinistic runs with uncomfortable leaps across the fingerboard for the strings. Janáček soon grew out of the thickly 'varnished' style; his mature works, on the contrary, show extraordinary clarity and transparency. With the minimum means they achieve the maximum effect, despite technical difficulties in various places.

It is questionable how far we, as exponents of Janáček's music, should alter the instrumentation to satisfy everyday practical requirements in performance, or should retain the *Urtext*. One reason why Janáček's music used to be so seldom played lies in the enormous difficulty of performance, and the sad state of the orchestral parts, which is mainly owing to Janáček's indifference about bowing and phrase marks and other small but important details. The attempts by several conductors to cope with these problems and make the music more acceptable to players may have been a necessary stage in the propagation of Janáček's music; without Kovařovic's version of *Jenůfa* maybe Janáček would never have come to fame at all, or given us the miraculous works of his old age. At the same time, however, such conductors have inevitably distorted the spirit of the music. Lovely and rich as Talich's reading of *Káťa Kabanová* is (and I hope he would have forgiven me my criticism), ironing out the grotesque and sometimes even ugly sounds has taken away something from the essential Janáček style. That furiously grotesque, that almost primitive element in the texture becomes too cultured, too sophisticated, in Talich's version. The opera depicts a class of landowners, but none of the characters apart from Káťa herself could be regarded as refined, just the opposite – and Janáček's rather stark, even rough sounds seem to me to represent the drama exactly. Even in the passionate love-scene in Act 2 the emotions of the two pairs of lovers are accurately expressed by the orchestra – the feelings of people that are trapped in the provincialism of their society. Any attempt to refine the orchestral sounds suggesting the emotions of these people transforms their world into that of Octavian and the Marschallin. Janáček's score would have seemed incompetent and gauche to a musician as habituated to the orchestral colours of his own time as Talich, despite his obvious admiration for the work itself. Taking little heed of fashions and instead concentrating on the dramatic aspects, Janáček expressed superbly just what he wished to express.

While today most people would agree that Talich's 'varnish', having served its function in promoting acceptance of the work, should be removed, we are left nevertheless with several problems which demand solutions. There are many places, for instance, where Janáček has a naturally weak instrument play a melody against a naturally strong one. His conception can be aided by modern recording and microphone technique. I can think of several passages in the Sinfonietta in which I have never been able to produce a satisfactory balance in normal concert performance, but which can be easily solved by 'faking' the balance in the recording studio. In my recent recording (1981), for instance, the viola d'amore was able to play the part originally intended for it simply with the aid of microphone. In the operas the question of balance is more difficult because it has not generally been considered feasible or proper to put a special microphone with a loudspeaker in the theatre pit in order to bring out particular sounds. The proper realization of Janáček's favourite combination of harp and English horn, or of his viola d'amore parts, will always be an insoluble problem until some conductor has the courage to make use of a discreet microphone technique in the orchestra pit.

Unconventional methods in composition have to be dealt with in an unconventional way. It seems to me that some of the problems of Janáček's instrumentation could be better solved this way than by strengthening the melodic parts with extra woodwind. Again, Janáček's extraordinary use of high flutes or piccolos to produce the effect of upper harmonics in ordinary chords, such as we find in the overture or at the end of the Prisoners' chorus in Act 1 of *From the House of the Dead* (before fig. 18), and particularly at the very end of *Makropulos* (Act 3, figs. 121–4), would perhaps best be realized by some artificial alteration of the orchestral balance, since no flute player could possibly play as inhumanly softly as the composer seems to require to produce exactly the right mysterious effect.

Like all Janáček operas *Káťa Kabanová* presents many problems when one tries to establish a correct text for it. Though a printed edition of the full score was published by Universal Edition in 1922, i.e. during Janáček's lifetime, Janáček seemed incapable of correcting the proofs and allowed literally thousands of mistakes to appear in it. In 1923 the publishers, painfully aware that the material was full of errors, gave out a list of errata, compiled by Břetislav Bakala (himself responsible for the piano reduction in the vocal score). It is not known how far Janáček supervised the compilation of this list, but it is itself far from complete and contains further errors. It is a comment on the quality of the opera that its greatness has shown through the mass of errors of notes, phrasings and dynamics that have been played more or less uncorrected for years.

A new edition of the opera was long overdue; my revised edition is designed not only to correct the vast numbers of mistakes in the first edition, but also to provide practical suggestions for the many problems of interpretation which might discourage others from performing the work at all. In my edition Janáček's text is clearly distinguished from editorial suggestions, which conductors can accept or reject as they please. For those wishing to delve deeper an extensive Revisionsbericht explains how the various sources differ and why particular readings have been adopted. Here, however, I would like to single out a few passages which raise special problems.

I referred earlier to passages found to be impossible on the instruments specified. Since this is a charge often made against Janáček it may be helpful to give a few specific examples. Here are eight brief extracts from *Káťa*, with suggested solutions.

Ex. 29. Act 2, last five bars (FS 291)

The original first flute part is unplayable *pianissimo*; it can be played by the piccolo.

Ex. 30. Act 3, bars 4–5 before fig. 8 (FS 317)

The horn solo is very high and exposed in the first two bars (it becomes more manageable as it descends) and could perhaps be given to the clarinet instead (which was Janáček's intention in the autograph – he changed it in the authorized copy).

Ex. 31. Act 3, bars 9–10 etc. before fig. 16 (FS 342–3)

The parts for second violin and viola are unplayable at this speed (dotted minim = 60) as the passage involves almost continual string-

Ex. 30   VS 124

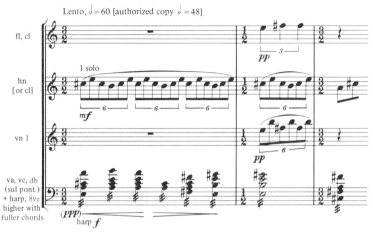

Ex. 31   VS 135

Ex. 32 VS 155

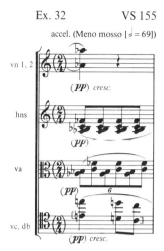

crossing in an awkward key for these instruments. The simplification I have suggested will be more audible if the second violin part (the main motif at this point) is played an octave higher.

Ex. 32. Act 3, fig. 31, bar 13 (FS 392)

Double basses used to find this passage impossibly high, so I suggested in the score that cellos could be divided in octaves with a solo double bass playing at the lower octave. However, technique has improved so much recently that most orchestral bass players now seem able to play this passage without too much strain.

As can be seen, most of the above problems in *Kát'a* are capable of fairly straightforward solutions. This is not so in those passages with problems of balance where important lines are given to instruments or groups of instruments unlikely to be heard against more heavily scored accompaniments.

Ex. 33. Act 1, fig. 29, bars 7–11 (FS 137)

The tune on the viola d'amore and flute (an octave apart) is heard against a sustained harmonic background of wind and lower strings, faster-moving ostinato figures on all the violins and harp, and an offbeat figure on the violas. Tichon sings against this for the first two bars. After another two bars this same tune is heard in octaves on the first violins and viola d'amore; there are sustained parts on lower

Ex. 33   VS 67

wind and lower strings; the ostinato is now on the harp and violas, and the second violins have the offbeat semiquavers. How much can be heard of the important tune, scored in both cases with a solo viola d'amore at the lower octave? In the first four bars the flute and viola d'amore play above the rest of the orchestra (fairly lightly scored at this point). If there are balance problems the second violins (simply doubling first violins) could be omitted. In the next four bars second violins and viola d'amore could exchange parts. The violins sound better in octaves anyway, and the viola d'amore, with the semiquaver offbeat figure, will stand out by virtue of its rhythmic differentiation.

The latter half of Act 2 Scene 2 presents many problems of orchestral balance, particularly in orchestras with insufficient strings. I have therefore made an alternative version (printed in the score, in addition to Janáček's original), which can be used by smaller orchestras. It consists mainly of added sustaining wind instruments to give cohesion to the restless accompanying repeated triplets and of rearrangement of some of the complicated divisi string passages (from fig. 24 onwards), particularly in the double basses.

Ex. 34. Act 2, fig. 34, bars 1–4 etc. (FS 260/289)

This tutti is the only loud music for most of the act and comes significantly at the end of the assignation scene with the stage direction 'Káťa goes up the path alone, with difficulty'. It is thickly scored for strings (subdivided violins), woodwind, a timpani roll, horns and trombones but not, surprisingly, trumpets. In the theatre trumpets could be added for a richer sound (otherwise this crucial passage could be an anticlimax), but they must not play as loudly as the trombones, otherwise it may sound vulgar rather than noble. I have also suggested changes in the bassoons and trombones for reasons of harmonic balance, and doubled the important melodies in the horn parts.

Ex. 35. Act 3, fig. 14, bars 1–2 (FS 338)

Harp and lower strings do not have the impact here (just before Káťa's confession) that Janáček may have imagined. There are several ways of solving this problem: by adding violins doubling an octave higher; by adding woodwind in wide-spaced harmony; by directing the harp to play an octave higher; or by a combination of any two, or all three, of these.

Ex. 34

Ex. 36. Act 3, 5 bars before fig. 28 (FS 382)

This is the final meeting of Kát'a and Boris. While their silent rapture
five bars later is memorably captured on the very soft muted strings,
Janáček allows himself this tutti climax for the moment when they
fall into each other's arms. Against a tutti G flat major chord the
main tune is played by oboes, English horn, clarinets, harp (thickened
in four-part chords) and a single viola d'amore. But this tune is
difficult to hear – it is apt to be drowned by the thick accompaniment. To strengthen this melody the violas, otherwise silent, could
double the viola d'amore, as could the flutes, which play only on the
first beat of the bar.

With players more accustomed to Janáček's unconventional demands and with improved standards of technique many of the
passages once considered impossible, for which I have devised alter-
natives, can now be played much as Janáček wrote them. Besides, our
ears have got accustomed to different sounds, and passages which
once seemed to me to require alteration when I was faced with the

Ex. 35   VS 133

Ex. 36   VS 151

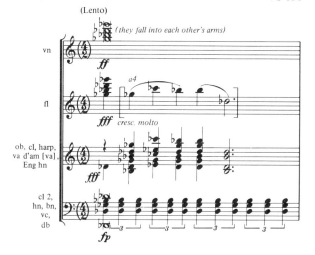

practicalities of performance no longer seem so extraordinary – Ex. 35, for instance, I now play in Janáček's original without the suggested retouchings. I should also stress that whatever retouching may be useful in the theatre (especially in those with smaller numbers of strings), my recording of *Káťa Kabanová*, relying on the artificial balancing of the modern recording studio, is played exactly as Janáček notated it in the score. Fashions in performance, in listening, and even in notation change, and it seems to me dangerous to tamper too much with the composer's *Notenbild*. In the end, one's desire must be to retain as much of Janáček's unconventional orchestration as is commensurate with the practical considerations of performance.

Janáček and the viola d'amore
JOHN TYRRELL[13]

It is well known that Janáček included a part for solo viola d'amore in *Káťa Kabanová* and other works such as *The Makropulos Affair* and the Sinfonietta. The recent recordings of these works by Charles Mackerras, using the instrument for the first time, have reawakened interest in this curious quirk of Janáček's. Why did he write for this rare, if not obsolete, instrument, and where did the idea come from?

It seems likely that Janáček's first acquaintance with the viola d'amore was through his reading, in Leipzig, from 1 December 1879 to 15 January 1880, of Berlioz's *Grand traité d'instrumentation*, which he knew in an abridged German edition.[14] It is clear from his numerous markings that he concentrated mainly on the brass and woodwind chapters; the only passages he marked in the string chapter deal with the double bass and the viola d'amore, which Berlioz discussed after the viola. Most of Janáček's markings are of a practical nature, suggesting that the twenty-five-year-old composer was still getting to grips with the essentials of instrumentation; it is not surprising therefore that the passages he marked concerning the viola d'amore deal with its tuning rather than with its character and sound.

Though the edition Janáček used omits the extensive music example from Meyerbeer's *Les Huguenots*, it retains Berlioz's comments on this, the most celebrated use of the instrument in the nineteenth century: a solo for the viola d'amore first as a prelude, then as an accompaniment, to Raoul's *romance* 'Plus blanche que la blanche hermine'.[15] Janáček not only heard the work, in Brno on 19 November 1890, but published a review of it in *Moravské listy* three days later.[16] Though the instrument is so exposed that no one could miss it, it is highly unlikely that the tiny Brno Provisional Theatre would have afforded such a luxury, and presumably it contented itself with the usual solution of substituting an ordinary viola. Janáček's generally favourable review, which mentions the 'brilliant orchestration', makes no reference to the instrument. Whether Janáček ever saw a score can only be a matter for speculation, as is the possibility, eleven years later, of his coming across an extensive article on the instrument by Jaromír Borecký in four issues of the periodical *Dalibor*.[17] Borecký offers none of the practical hints for using the instrument that we find in Berlioz – there is only one tiny music example; instead he provides a wide range of references to the instrument in both general and scholarly literature, comparing, for instance, information on sizes and tunings. Of particular interest are his final lines: 'I have just learnt that the Brno virtuoso Mr Karel Reissig has for some time now been concerned with the study of the viola d'amore, assembling and preparing its literature, and that he intends giving concert performances on this interesting instrument.'

I have not been able to trace a Karel Reissig in Brno and assume that Borecký in fact meant Rudolf Reissig (1874–1939), well known for many years in Brno as a violin teacher, and as a performer on the violin, viola and, particularly, the viola d'amore. That Janáček knew Reissig is attested not only by their correspondence (now in the Janáček Archive), but by the fact that Reissig was a member of the Klub Přátel Umění (Club of the Friends of Art, of which Janáček was a prominent member) and from 1903 to 1909 taught at Janáček's Organ School. It seems likely that Janáček gained first-hand knowledge of the instrument from him.

A few months before Reissig joined the Organ School staff, however, Janáček had a further opportunity of hearing the instrument, when he saw Charpentier's opera *Louise* for the first time in Prague, on 21 May 1903.[18] Janáček's enthusiasm for the opera is well documented; it is less well known that the fourth act contains a small but prominent part for viola d'amore in the accompaniment of the song with which the father attempts to soothe his daughter Louise to sleep: 'Reste, repose-toi, comme jadis toute petite'. As with *Les Huguenots* we are faced with the questions whether the viola d'amore actually used in any of the performances Janáček heard (*Louise* was a mainstay of the Prague repertoire until the Second World War and was heard in Brno's German Theatre from 1906 and in Brno's Czech National Theatre from 1913)[19] and whether Janáček ever saw a score. In 1922 he asked Universal Edition to try to get him a full score[20] (they failed), and this suggests that he had never had one earlier. Yet his students studied the work in 1910, so a vocal score at least was available then – though none exists in the Janáček Archive today.

A byla jedna z nejkrásnějšich paní. Hlas její byl jako violy d'amour.

And she was one of the most beautiful of women. Her voice was like violas d'amore.

With Reissig and possibly *Louise* in mind, these famous words with which Janáček described Kamila Urválková in his Autobiography[21] take on a rather more concrete meaning. For there seems good reason to suppose that by the time of his chance meeting with Mrs Urválková in Luhačovice in August 1903, which set him working on his opera *Fate*, he had actually heard the instrument (rather than just liked the name) and knew how it sounded. Kamila Urválková's character and name, at first as Míla Válková, then simply as Míla, were taken over into the opera;[22] was her voice – the violas d'amore – there as well? Though the authorized score of *Fate* itself contains no viola d'amore part there are some passages for two solo violas. On closer examination the designation of these can be seen to have been changed, in Janáček's hand, to '2. violy solo' from the copyist's '2. viola d'amour'. The passages in question are Act 1, fols. 97b–134b and Act 2, fols. 26b–30a, all from the score copied by Stross, completed on 12 June 1905.[23]

It is reasonable to suppose that Act 1, fols. 144a–150b, containing similar passages for '2 violy solo', written in a copyist's hand, were also originally for viola d'amore and, since these pages date from the 1906 revision of the work, that Janáček had changed his mind about using the instrument before then. Though there is no viola d'amore in the authorized score of Act 3, one of the few pages of Janáček's original manuscript score that has survived, p. 15, has a part for '2 violy d'amour'. It could not have continued long: by p. 18, the next page that survives from this sequence, it has disappeared again. Though the first four bars of Janáček's p. 15 correspond approximately to those on fol. 14a of the Stross score, the remainder is so different that Stross clearly could not have copied directly from it but must have had some replacement, and this page must represent an earlier stage of Janáček's work on the opera.

The dwindling role of the instrument – from a big scene in Act 1, to twenty-one bars in Act 2, to a discarded sketch in Act 3 – suggests the composer's growing doubts about using it in the orchestra, culminating in its complete elimination from the score during the first revision. Though replacing the viola d'amore with the viola may seem an eminently practical measure, it may not be too fanciful to suggest that the instrument disappeared from the work at the same time as the direct references to Mrs Urválková, while the central interest in the opera switched from its heroine to the composer Živný, with autobiographical references to Janáček himself. After *Fate* Janáček seems to have left the instrument well alone until *Káťa Kabanová*. In the meantime he had the opportunity to hear at least two more operatic examples of the instrument's use: in Puccini's *Madama Butterfly* (which he saw in the Prague German Theatre in 1908 and which remained in his mind many years later),[24] and in Kienzl's *Der Kuhereigen*, performed in Brno in 1912. There were important differences when Janáček returned to the instrument: whereas in *Fate* he wrote not for one but for two violas d'amore, always in the treble clef, sometimes above the violins, from *Káťa Kabanová* onwards he conformed to the usage of Meyerbeer's, Charpentier's and Puccini's printed scores by writing for a single viola d'amore, generally in the alto clef, and above the orchestral violas. In none of Janáček's viola d'amore parts does he ask for anything that an ordinary viola could not play equally well. In *Káťa* the arpeggio runs of the overture[25] are the nearest he comes to the more idiomatic writing that Meyerbeer used; there are few uses of another viola d'amore speciality, double stops, let alone the chords formed by its possible tunings; there are no harmonics, so much recommended by Berlioz. For all practical purposes Janáček had written a viola part. Should we then be looking, when trying to determine why he used the instrument, not at its technical capabilities but at the inspiration of its name or the distinctive tone produced by its sympathetic strings?

In his recent book on the composer Bohumír Štědroň comments on *Káťa Kabanová*: 'And a viola d'amore – as in the Second String Quartet "Intimate Letters" – was meant to underline Janáček's views about Káťa Kabanová's love. In these love-scenes Janáček had his friend in Písek [i.e. Kamila Stösslová] directly in mind.'[26] Both Káťa Kabanová and Emilia Marty in *Makropulos* were associated with Kamila Stösslová, in the same way that *Fate* was associated with Kamila Urválková, and this led to the use of the viola d'amore in all three operas. It is not used in Janáček's two other late operas, *The Cunning Little Vixen* and *From the House of the Dead*, which both seem to lack a suitable erotic role for the instrument. Because of the extensive doubling little of the viola d'amore parts in *Káťa Kabanová*, for instance, would ever be heard in the theatre: at times Janáček seems rather to be weaving the instrument into the texture almost as a secret code than making a real contribution to the orchestral sound. It does indeed seem that the name of the instrument was more important to Janáček than its technical possibilities.

It is surprising that not all the passages written for it have the clear erotic connotations that we find in the Act 1 love-scene in *Fate*, in the love-song in Act 2 of *Fate*, or in the first and last meetings of Káťa and Boris. In the sketch for Act 3 of *Fate*, for instance, the two violas d'amore were to have accompanied the chorus's awed response to the words 'Opera celá bez posledního aktu! To je divné a směšné!' ('An opera without a last act! That's strange and comical!'). This idea of mystery is perhaps what Janáček had in mind in the distinctive motif he gave to the instrument at the first appearance of Marty and at other important moments in Act 1 of *Makropulos*, an impression enhanced visually by the request for a 'strange light' in the stage direction that he added.

The use of *two* violas d'amore in octaves for almost all the instruments' appearances in *Fate*, generally in slow-moving sustained melodic parts, perhaps gives us the best clue to how Janáček wanted the instrument to sound. He seems to have imagined a somewhat mournful, plangent sound, which could easily have been suggested by Charpentier's use of it in *Louise*. (He clearly regraded it as a soft sound: describing a lecture by Josef Zubatý in October 1925 he refers to his 'weak, thin voice . . . with the colour of a viola d'amore'.)[27] The slow tunes in *Káťa* belong to this type, e.g. the tune which accompanies Tichon as he repeats his mother's instructions to Káťa at the end of Act 1 (Exx. 9 and 33).

Janáček wrote for the instrument in two non-operatic works. The erotic association in the Second String Quartet 'Intimate Letters' has already been mentioned. In one of his letters to Kamila Stösslová about the progress of the work (1 February 1928) he writes 'Celek bude obzvláště držet zvláštní nástroj. Jmenuje se Viola d'amour – Viola lásky.' ('The whole piece will be held together particularly by a strange instrument. It is called the viola d'amore – the viola of love.')[28] On the other hand it is hard to see what he intended in the Sinfonietta's third movement (originally entitled 'The Queen's Monastery'), where a single viola d'amore originally substituted for the entire viola section; perhaps to express the relationship between the foundress of the monastery, the widowed queen Eliška Rejčka, and the Czech baron Jindřich z Lipé.[29] Did Janáček really intend the instrument to be used? According to Dr Milan Škampa (violist of the Smetana String Quartet and editor of the forthcoming edition of Janáček's Second String Quartet), the members of the Moravian Quartet played through the first and third movements of his Second Quartet to Janáček at the first rehearsal on 18 May 1928. One member of the quartet was able to play the viola d'amore and tried to convince him of the unsuitability of the instrument in this context. At first Janáček insisted that at least some of the viola part be left on this instrument. The second day, however, he pronounced: 'So I've cut it out – but it was terrible!'[30] There is no firm evidence that a viola d'amore was ever used at any performances of his operas,[31] or that Janáček ever complained about this: his extensive correspondence over productions of *Káťa Kabanová* deals with many problems but none concerning the viola d'amore. But while Janáček changed his mind about the viola d'amore in *Fate*, the Sinfonietta and the Second String Quartet, he actually added to the part for it in *Káťa Kabanová* in the authorized copy.

How are we then to regard Janáček's use of the instrument? His writing for it is unidiomatic, apart perhaps from aptly capturing its tone; its use is impractical; his whole approach is a trifle absurd. It would be rash, however, to dismiss as an aberration something which haunted Janáček for the last twenty-five years of his life and which has its place in some of his greatest music. While there is much to be said for authentic recordings with the viola d'amore included, it is clear that it will never be used for ordinary performances. I believe that in general we should regard the instrument as one of the inspirational devices which helped Janáček to compose. In the same way that we see him underlining all references to music in his copy of Svatopluk Čech's novel *The Excursion of Mr Brouček to the Moon*, or writing the sound of anvils, chains and saws into *From the House of the Dead*, we see him laboriously writing 'viola d'amour' into his scores. Janáček's genius lies in the way he was able to transmute these crude and naive beginnings into great music.

Janáček's use of the viola d'amore in 'Kát'a Kabanová'

Location

Act 1   a   FS 8–11, 17–19; VS 9–12 (16 bars)
         b   FS 130–9; VS 64–7 (41 bars)

Act 2   c   FS 166–7; VS 79 (13 bars)
        d   FS 225; VS 101 (4 bars)
        e   FS 241–4/273–5; VS 107–8 (12 bars)
Act 3   f   FS 358–9; VS 142 (14 bars)
        g   FS 379–80; VS 150–1 (5 bars)
        h   FS 382–5; VS 151–2 (8 bars)
        j   FS 394–5; VS 156–7 (5 bars)

Appropriateness

The viola d'amore is distinguished from the viola by having more strings (usually seven, with no standard tuning), and by its set of sympathetic metal strings. Berlioz considered the larger number of strings and the flexible tuning suitable for rapid arpeggios and double stops, while the sympathetic strings, he suggested, help to give it a sweet, seraphic tone, particularly appropriate to dreamy melodies and the expression of ecstatic or religious feelings.

Janáček employs a range virtually identical to that of the viola. It lowest notes are the low C sharp and D flat in the overture (i.e. a semitone above the viola's open C), and the favourite tessitura is in the octave or tenth above middle C. He uses arpeggios only in the overture (a) and prominently in the last example (j); the only double stops are also in the overture (seven two-note chords, in a). On the other hand many of the melodies he devises for it (particularly in a, b, c, f and j) would certainly fit Berlioz's suggestions for dreamy or ecstatic melodies.

Aubidibility

Generally Janáček uses the viola d'amore in a slightly reduced orchestra (see Ex. 33); on the other hand he takes no pains to omit the orchestral violas (the instruments nearest in tone and most liable to cause confusion), when the viola d'amore is playing, and furthermore it is almost always doubled by other instruments. Favourite doubling instruments are the clarinet, English horn and harp, although bassoon, flute, oboe and violin are also used (see Exx. 9 and 33).

The viola d'amore as symbol

All the examples could be said to be 'Káťa' music. In all the Act 3 examples (f–j) and in two from Act 2 (c, d) she is on stage, and the centre of attention. The overture (a) is, by association, also 'Káťa' music, though it is curious that no viola d'amore is called for when this music is played again when Káťa first sings (FS 55, VS 29). Káťa does not sing during the most extended use of the instrument, Tichon's repetition of his mother's instructions to her (b); but just as the abrupt, whole-tone outbursts would seem to represent Kabanicha, so the serene tune could represent Káťa's calm reaction. The only possibly 'non-Káťa' example is in Act 2 Scene 2, when Varvara and Kudrjáš discuss Kabanicha's sleeping, and the viola d'amore contributes to what has been described as 'snoring music' (e). But when this music recurs a few bars later, the offstage voice of Boris (singing to Káťa) is added to it, so perhaps the viola d'amore was meant to depict not Kabanicha sleeping but the distant presence of Káťa.

It is possible, then, to argue a 'Káťa' connection with all the viola d'amore music, but not a particularly consistent one – which is of course no surprise in Janáček. In other words the viola d'amore is not Janáček's only way of articulating his feelings about Káťa and her love.

8 Interpretations

'Katja Kabanowa'
MAX BROD (1924)[1]
Translated by J. B. Robinson

The libretto [of *Káťa Kabanová*] is based on Ostrovsky's drama *The Thunderstorm* – a Russian *Madame Bovary*. As in Flaubert's masterpiece, the entire plot hinges on the adultery of a romantically inclined woman no longer able to bear the pressures of a repugnant and constricting environment.

Several characteristic differences emerge between the French and the Russian versions of this theme, tempting us to trace them back to differences in national character, or between East and West. Mme Bovary's vein of romanticism is primarily poetic and hedonistic, Káťa Kabanová's more religious and introspective – which is not to deny Emma Bovary's very real religious traits. The winning quality of both figures is an artless nobility. By their very existence they protest against the narrowness of their surroundings, against provincialism and small-mindedness. In Mme Bovary's case these surroundings are marked by boredom, philistinism and imposture. Káťa bears the greater burden, for she is enslaved – what is worse, enslaved to her own family. Her husband is a weak man whose mother, the sinister Kabanicha, is the true driving force behind the drama. She rules with the conventions of so-called 'good breeding' – in reality nothing more than traditional mores. Her absolute tyranny within her family mirrors in miniature the ruthless power wielded by the tsars to keep the whole of Russia in bondage. From above came oppression by government, officialdom, a superstitious clergy; at home an entire household stood in thrall to the eldest family member. The aged Kabanicha is more than that time-honoured harridan, the 'wicked mother-in-law'; she stands symbolically for tsarist Russia, with its morality of blind obedience to arbitrary command.

162

In their final dénouements the French novel and the Russian play – which, though of the same generation, were probably written with no knowledge of each other's existence – are fundamentally different. Emma Bovary is the victim not merely of her disappointments, but of her straitened finances as well (bitter though this sounds, the bitterness fully accords with Flaubert's sceptical turn of mind). Káťa, however, does not face disappointment; Boris is hers alone. There is no outward cause for her ruin, and in this respect the Russian work is the more powerful and gripping of the two in rendering the turmoils of human passion. Káťa's death is brought about by inner forces, the lie and the sin simply overmastering her. Her very death makes her as pure and as lovely as she ever was. Unable to bear the burden of her conscience she brings about her death, very much like Kleist's Penthesilea, by her own words: with no one pursuing her, in no danger of discovery, she throws herself at the feet of her husband and her mortal enemy Kabanicha, confessing to all humanity her infidelity and openly demanding punishment.

It is this great scene of public confession that forms the psychological link between Janáček's *Káťa* and his *Jenůfa*, or *Její pastorkyňa* [*Her Foster-Daughter*]. *Jenůfa* likewise culminates in a similar repentant unburdening of guilt before the assembled villagers. Other analogous works from Slavonic literature suggest themselves, such as Tolstoy's *Power of Darkness*. I think I would not be wide of the mark in suggesting that, besides the play's impassioned plot, it was the scene of penitence which prompted Janáček's choice of this material. In addition, through his close family ties with Russia, and after two long study tours of the country,[2] bringing him to the very banks of the River Volga where Ostrovsky's drama is set, he was especially receptive to the subject-matter and atmosphere of this work.

The River Volga figures in each of the six scenes that remained after Janáček's compression of the somewhat clumsy stage play. One sees the mighty river now from the quayside, now through the windows of a merchant's room, now again from the still uncharted river banks. This broad watery expanse flows through the entire work; clearly it is symbolic, but – of what? Symbols should always be unambiguous to the senses while remaining slightly beyond the reach of reason, lest they sink to the frigidity of allegory and its imprisoning system of meanings. From this standpoint the Volga, both in Janáček's libretto and in his music, is the perfect example of an effective – because, at root, inexplicable – symbol. Perhaps if one saw in the monstrous, ceaselessly flowing masses of water churning headlong in the Volga a symbol of the inexorability with which life in tsarist Russia, unchanging and invincible, marched with relentless tread over the corpses of its children – perhaps then one would approach its meaning, or some shade of it. What can Káťa, pale and fragile, this pious rebel, do in the face of the timeless Volga? – this, or something like it, seems to be the message of each scene, a message repeated so often that, in the end, the unhappy woman flings herself into the river, perishing in its timeless depths. The Volga has triumphed, tsarist orthodoxy can continue on its way unimpeded. And even in the opening bars of the overture, in the ominous timpani strokes, one senses the remorselessness, the inexorability of this mighty, cruel, Russian world that has astounded us from time immemorial by its ruthless inflexibility.

Against this sombre background of an enslaved people one figure stands out – old Kabanicha, the work's true central character and prime motivating force. She embodies the tsarist ideal of absolute authority and unflinching obedience, projecting it into the domestic sphere where its effects are even more agonizing than in the wider canvas of public life. Kabanicha dominates her weak-spirited son Tichon, her domineering ways upsetting his marriage to the succeptible Káťa. Gentle Káťa rebels and, against her better judgement, falls for Boris, a young city-dweller of dubious noble ancestry who endures similar shackles to her own, being as much tyrannized by his uncle as she is by her mother-in-law. Destiny forces the two together, and the most riveting scene of the drama (left unchanged by Janáček) occurs when Káťa and Boris sink into each other's arms, neither a free agent, each handing the guiding responsibility over to the other in the tumult of their feelings. But Káťa cannot endure the lie that must follow. Normally a creature of pure heart and delicate religious sensibilities, she could momentarily forget herself as long as her husband was away. He returns and, under no compulsion, she confesses everything and seeks death in the Volga. Seduction against the voice of reason, a chaste, self-inflicted punishment – these link this work in spirit with Janáček's last[3] song cycle, *The Diary of One Who Disappeared.* 'Love against one's will' might appropriately head either of these works, and in each of them it is just this triumphant unleashing of elemental forces, sweeping aside the barriers of custom and reason, that inspired the composer in the most poignant passages of his score.

The opera races by with all the strength of youth as though in a single breath. Janáček himself, in conversation, described the highest aim of his music as being to engage the listener's attention so completely that, at the end of an act, he would be hard put to explain what had happened, or why it had to happen in this way and no other. From climax to climax, outburst to outburst, this music of pure feeling intensifies with a tightness of construction never heard before. Right from the start, the overture, built from Káťa's noble motif, augurs something extraordinary. After a subdued introduction from the plaintive, almost inaudible, strings, a darting flute motif[4] is heard, accompanied by sleigh bells [Ex. 10]. It conjures up the endless steppe, parting, loneliness. This motif is heard again at Tichon's departure, as are the bells on the horses of the carriage waiting outside the door. At the beginning of the work a slowed-down version of this 'departure' motif, in augmentation, can be heard on the timpani [Ex. 11]; thereafter it permeates the entire piece, recurring again and again until finally, in the confession scene, it flares out in thunderclaps and lightning flashes. Despite the forward surge of the opera, Janáček finds time for several other self-contained 'numbers' with the same effective immediacy as the overture, though there are fewer such numbers or arias here than in *Jenůfa*.

Both in emotional force and technical finish this opera surpassed everything Janáček had written to date. Even Janáček's disparagers have had to admit the mighty unity of its construction. It is the ripe fruit where *Jenůfa*, with its occasional inconsistent patches of dreamy colours, was the budding flower – though I hasten to confess my weakness for first flowerings, notwithstanding the many blessings of full summer. It is impossible to list the many lovely moments that stand out against the – to my taste – perhaps slightly contrived parlando style. The introduction to Act 2 speaks directly to the heart, as does, earlier, the great scene [in Act 1 Scene 2] in which Káťa recalls the happiness of childhood and her rapturous visions in church. Here, as the horn enters and the woodwinds slowly begin to span their giant musical arch over its melody – surely this moment should bring tears to the eyes of anyone sensible to music. Then comes the nighttime love-scene on the Volga [Act 2 Scene 2], with the two contrasting couples: Kudrjáš and Varvara – vulgar, merry, drawn in folk tunes; and Káťa and Boris – heroic, their thoughts transported to realms of death and eternity. Both text and music of this scene make it worthy of a place in world literature, perhaps even a place of honour. There is a second love-duet in the last act, and here, as the muted strings lift up their mystical lay over the strangely altered harmonies, the two lovers kiss, and the listener thrills with them in sweetness and surrender.

As to the opera's technique, it is notable that its motifs, even more so than *Jenůfa*'s, are frequently orchestral in origin, so that the theory that Janáček has pasted together 'speech-melodies' into operas is here less tenable than ever and deserves to be dismissed once and for all as absurd. The long *cantabile* oboe melody (VS 24) that refers to Káťa, passing to the flute at her entrance [Ex. 12], is, for instance, a motif that appears solely in the orchestra; a similar instance is the 'swallows' flight' motif[5] that opens Act 1 Scene 2 and forms a background to the ensuing dialogue up to Káťa's narrative. The cheerful Varvara is given a motif consisting of chords in quadruple flutes and celesta [Ex. 14]; it suggests a transparent hedonism kept within limits. It is interesting that this motif, which is confined to the orchestra at its first appearance at the beginning of Act 2, later passes to the voice parts at the end of this act, appearing in free inversion, to form the melody of Varvara's and Kudrjáš's strophic song [VS 111–12]. Here what seems like a folk tune in its own right has in fact emerged organically from the motivic tissue of the work as a whole.

The abundance of sheer musicality that found expression in *Káťa Kabanová* could hardly have been exhausted in this terse, almost epigrammatic opera, fairly bursting though it is with musical invention. Indeed, it seems that in his old age, with many external obstacles now finally removed and even the public's and critics' disheartening lack of understanding beginning to give way, Janáček worked with greater ease, vigour and fruitfulness than when he was in the prime of life, with its many struggles and sorrows. Perhaps this was also partly due to the recent upsurge of cultural activities in Brno, and further to the strengthening of artistic ties between this city and Prague, which freed his work from the curse of provincialism and opened up the path to the rest of the Czech nation and to humanity – a path which, with all his genius, Janáček would have traversed long before this, if circumstances had permitted.

Les autres oeuvres dramatiques: 'Katia Kabanova'
DANIEL MULLER (1930)
Translated by Caroline B. Lloyd

With *Káťa Kabanová* we return to the Janáček of *Jenůfa* with all its melodic qualities and dramatic appeal. A journey to Russia in 1896 may have been the starting-point of this sinister drama taken from the famous play by Ostrovsky *The Thunderstorm*. A young woman with a sensitive inner life is unhappily married to the merchant

Tichon, who does not understand her and is entirely dominated by his mother, old Kabanicha. During her husband's absence, Káťa yields to the advances of the young Boris, another unhappy soul who is ill-treated by his uncle. On Tichon's return, she confesses her unfaithfulness and goes away to throw herself in the Volga. In spite of the title, it is not Káťa who is the principal character of the play. Janáček saw in the bigoted little town of Kalinovo an epitome of the old Russia of eighty years ago. The iron bonds of tradition, the tyranny of the family, the abject subjugation of married women, a punctilious piety with its strict observances and crude superstition, the whole inflexible code of moral rules which confines its adherents like a strait-jacket, all this is personified in the extraordinary figure of old Kabanicha (a successor to the Kostelnička of *Jenůfa*), who, in the name of the old customs, tyrannizes over her son, her daughter-in-law, her friends, over everyone around her. It is to her that we owe a series of scenes which are certainly dramatic but are rather too disturbing for us because they offend our western sensibility and our modern sense of personal freedom. The intensity of this forceful figure worthy of Balzac makes the other characters in the play seem weak by comparison. In this opera, whose Russian original has clear revolutionary tendencies, we are transported into a truly Slavonic atmosphere of moral laxity, despairing fatalism, destructive nihilism and spiritual death – which was precisely what attracted Janáček, whose technique was ideally suited to depicting this noxious environment with its festering corruption and morbidity.

A further attraction was that the libretto offered him a sharp contrast to all this in the uninhibited pair of lovers: Kudrjáš, an educated young man who knows what causes lightning, and Varvara, his mistress, who has taken over his principles. Throughout the opera they spend their time heaping sarcasm on the old customs and their representatives and finally, sickened to death by this repressive company, they bid farewell to the little town to seek their fortune in the capital, thus giving us a fine example of courage: chains are only made to be broken.

For this libretto Janáček wrote an admirable score, saving his harshest strains of terror and anguish for the old Russian side of the play and his sweetest melodies for the pair of emancipated lovers. In particular, there resulted from this contrast an important passage which has no equal in all Janáček (with the exception of the love-scene from *The Diary of One Who Disappeared*); it has an assured place amongst the most beautiful musical creations of any land. I refer to Act 2 Scene 2, which is, on a larger scale, the counterpart of the garden quartet in *Faust*. A marvel of grace, of expression and of skill, this astounding quartet, comprising nearly six hundred bars, is constructed on the best classical lines and its harmony shows all the resources of the most subtle technique. In it we see by turns the two pairs of lovers against the backdrop of the moonlit park. We have on the one hand Káťa and Boris, over whose sensitive and sombre passion hangs a presentiment of death, and on the other Kudrjáš and Varvara, whose love reflects only the happiness of their carefree youth. This is one of those almost perfect musical creations and, as an example of what modern art can achieve, it can be compared to the finest creations of classical art. The exquisite poetry of the last fifty bars, the wisps of themes floating like perfume in the clear summer night, the chromatic sigh breathed by the orchestra before the final chord, have the poignant charm of the best of Mozart in this genre: we have here all the languor and voluptuousness of the balcony trio in *Don Giovanni* but loaded with all the *morbidezza* of our times.

Indeed, when we look at the evident sympathy with which the composer treated the two characters Varvara and Kudrjáš and the aura of black pessimism in which he steeped the other roles, we may even be tempted to suspect that his real intention was to satirize this whole world of old Russia and induce us to share the horror it inspired in him.

Looked at from this angle, the principal leitmotif of the work is full of significance. It appears at the beginning of the overture and has been labelled by Czech and German critics[6] the 'departure motif'. In fact it is something very different. In its complete form [Ex. 10], as it is enunciated by the oboe in bar 33 of the overture, it is a theme with religious overtones consisting of eight bars in 2/4 *allegro* in F minor[7] with a flattened leading note (aeolian mode), accompanied by rapid arpeggios on the flutes (and even by bells). It is the flutes alone which represent Tichon's journey. Janáček has detached from the theme the first two bars consisting of eight notes of equal value, the last four of which are a fourth above the first, and out of these eight notes he has made one of the two basic motifs of his opera [Ex. 10], the one representing old Russia and the iron circle of tradition; it [i.e. Ex. 10] appears nearly fifty times in the opera unmodified, deliberately inserted into every sort of movement but always with the same overriding rhythm, most often on the timpani *fortissimo*. This means it is clearly recognizable. It is heard eleven times in the overture and seventeen times in the scene of Tichon's departure [Act 1 Scene 2]. It is heard in close connection with thunder, lightning and the rain squalls of the storm, during Kát'a's confession [Act 3 Scene 1] and in the last scene (the suicide); it is with this theme that the opera closes. This is one of those dynamic mechanisms which Janáček used in *Jenůfa* and for which he has been so severely criticized; nevertheless it is the constant repetition of these eight notes that finally induces in one a feeling of abject terror.

Directly related to this same oboe theme in F minor, which gives us this principal motif, we find Kát'a's theme, which forms the subject of the overture and which reappears in the first words she pronounces [Ex. 1]: this theme, cast in a gloomy minor and composed of sixths, fourths and sevenths, is as cold as the grave; the delicate arpeggios of a poetic viola d'amore [in the overture] only seem to give it a more sinister expression, and it reminds one of the accompaniment to part of the Kostelnička's dialogue with Števa in *Jenůfa*.[8]

From the oboe theme, too, comes one of the oddest passages of the opera; it is one of those passages in which Janáček gives free rein to his bizarre sense of humour. Kát'a's corpse has just been brought back to the bank; the only funeral oration which old Kabanicha delivers is to thank the boatmen[9] with a ceremonious bow, singing to them in a sanctimonious tone 'Thank you, thank you, my good people, for your kind services!' ['Děkuji vám, děkuji vám, dobří lidé za úslužnost!', VS 164], in a sort of chant taken from the fourth bar of the aeolian oboe theme which reproduces note for note the beginning of the Dies irae. Suddenly and shrilly the orchestra takes up Kabanicha's theme *prestissimo rubato* and performs a sort of dia-bolical gallop of semiquavers, ending, after a descending march, in a hellish frenzy of sextuplet semiquavers over six slow bars in 6/4, in which the motif is repeated very rapidly thirty-six times; beneath this frenzy, the mysterious voices of the Volga sing their sinister chant [VS 165, fig. 40] one last time to the accompaniment of the brass, and the timpani beat out the strokes of the eight imperious notes of the theme of the slavery of tradition. We seem to hear all hell let loose and it is difficult to explain why Janáček used this satanic effect unless he had the clear intention of inspiring in his listeners a horror of the code of rules which, however respectable it may once have been, has here been the cause of so much cruelty.

The other basic theme in *Kát'a* is Varvara's motif [Ex. 14], consist-ing of two bars in 2/4 *allegretto*, the beginning of a melody full of freshness; it is enunciated first by the bassoons accompanied by charming chords in cross-rhythm on the flutes and celesta, which give it its true character; it underlines Varvara's first words [VS 30] when she fires off her first sarcastic jibe at old Kabanicha who, as soon as she is out of church, has angrily begun to scold her daughter-in-law. This theme, contrasting as it does with the tradition motif (between them they encapsulate the meaning of the opera), appears about fifty times in the course of the work. Janáček made the best of it, dissecting it, prolonging it or sometimes inverting it.

It is used wittily when Varvara, whom Káťa still believes to be pure, tells her guardedly that she already has much to reproach herself with [VS 51]; a little later, when Varvara gives Káťa the key she has stolen from the old woman, the theme, with its alternate thirds and fourths, so curiously suggestive and insinuating, evokes the idea of temptation [VS 74–6]; this time it is embellished first by an additional bar giving it the air of a folksong, then by captivating trills, and in the end it becomes languid, *pianissimo*, with delightful chords on the harp [VS 75]. Later again, in the celebrated nocturnal quartet in the garden, it is openly transformed into a folksong with a refrain sung by Kudrjáš, who is coming to meet the lovely Varvara [VS 93–4]; at the end of the quartet, giving Káťa and Boris the signal to leave, the composer conjures from his motif a second folksong, a charming piece with its gracious descent on the weak beat [VS 110–12]. Finally the theme appears for the last time when Varvara decides to quit the little town with her lover [VS 140–1]. One feels that Janáček, despite his sixty-seven years, worked on this theme *con amore*, a fact which would tend to prove that the couple Kudrjáš and Varvara had all his sympathies.

There are many other beautiful passages which still deserve a mention: the delicate swallow[5] theme which accompanies Káťa's confidences to Varvara, a magnificent answer to the daydream woven in *Salammbô*:

> Qui me donnera comme à la colombe
> Des ailes pour fuir dans le soir qui tombe?

Then there is Káťa's account of her religious ecstacies as a child in church, a companion piece to the Salve regina in *Jenůfa*,[10] a beautiful passage where the solo horn echoes so movingly Káťa's voice above the pure chords of the harps and the delicate ethereal tracery of the flutes [VS 42ff]; the scene of Káťa's farewell to her husband, with the awe-inspiring chords of the vow [VS 55ff]; the heartbeats of the young student Boris as he awaits the arrival of the woman who is to be his first lover [VS 96ff];[11] the storm scene [Act 3 Scene 1] in its romantic setting of ruins painted with ancient frescoes of hell, and Káťa, terrified by the lightning, impelled to her confession; the final scene with the voices of the Volga [VS 145ff] (hummed by the chorus, whose theme [Ex. 15] has begun to emerge during the storm [e.g. Ex. 30]), voices which ring in the ears of the despairing Káťa, a new Alcestis calling upon the divinities of the Styx; her last appeal to Boris in the night on the banks of the river [VS 150–1]; their last kiss . . . A sombre drama this, and one which, in spite of the imperfections of the libretto, contains such beautiful music that surely it must take first place after *Jenůfa*. Mr Max Brod calls *Jenůfa* the flower of Janáček's genius and *Káťa* the ripe fruit;[12] he adds, however, that he prefers the flower to the fruit and I am entirely of his opinion.

Janáček and 'Katya Kabanova'
WINTON DEAN (1954)

There is a modern danger that the work of art that fits neither the pigeon-hole nor the pillory may go by default, and 'Katya Kabanova', while it has no scandal value, does not hang comfortably on any of the traditional pegs. It has affinities with 'Pelléas et Mélisande' and still more with 'Boris Godunov', not on account of its Russian subject (it is based on Ostrovsky's well-known play 'The Storm', for which Tchaikovsky wrote a concert overture), but because Janáček, like Mussorgsky, was much concerned with folk style and the rhythms of popular speech. Indeed his interest extended to the sounds of nature as a whole; he recorded in musical notation the voices of apes and walruses.[13] But by the time the opera was written (1919–21) most of musical Europe had long turned its back on nationalism. It is true that Bartók, with whom also Janáček has not a little in common, won world fame between the wars, but the new music that made most stir was that of the expatriate Stravinsky and the doctrinaire Schönberg and their followers. And it was the experimental rather than the national and traditional elements in Bartók that generally claimed attention. History may well disturb these judgements. We have suffered a good deal from the critical heresy of judging contemporary music by the adjective rather than the noun. Some of the greatest composers of the past have been denounced as reactionaries in their own lifetime.

No one could possibly call Janáček a reactionary, but he was undoubtedly eclectic. He worked to no system, brandished no slogans, and attracted no pressure group. He inconveniently proved the continuing vitality of the tonal tradition just when it was to the interest of many to suppose it exhausted. His freedom from technical preconceptions annoys the academic traditionalist without satisfying any of the fashionable types of doctrinaire. He repeatedly does things that look wrong on paper but (except to an ear stopped with prejudice) sound right in performance; and to this must be added that stumbling-block peculiar to the born opera composer (Verdi, for instance), the perpetration of effects that fall flat in the study but are brilliant and moving in the theatre. Although he wrote much other vocal and instrumental music of high quality, Janáček stands or falls by his nine operas. And 'Jenufa' and 'Katya Kabanova' alone are enough to place him among the few great opera composers of the century.

An instructive comparison can be made between 'Katya Kabanova' and the almost exactly contemporary 'Wozzeck'.[14] Both operas are intensely concentrated and tragic in tone; both handle nineteenth-century plays in a manner that owes a good deal to the modern science of psychology; both composers reveal a profound compassion for the sufferings of their chief character. But in technique and approach they are poles apart. Where Janáček combines many traditional elements in a free and empirical style, Berg creates his stresses in the main by circumscribing a revolutionary language with the strictest logic. Janáček works outwards from his dramatic data, Berg inwards from his musical premises. And while 'Wozzeck' has not a little of the obsessional quality of Strindberg – a pity so ferocious that for some listeners it may defeat its own ends by escaping their notice altogether – Janáček treats his theme with a detachment, at once intense and ironical, that strongly recalls Chekhov. His range of sympathy is far wider than Berg's, whose two operas are preoccupied with the sordid side of human nature. Janáček's characters – and also the subjects of his operas – are remarkably varied, and although he can draw persons who are contemptible and even repulsive, like Katya's husband and mother-in-law, he never weights the scales so as to make them incredible. They are comprehended with the same vision and lapped round with the same musical essence in which the rest of the drama is distilled.

This sense of background, of the locality, both physical and spiritual, in which the characters have their being, is one of Janáček's greatest (and most Chekhovian) gifts. It is doubtless connected with his peasant origin and the strong feeling of community he derived from contact with his own people and their environment. At the same time he shows an exceptional penetration into the motives of individuals, particularly of women; his portraits of Jenufa and Katya, neither of them simple characters, have an extraordinary subtlety and vitality. Katya, a passionate heroine whose power to break with her constricting environment is inhibited by her conscience, is unique in opera. Wilfrid Mellers has suggested that all Janáček's mature art springs from the intensity of his sympathy with nature and his consciousness of sin.[15] Certainly his vision of human nature is not only localised but universal. He is as free, both in style and outlook, from the homespun folkiness of some national art as he is from the dreary realism of *verismo*. Although his fruit springs from good rich soil, it never tastes of the farmyard. He was in fact an experienced practical musician with a thorough knowledge of many styles and periods. In this he differs from Mussorgsky, who in some of his songs was in greater danger than Janáček of allowing his interest in linguistic inflections to drain the lyrical power of the music.

It is this lyrical quality that should commend Janáček's music to a wide public, provided they do not expect the more leisurely expansiveness of Strauss or Puccini. Janáček stands in relation to those composers rather as Verdi's 'Falstaff' stands to 'Rigoletto'. Music and action move with such swiftness and economy that the sudden soaring phrases in the voices (and still more in the orchestra) must be caught at once before they escape. The extreme flexibility of the style forbids set-pieces, and the recurring motives, though skilfully used, do not bind the music together in a Wagnerian manner. Many technical features – the treatment of the dialogue, which may sound clipped and breathless until the ear grows used to it, the comparative absence of counterpoint, the lack of transitions, and in particular Janáček's fondness for unprepared modulations into adjacent rather than related keys [e.g. Ex. 12] – would appear at first glance rather to tear it apart. Nor does the rhythmic complexity, with a preference for compound, irregular, and swiftly changing metres (there is very little common time)[16] and a tendency to avoid accents on the first beat of the bar, always carry conviction on paper.

But such suspicions are confounded in practice by the same qualities that dispel the obvious objections to 'Pelléas et Mélisande'. Janáček's sensitiveness to every nuance of the drama, the shimmering and multi-coloured beauty of the orchestration, which is integral and not applied, and the very personal use of harmony contribute to an impression at once unified and urgent, if not positively overpowering. Janáček's chromaticism, thanks partly to its modal tinge, is always mobile and utterly unlike the chromaticism of the German romantic tradition from Spohr to early Schönberg, which tends to bring movement to a standstill. Such a style, of course, is apt to break down in any other hands than those of genius. Even in Janáček it produces occasional incoherence; for instance the comic scenes, such as that between the mother-in-law and the drunken Dikoj in Act 2, though their dramatic intention is plain, are not quite in focus with the rest.[17] But the score is so rich in invention, psychological insight and haunting sensuous beauty that it reduces many of the *enfants terribles* of our age to the status of nursery bogies.

Leoš Janáček

K.-H. WÖRNER (1969)
Translated by J. B. Robinson

Now mysteriously, now conspicuously, the Volga is constantly drawn into the action of the opera *Káťa Kabanová*, whose libretto, written by Janáček himself, derives from a realist drama *The Thunderstorm* by the Russian poet Alexander Nikolayevich Ostrovsky, the founder of Russian national theatre. As the curtain rises we see Kudrjáš sitting on a bench, lost in contemplation of the river; he cries, 'Marvellous sight! You must admit it's a marvel!... I've been looking at the Volga every day for twenty-five years and I can never see enough of it!... A fantastic sight! The beauty of it! It makes your very soul glad!' 'A marvel' – these words sound almost strange[18] coming from him since, in the stage piece, he plays an enlightened figure among conventional men, a revolutionary surrounded by bigotry and superstition, a 'teacher, chemist, engineer', as he is referred to in the list of characters. 'It's Nature that we should do homage to' – that, in essence, is his thought, the wisdom of pantheism.

For Káťa, the opera's title role and heroine, suicide – her liberating plunge into the waters of the Volga – is a means of returning to Nature. Her last words, after steeling herself to face death, are these: 'The birds will fly to my grave, bringing their young with them; and flowers will blossom – red, blue and yellow. How quiet! How lovely! How lovely! And to have to die!' And here, in her last moments of consciousness, a human being rises far above all the suffering and humiliation she had to endure in her life, reconciling herself with the world by returning to Nature. Thus – however little Janáček, and perhaps Ostrovsky, may have been aware of it – the beginning and the end of the drama are spanned by an arch, extending from the contemplation of the Volga, through the eyes of the enlightened Kudrjáš, as a vital element in the continual ebb and flow, to Káťa's self-sacrifice in this primordial element.

Water as an element, the Volga as an eternal cycle, an event of perpetual grandeur in the lives of those inhabiting its shores – this metaphor permeates the whole of Janáček's music. The listener senses its movement, but only the musical analyst can approach its secret. This secret resides in Janáček's having equated the principal theme assigned to Káťa with one that characterizes water.

The musical technique used to bring about these resemblances and connections, as well as their transformations, is based on the principle of 'modular variants'. Janáček does not presuppose a fixed form for his themes, with their first appearance being definitive; rather, the first instance of a theme (keeping in mind the one for Káťa and water) is itself merely one of many possible transformations, or 'variants' (in the hands of a genius of thematic transformation like Janáček the possibilities may well be limitless), of a particular 'module'.[19] This module is composed of three pitches so arranged that the first two form a descending scale step, usually a major second, while the second and third pitches span a larger interval, usually a perfect fourth. At its various occurrences the module can be extended, as for example by prefixing two steps to the descending fourth; it can also be presented in inversion, in retrograde, or in retrograde inversion. The table of musical examples [Ex. 37] shows the principal variants that Janáček happened to light upon. Yet each of the main transmutations here compiled (there are forty-nine in all) is characterized as such in a highly individual manner within the context of the drama. It is thus toward the drama that we must now direct our scrutiny.

Ex. 37.1–3 shows how a group of four pitches is subjected to extension by the particular device of eliding and telescoping the group in the course of repetition. The examples cited form the musical background to Kudrjáš's above-mentioned lines, at the opening of Act 1 Scene 1, as he expresses his admiration for Nature. The extension of the group has, appropriately, a quality of organic growth, equally in harmony with the subjective feelings toward Nature and the mighty ebb and flow of the Volga.

Kudrjáš has withdrawn; Dikoj and Boris appear, quarrelling. The backdrop supplied by Ex. 37.4 is derived from a motif taken over literally from the first act of *Siegfried*, with the same emotional connotations.[20] Its relationship to the module is remote, but nevertheless evident: the descending pitches now fall in wide leaps, just as happens in Ex. 37.20, 26, and 35 and subsequently in 48 and 49.

Ex. 37

11 VS 29: fig. 34

ACT 1 SCENE 2

12 VS 37: fig. 1

13 VS 40: 12 bars after fig. 5

14 VS 42: 4 bars after fig. 7

15 VS 44: 3 bars before fig. 9

16 VS 49: fig. 14

17 VS 51: fig. 16

18 VS 57: 2 bars after fig. 21

19 VS 58: 11 bars after fig. 21

20 VS 59: 3 bars after fig. 22

VS 65: fig. 27

21

ACT 2 SCENE 1

VS 71: bar 2

22

VS 74: 15 bars after fig. 3

23

VS 75: 14 bars after fig. 4

24

ACT 2 SCENE 2

VS 86: bar 1

25

VS 92: fig. 8

26

VS 98: fig. 15

27

VS 99: 5 bars after fig. 16

28

VS 101: fig. 18

29

VS 101: 14 bars after fig. 18

30

ACT 3 SCENE 1

VS 113: bar 1

31

VS 119: fig. 4

32

VS 120: 8 bars after fig. 5

33

VS 133: fig. 14

34

VS 137: 8 bars after fig. 16

35

ACT 3 SCENE 2

VS 141: 4 bars after fig. 19

36

VS 142: 9 bars after fig. 19

37

VS 145: 9 bars after fig. 21

38

VS 145: 11 bars after fig. 21

39

VS 145: 19 bars after fig. 21

40

VS 147: 2 bars after fig. 24

41

VS 148: fig. 25

42

VS 149: 13 bars after fig. 25

43

VS 149: 5 bars after fig. 26

44

VS 151: 12 bars after fig. 27

45

VS 152: 2 bars after fig. 29

46

VS 154: 10 bars after fig. 30

47

VS 156: 7 bars after fig. 32

48

VS 161: fig. 35

49

Dikoj has now left, and Boris, deeply wounded by his uncle's up-braiding, speaks his mind to Kudrjáš. Here, for the first time, the thematic module is provided with lyrical variants (Ex. 37.5, 6, 7) depicting Boris's depression in the face of his present inescapable plight. The church service is over and the congregation return to their homes; Káťa appears on stage as one of their number. Her first entrance is accompanied by Ex. 37.8, played by the flute; this is Káťa in all the intimate tenderness of her nature, the wealth of her powers of feeling, her hidden passion. And beside her, in direct contrast (Ex. 37.9), is Kabanicha – tyrannical, splenetic, fierce; both themes belong together, being distant relations of one and the same module. A conversation then follows between Kabanicha and her son in which she asserts her rights as his mother, as depicted in Ex. 37.10. Disarmingly, Káťa enters the dispute (Ex. 37.11). Even these few variants from the opening scene of the opera show the far greater flexibility of the principle of modular variants as compared to the techniques of motivic variation.

Act 1 Scene 2 opens with a conversation between Káťa and Varvara. In the very first bar (Ex. 37.12), with its flowing thirds, there is a new variant of the module, referring in this instance to Káťa's notion and hope of flying, and thereby to the deepest yearnings of her spirit. She returns immediately thereafter to her former dejection (Ex. 37.13), then recounts incidents from her happy childhood (Ex. 37.14 and 15), before her boundless longing finally breaks forth in all its passion (Ex. 37.16), bringing with it a confession to Varvara of her hidden love. Varvara now shares her secret. Ex. 37.17 shows the module in a new variant with a rhythmic structure closely allied to the folk-like theme given throughout the opera to Varvara and her admirer Váňa Kudrjáš. And Varvara is the source of the fateful suggestion that Káťa and her lover meet in secret.

The next scene, Tichon's departure on a journey of some distance, reveals a truly remarkable broadening of the psychology. Káťa, sensing the danger that threatens her, clings to her husband, who reacts with incomprehension to her passion and strange demands. Káťa's request to be allowed to accompany Tichon on his journey is clothed in variants 37.18 and 19. The module, by now so extended as to span two octaves (Ex. 37.20), embodies Káťa's desperate fear of the encroaching entanglements of her fate.

Tichon's mother, Kabanicha, enters, and Káťa now stands confronted by both mother and son. Tichon commands his wife to obey his mother (Ex. 37.21).

Act 2 opens with a fairly lyrical orchestral prelude in which, at bars 2 and 3, a new, sensitive variant of the module rings out on the oboe; it is Káťa, lost in thought, introspective, silent – not at all as her mother-in-law had wished her to be (Ex. 37.22). Once again Varvara and Káťa are alone, and now Varvara hands her friend the key to the garden gate. Káťa's violent inner turmoil is depicted in variant 37.23 and, further expanded, in 37.24. The new element in these themes is the ascending semitone that precedes the module, effecting an extraordinary increase of intensity. The new variant thus created dominates Káťa's subsequent monologue, the desperate struggle in her soul against 'temptation'.

Act 2 Scene 1 concludes with a dialogue between Kabanicha and Dikoj the merchant. Here it is difficult to overlook a certain want of consistency as Janáček reverts to the module without having a compelling reason in the drama for doing so.

Now follows the second scene of this act – the first nightly tryst of the two lovers, Káťa and Boris, on the banks of the Volga. The music accompanying the scene-change portrays the state of Káťa's mind – her rapture, her doubtful hesitation. The intervals of the module are now filled in, first with scale steps (Ex. 37.25), later in bold, leaping fourths as Boris speaks ecstatically of Káťa to Kudrjáš (Ex. 37.26). The love-scene between Káťa and Boris offers the richest elaborations of the module (Ex. 37.27, 28, 29, 30) to be found outside Káťa's concluding monologue shortly before her death; Janáček reaches these further degrees of intensification by prefixing an ascending phrase to the module, whose sequence of pitches has till now usually been directed downwards. Throughout the scene Janáček achieves music of a sublimity that bears comparison with the greatest exemplars of the genre, thereby completely winning over our sympathy to the lovers as, after much internal struggle, they break through the strictures of conventional standards.

Act 3 Scene 1 proceeds on two levels, its external structure being determined by the gathering and ultimate unleashing of the thunderstorm, and its internal logic paralleling these external events; just as, externally, the storm clouds assemble, so the burden of guilt mounts in Káťa's conscience, seeking release in a confession to the entire world of her adultery. What takes place in Káťa's mind may perhaps be fully understood only if one extends to her the view first uttered by Dikoj, and later taken up by the whole assembly: that thunderstorms are a punishment inflicted on men by God. And before the confession has escaped her lips Káťa admits to being terrified by lightning.[21]

The music is a single *crescendo*, relentlessly unfolding. It begins with the pre-pentatonic descending group E flat, D flat, B flat and A flat, a new variant of the module (Ex. 37.31), and from the Nature theme of this group Janáček derives a series of themes (Ex. 37.32, 33, 34, 35) intimately related to the psychological progress of the scene as a whole. 'Káťa's Death' might be an appropriate title for the concluding scene of this work.

It is, after the love-duet, the opera's second great climax, a scene dominated by the figure of Káťa who, in her greatness of spirit, seeks death as she reaches out across and beyond it; it is one of those scenes in operatic drama in which a female figure brings the work to its final resolution, as do Isolde, Brünnhilde, Salome, Electra or the Woman in Schoenberg's *Erwartung*. At the very end Ostrovsky, a realist, hints at a pantheistic afterlife; Wagner's mystical, metaphysical interpretation of death means nothing to the Russian playwright. In Janáček's opera Káťa is a completely unreflecting being of artless naivety; the compelling beauty of this figure lies precisely in her spontaneity.

What Janáček has at his disposal here is quite extraordinary; one must turn to Verdi's great death-scenes for anything immediately comparable. Káťa's entrance in the final scene is accompanied by Ex. 37.36, comprising the first three notes of the module in retrograde. Her desire to see Boris once more is set to Ex. 37.37; the final three [intervals] of this example are identical to the first three of Ex. 37.8, the motif that accompanies her first entrance in Act 1 after attending church. The voices of the Volga (Ex. 37.38 and 39) resound in Káťa's profound fear of darkness and solitude. The burden her spirit has to bear finds expression in Ex. 37.40; Ex. 37.41 underpins her questioning, in deep depression – why she should go on living? She cries out for death (Ex. 37.42 and 43). Once again she thinks of Boris (Ex. 37.44); her cries become more impassioned (Ex. 37.45).

Boris enters; the couple remain in silent embrace, Káťa sobbing on his shoulder. Ex. 37.46 derives from Ex. 37.44 by a mere interchanging of its two bars. Boris mentions his forthcoming journey to Siberia (Ex. 37.47). Káťa's words of farewell – warm, compassionate, yet so full of yearning – are borne by the great solo cited in Ex. 37.48, with the module soaring forth once again, here in its most widely divergent variant. The voices of the Volga, now with ever greater insistence, reverberate in her parting words, as does Ex. 37.34, here in a full harmonization with the melody doubled by a unison chorus. In Káťa's final gaze beyond the grave the module is heard for the last time in a new variant (Ex. 37.49).

Káťa Kabanová could be used to demonstrate how important the constitutive aspect of a module was for Janáček in composing a full-length opera, and how, in the composer's hands, the module can be freely adapted in accordance with the demands of any given moment in the drama, by recourse to individual variants. Yet the module that we have extracted from this opera is in no way unique to this particular work of Janáček's. We also find it in *The Diary of One Who Disappeared*, *The Cunning Little Vixen*, *From the House of the Dead*, the Glagolitic Mass, the string quartets and the Sinfonietta, to cite just a few examples from Janáček's later works. The module formed by the combination of a second with a subsequent third or fourth – or its inversion – has been traced by Hans Hollander [1963, pp. 99–100] directly to the folk music of eastern Moravia. Hollander calls the module a 'typically vocal intonation formula' which was 'ever-present in Janáček's subconscious' and appears 'in numerous instances as a germinal cell in effecting melodic cohesion'.

If, as above, we note a certain inconsistency in Janáček's drawing upon variants of the module in the scene between Kabanicha and Dikoj, our interpretation has, of course, been biassed by Wagner's use of leitmotifs. But Janáček's very methods show that he did not have a system, in the Wagnerian sense, in mind. To be sure, the module and its numerous variants are primarily connected with the character of Káťa and with the Volga as a natural phenomenon representing the ebb and flow of life. But for just this reason these modular variants cannot simultaneously function as 'leitmotifs' for Káťa and the Volga. Rather, they are something greater than this: they represent an indispensable, perhaps the essential, structural device in composing by means of thematic manipulation; only secondarily do they serve to delineate the psychology of the characters.

Producing 'Káťa Kabanová'
DAVID POUNTNEY (1982)

The first matters in which a producer must commit himself well before rehearsals begin are the visual ones. In the case of *Káťa* the decisions to be taken about its milieu and visual atmosphere are not simple. The interaction of Janáček's advanced 1920s attitudes with Ostrovsky's of the 1850s throws up some interesting questions. Is the opera a work of social criticism in the nineteenth-century naturalistic tradition? Or is it rather a modern drama about psychological destruction? Is the fate of Káťa intended by Janáček to be seen as a 'beacon' for social progress and humanitarian reform? Or is it a personal account of neurotic collapse? Is the reality of the social background crucial or incidental? Do Russia, the Volga, the date, matter? Music invariably shifts the emphasis of a play on to its emotional and spiritual content. These are the areas about which music has most to say. It is therefore no suprise that Janáček chose to omit much of the precise social criticism that was a principal feature of the original play. In fact, he swept aside all incidental detail with such ruthlessness that he left a trail of minor if obvious inconsistencies behind him. The somewhat pedantic Brod had to come puffing along in the wake of Janáček's streamlined inspiration, vainly trying to clear up a host of petty imprecisions (see above, pp. 64–8).

Janáček's concentration on his heroine and the figures who immediately determine her fate is so absolute that when he does include a minor figure, or item of social background, it is usually in a most offhand manner. Fekluša is a good case in point. In the play her sycophantic adulation of the pious Kabanov household makes sense, as she is clearly portrayed as one of the bands of parasitic pilgrims who would have been a familiar figure in provincial Russian households. In the opera she is so deprived of space and time that she merely hobbles across the stage muttering something inaudible which apparently annoys Boris.

Similarly, the perfunctory interjections of the chorus in Act 3 are treated wholly as they might have seemed to Káťa – disjointed cries penetrating her own confusion. They are not allowed an independent existence of their own. The traditional Russian ceremony of departure at the end of Act 1 is mercilessly compressed almost to the point of incomprehensibility. But Janáček is pursuing his unerring sense of dramatic pace towards the act curtain, and no item of ethnic social behaviour is allowed to delay him.

Janáček treated the social background almost with contempt. The producer is left to decide whether he should strive to clarify the social milieu by concentrating on the kind of detail which staging rather than music can excel at, or whether he should echo the music and create a stage picture which brings the expressionistic and psychological elements to the fore, and leaves the social background more abstract and blurred. The tendency in most post-war productions has been in the latter direction. This is partly because that has in any case been the general trend of stage design, especially as pioneered by the great Czech designer Svoboda; but also because the visual atmosphere of the late expressionist movement, and perhaps especially

Munch, is not only contemporary with Janáček, but very close to his work in feeling.

Nonetheless, I am also convinced that the work could be most interestingly interpreted along detailed naturalistic lines – in the style of an Ibsen play, for instance. A meticulously detailed and restrained bourgeois setting could create a startling tension with the music: absolute Victorian probity and order on the stage, whilst the music betrays the psychological turmoil underneath. As far as I know, this interpretation has not been attempted recently, probably for technical reasons. Even with Janáček's added interludes (see Chapter 7) both the first two acts involve changes from exterior to interior in about two and a half minutes. During the interval between them, however, no scene-change is necessary! In the last act, Janáček has allowed forty-five seconds for the scene-change, though he has at least had the grace to supply loud music for it. A naturalistic interpretation therefore demands very sophisticated stage equipment.

The temptation also exists to use Janáček's strikingly modern psychological grasp as an excuse to interpret Káťa as a 'modern woman' haunted by a typically twentieth-century urban neurosis. But the religious element, with its crucial expressions – guilt and confession, ecstasy and abasement – cannot be ignored. The producer must preserve enough of Ostrovsky's background and period to enable the essential religious element to be readily convincing.

Two awesome natural elements dominate the work: river and storm. They are both extremely difficult to realize effectively, and capable of great variety of interpretation. The presence of the Volga is inescapable in the score, more in overall atmosphere than by any precise motivic identification, even though the 'voices of the Volga' motif (Ex. 15) dominates the whole of the last act, emerging from accompaniment to full melodic prominence. The symbolic function of the Volga in both play and opera has been the subject of widely differing interpretations. It has been seen as a symbol of love and freedom – especially of the everlasting freedom to which Káťa escapes. Others have seen it as a symbol of the perpetual despotic cruelty of Russian life – brutal, savage and insensitive. Any interpretation of its function in the opera must hang to a large extent on one's view of the end of the opera, since the Volga unmistakably has the last word. The eerie and plaintive cry which we hear earlier in the act almost becomes a cry of rage in the opera's closing bars. I say 'almost' because though the effect is most powerful, each listener will, I think,

Fig. 9 Glasgow 1979: Act 1 Scene 1, set model (see also Fig. 2). A silver swirl, growing from top right to bottom left, dominates the panorama to suggest both the omnipresent river and Munch-like eddies of emotion (see p. 188) (photograph Donald Southern)

have his or her own view about the attitude to the opera's harsh dramatic conclusion that it conveys.

My own view is that the Volga is an antithesis to the frailty and insecurity of the human society along its banks. It is therefore a mighty rebuke to those like Kabanicha who, in their arrogance, forget that frailty. On a social and human level Kabanicha is triumphant and unrepentant at the end, but the Volga mocks that triumph. It asserts the truth that Káťa has escaped to her freedom, and that her death is therefore not a loss. The Volga is the atmospheric basis of the opera. It is also a metaphor for its inner emotional dynamic: the sensation of something of great weight and depth travelling at speed. This is the key to the emotional excitement, the sense of danger, in the work. Munch's paintings constantly employ a similar device: a swirling pattern of ebb and flow in the background which instantly creates a sense of emotional stress. It is not essential to represent the Volga on the stage, but the visual impression must be such that the presence of the river is strongly felt.

The storm is less contentious, partly because Janáček himself has reduced its importance in comparison to the play. He has avoided what could perhaps have seemed a cliché of Romantic opera (the inevitable 'lampi e tuoni'), but by confining it to the third act he has made it more difficult to establish as a symbol of the fundamentalist religious tyranny which dominated Russian provincial life.

Ostrovsky prepares the storm idea at the end of his first act; Janáček replaces this with an even more awesome storm – but a psychological one, based on the insistent rhythm of his so-called 'fate' motif (Ex. 11). When we reach the real storm in Act 3, it seems that for the first time Janáček's primarily psychological approach meets the superstitious 'Russian' element in the story head on. Clearly the ruined building with its frescoes of hell and damnation was intended by Ostrovsky as a further symbol for the age-old moral world of provincial Russia. The merchants' wives may be 'dressed in their finery', but they still shelter here when it thunders. Hence its function, in conjunction with the storm, as a trigger for Káťa's guilty conscience.

In the opera, however, the intensity and accuracy with which the music has depicted Káťa's inner storm throughout the work make the somewhat creaky dramatic devices of stage storm and gruesome fresco almost unnecessary. The storm as such in the opera is not of central importance. Rather it should be seen as part of the overall balance between the cramped and squalid conditions of human society, and the larger forces of nature – river, sky and steppe – whose presence, whether actual or imagined, is indeed important.

This puny town, dwarfed by the nature that surrounds it and ruled by petty provincial tyrants, is not likely to be a place of great beauty. In the first scene, the aimless and dispirited conversation of Boris and Kudrjáš has all the atmosphere of a drab provincial Sunday – two men loafing on a draughty corner. It is almost as though Boris was infatuated with Káťa for want of anything else to do. Likewise it is hard to imagine that Kabanicha keeps a comfortable and friendly house. Both the interior scenes speak of a comfortless claustrophobia in which the two young women, Káťa and Varvara, voice their dreams in hushed tones. Varvara is appalled when Káťa gets carried away and lets her real feelings show.

Only the garden scene promises any element of comforting seclusion and beauty, though the setting of this should not be over-romanticized. Part of the special poignancy of the scene is the astonishing brevity of its lyrical outbursts. The music makes it clear that the passion which is enjoyed here is clutched at only for a moment; hence its desperate intensity. But this implies that the setting, though it may transiently appear romantic under the moonlight, should in fact be no paradise.

The ruined building in Act 3 Scene 1 is a particular problem, aggravated by there being only forty-five seconds in which to dispose of it. If it is too small, the frescoes will not be clearly visible, and the already obscure conversation between Kudrjáš and Kuligin will be even more incomprehensible. Furthermore it is supposed to be capable of sheltering several passers-by. In any case, there is a stylistic problem about this scene in relation to the rest of the work, to which I shall return later. The last scene should be as empty as possible. Some means has to be provided for Káťa to drown herself, though Janáček, by his perfunctory treatment, has himself dismissed this event as by then inevitable and therefore unimportant! As with the end of all his mature works Janáček manages, more than any other composer, to create an overwhelming sense of apotheosis – a sense that the consequences of the action shown have burst the bounds of the theatre – a sense of the universal application of the work. The attempt to match these cathartic climaxes with any kind of stage device which explodes the work out of its 'here and now' limitations, in the way that the music does, will almost certainly fail. But it should be clear that there is nothing Brechtian about these works, and the audience should have continual encouragement to respond imaginatively rather than factually.

Having crystallized Ostrovsky's richly detailed social drama into a tightly knit moral one, Janáček defines his characters in musical terms with a high degree of precision. As Michael Ewans has pointed out (pp. 108ff), the three pairs in the drama each enact a particular moral approach: the idealistic, the amoral, and the hypocritical. It is the last, the Dikoj/Kabanicha pair, which represents Janáček's sharpest move away from Ostrovsky.

His musical method with both of these unsavoury types is primarily satirical – a vein he had recently developed in *The Excursions of Mr Brouček*. It may seem surprising that Kabanicha, conventionally viewed as a venomous tyrant, should be characterized in a slightly humorous manner, but it makes the point that her tyranny is after all only on a domestic scale. The results are tragic; her behaviour is despicable; nonetheless, she is not a grandiose tyrant on the scale of Ivan the Terrible. In fact, Janáček goes to some trouble to make both Kabanicha and Dikoj slightly ridiculous in their inflated view of themselves. Dikoj's entrance is heralded by grumbling trombones and trilling woodwinds, and he himself stomps down whole-tone scales almost in a parody of Russian 'Ivan' bombast. Kabanicha nags at her pathetic son accompanied by angular squawkings which are contrasted with the nobility of Káťa's replies.

The most controversial change from Ostrovsky is the veiled implication that these two provincial ogres enjoy some kind of grotesque sexual relationship. It is possible to argue that no such thing is implied at all, and indeed there is no specific mention of it in the stage directions, which end with Janáček's addition 'she repulses Dikoj'. Nevertheless, the combination of the maudlin self-abasement of Dikoj with the severe disciplinarian reproaches of Kabanicha is full of innuendo. The music adds its own kinky flavour, beginning by wonderfully mocking Dikoj's drunken self-pity, and ending with a sinister and patently suggestive trombone solo. Janáček's reordering of scenes also adds some circumstantial evidence. In Ostrovsky, Dikoj converses with Kabanicha outside her house, and is then invited in for dinner. But in the opera, their scene seems to take place later at night, and Janáček actually adds[22] a line not in Ostrovsky for Varvara during Act 2 Scene 2 explaining why Kabanicha will not notice their absence: 'And then Dikoj is visiting her. Such brutes, but they understand one another.'

Although Kabanicha and Dikoj have a genuinely tragic influence on the lives of Kát'a, Boris and Tichon, they are nonetheless depicted by Janáček with a certain sarcastic humour. The music mocks and derides these petty provincial tyrants and resolutely refuses to do them the honour of inflating their importance. They are as brutish and trivial as their milieu, but nonetheless impregnable in their despotism. Janáčck has bccn careful to show us both their pettiness and their power, and this enables him to evoke such a strong sense of outrage at the end of the opera.

At the end only Dikoj, Kabanicha and Tichon are left. Everyone else has escaped in one way or another. Kudrjáš and Varvara, untroubled by moral qualms, and concerned only with the practicalities of the eleventh commandment (Don't get caught), conclude their story by fleeing to Moscow. We don't doubt that they prosper there. Their unforced sensuality and easy-going amorality are pinned down very early in a more or less free folksong style. Their music does not change or develop. Varvara only becomes a little breathless under the impact of events; as soon as Kudrjáš suggests elopement to Moscow, she reverts to her lightly floating melody with its delicious accompaniment of four flutes. Her most passionate line is reserved not for Kudrjáš, but for Kát'a, when she cries out at the end of Act 1 Scene 1 'Proč bych ji neměla mít ráda?' ('How could I not love her?'). This second couple, balanced between the highly strung and the loathsome, is perfectly done. They have the right amount of spirit, life and warmth to be charming without being insipid. Their cynicism is not deep enough to be unattractive, and we are grateful for their survival. It is an important ray of optimism in the work.

The last pair – Kát'a and Boris – is so imbalanced that it is scarcely a pair at all. One might consider Boris and Tichon together as the two half-men between whom Kát'a is lost. Both are in their way hopelessly ineffectual and unable to deal with the emotional commitment that Kát'a brings to her relationship with each of them. We are tempted to wonder if this is not a serious criticism of Kát'a herself. Must she not be a shocking judge of character to become involved with two such inadequate men? This kind of question exposes the danger of attempting to analyse the character of Kát'a from a modern point of view, even though Janáček's acute psychological intuition continually tempts one to do so. There is an uncanny way in which the role of

Káťa transfers itself directly into flesh and blood, and defies commentary. It is a role that demands to be performed, rather than explained verbally. This is largely because what Káťa stands for is precisely what cannot easily be rendered into words: spiritual beauty. In contrast to the hypocritical or the amoral, Káťa stands for what is pure. This is not a clinical purity, but a radiant one; hence the title of Dobrolyubov's defence of the play, 'A Ray of Light in the Realm of Darkness' (see above, p. 39). This quality of radiance, of light and ecstasy, shines out of her music throughout the work. Although she is an anguished and tormented woman, there is nothing morbid or introspective in her nature. Instead, she is a child of nature – she longs to fly like a bird, and dies thinking of the birds above her grave. Her ethereal beauty and nobility of soul are eloquently drawn in Janáček's music. The town itself may be squalid, vile in its customs, mean in its spirit, a debased community huddled on the mud of the river. But Káťa redeems all these people, because she unwittingly shows us the possibility of the existence of finer things, even in these surroundings. Her fate is a 'beacon' of individual spirituality, rather than a plea for liberal social change. Ironically, Káťa herself is the only true conservative of them all. Others mouth the old values; Káťa determines to die by them.

Káťa is in fact much closer in attitude to Kabanicha than to Varvara. She has clearly grown up and married with implicit faith in the old values which Kabanicha purports to represent. The inability of her husband to fulfil his duty towards her – to dominate and satisfy her – frustrates Káťa as much as it exasperates his mother. In the first act we hear about the dreams and visions of her childhood. We may be sure that for a girl reared in a deeply devotional and traditional manner these dreams would include a husband who would justify implicit faith and devotion. Her disappointment in Tichon is fundamentally that he cannot receive what she loves to offer him. Her religion has taught her to give and to obey. Tichon cannot handle her gifts, and has not the stomach for giving orders.

Káťa is thrown off course not because of any kind of selfish hedonistic desire for sensual gratification, or because her husband is an uncouth and ineffectual drunkard, but because she instinctively senses the absolute values in which she had put her trust to be shifting under her feet. This is why the implications about Kabanicha and Dikoj are so important. It is the disintegration of the old values, their corruption and decay, which permit Káťa's sensual and passionate impulses to rise to the surface and torment her. This disintegration is embodied in the pathetic figure of Tichon. He has been so effectively crushed and enfeebled by his mother that he does not even have the spirit to play the tyrant in his own home. His recourse is alcohol, and the ranting self-pity that it so often produces. Only at the end does he find some spark of independence, when he dares to accuse his mother of murdering Káťa. His total inadequacy when faced with the conflicting demands of his mother and his wife are particularly sharply drawn in Act 1 Scene 2. Káťa desperately needs the protection of his love and authority to stave off her adulterous longings. She begs Tichon to make her swear an oath of fidelity; she wants him to exercise absolute authority and domination over her: to wield the full weight of Old Testament patriarchy. Tichon is quite incapable of this charade. But Kabanicha also insists that nothing shall be left unsaid, and the mother extracts the words that were denied the wife.

The musical 'storm' with which Janáček ends Act 1 indicates that Káťa, denied this last possible protection, already knows that she will in turn succumb to her temptation, and pay the price. It is, incidentally, a typical device of Janáček's to allow the orchestra to conclude an act with a substantial postlude of its own (e.g. *Makropulos* Act 1, *Jenůfa* and the *Vixen* Act 3). In such cases he does not confine himself to summing up what has happened, but invariably allows the orchestra to develop the situation.

By the end of Act 1 Káťa has acknowledged her feelings for Boris to an extent which, for a woman of her honesty, means that there can be no turning back. All her deeply felt convictions about married life and love have been steadily dismembered. Finally, even the basic machinery of obedience within this holy state has not been sufficient to save her from sin. And Káťa knows that now that she has sinned in thought, if not in deed, her married life is over. When she does go to meet Boris, she tells him at once that he has already ruined her, and that if she truly had a will of her own she would not have come. The climax of the scene for her is at the words 'Tvoje vůle nade mnou vládne' ('It is your will conquering my will', VS 101) – it is precisely this experience which she seeks and does not receive from Tichon.

At each stage, Káťa acts without compromise. She has sought to give herself absolutely to Tichon, but he has not the strength to accept her. She gives herself utterly to passion, and then in turn to guilt and ruin. She has sinned, and throws herself into the mud in public and demands penance. Her confession in particular makes it necessary for the interpreter to stress the religious concepts of guilt and sin. The confession is the act that separates Káťa from countless other adulterous lovers, and places her firmly within the context of a certain society and period. The gesture of public self-abasement and confession is a familiar Russian trait, though it is now reserved for political 'sinners'.

Janáček introduces all his major characters in the first scene, giving each a lightning 'snap-shot' sketch. The three male admirers arrive first, the latter two hoping to catch a glimpse of their counterparts as they emerge from church. Kudrjáš, the first, is placed as the progressive 'teacher, chemist and engineer', Dikoj as the bully, and Boris as the hapless victim of family circumstances. The women are placed with the same precision. Káťa is introduced with a tune of radiant beauty, which is both serene and pulsing with nervous energy. Kabanicha wastes no time in nagging her son and daughter-in-law; the quiet nobility and restraint of Káťa's replies complete her picture. Her graceful beauty, her volatility and her sensitivity are established immediately. Meanwhile Varvara makes slyly cynical comments, and at the end takes up the cudgels on behalf of Káťa by rounding on Tichon, taunting him with his propensity for drink.

The first part of the second scene is devoted to a substantial *scena* for Káťa, in which the details of her character are filled out. She begins by recalling the visionary ecstasy of her childhood. She still longs to fly, to soar, and the music soars with her, luminous and ethereal. Gradually, she reveals the demons that haunt this natural creature of bliss. Her visions are interrupted and distorted by increasingly agitated alternations between hysterical anxiety and voluptuous surrender. The more warmly and insistently she is tempted, the more frenzied is her resistance. By the time Tichon enters, we have seen the extent of Káťa's inner torment. From this point onwards, Janáček uses the dramatic imminence of Tichon's departure to drive the act to its conclusion with unremitting concentration. The occasional pauses and moments of silence caused by the great strain between the characters only serve to emphasize the ruthless ferocity of the 'storm' which Janáček builds round Káťa at the end of this act. Though it may be true that Janáček wished to continue directly to Act 2 (see above, pp. 140–1), few audiences will want to surrender the respite of an interval after such a fierce conclusion.

Act 2 begins with two motifs which are to dominate its first scene; they represent the debate within Káťa. The rising and falling motif (Ex. 38a) is used with remarkable versatility, and appears beguilingly sensual, exultant, nervous or sinister according to the situation. It is generally linked to the idea of temptation. Its answering theme (Ex.

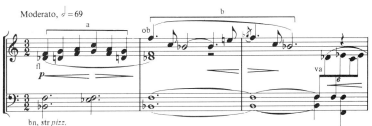

38b) corresponds more to the yearning/defiant aspect of Káťa's character. However, it is worth remarking here that Janáček never locks himself into any kind of motivic system which is not malleable enough to express the dramatic or psychological situation on the stage. This accounts for the striking subtlety of the ebb and flow of character and situation in his operas, of which this scene is a particularly good example, and worth considering in detail.

The scene opens with Kabanicha lecturing Káťa on her insufficient display of grief at Tichon's departure (VS 72). Káťa replies with her usual restraint, and Kabanicha leaves, giving orders that she is not to be disturbed. Immediately the orchestra breaks out with Ex. 38a at its most passionate and defiant – a marvellous expression of Káťa's pent-up rage (VS 73, fig. 3). This is instantly contrasted with Varvara's delicious 'folk' theme, as she begins to tempt Káťa (Ex. 14). Even her first, seemingly innocent, remarks about going out for a walk produce another explosion of Ex. 38b – Káťa's mute envy of Varvara's freedom. Varvara continues with her tempting story about the key. As soon as the key is mentioned Ex. 38a appears in a quickened-up version – Káťa has already realized where this is leading. Varvara's folk theme becomes increasingly voluptuous (e.g. VS 75, second system) as she gets to the point where she suggests inviting Boris to meet Káťa there. The temptation theme doubles its tempo again with Káťa's internal agitation (VS 75, fig. 5).

Varvara trips away, delighted with her plot (VS 76), and taking her bouncy little theme with her. She of course has no idea of the serious consequences she has set in train. The music shows this, however, by the dramatically increased contrasts between Ex. 38a and 38b. Ex. 38a is now literally removed from Ex. 38b in pitch – one is placed at each extreme of the compass (VS 77) – and their orchestration is further contrasted, Ex. 38a becoming increasingly sinister (on low strings, bassoons and muted trombones). Furthermore, the text is spread out, with several bars of this orchestral debate between short agitated lines for Káťa. It is the internal debate which matters. At the conclusion of this, Káťa's indecision becomes almost unbearable, and Ex. 38a grinds slowly down until it is interrupted by the sound of Kabanicha and Dikoj offstage (VS 78). The device is typical, in that it serves the psychological purpose of breaking Káťa's stalemate extremely well, and yet does not stand up to very close examination in realistic terms. When Kabanicha and Dikoj do appear after Káťa's exit, it is hard to imagine what they have been doing meanwhile. But Janáček is right, of course; the audience will have no time to consider such problems.

For Káťa, however, the interruption is crucial, and enables her for once to begin to deceive herself. The shock and feelings of guilt aroused by Kabanicha's voice dissipate the real terrors of her temptation, and she begins to toy with the idea of a harmless meeting with Boris. The music plays with her, and the two themes alternate more freely, Ex, 38a even acquiring a springy, dance-like rhythm (VS 78). Finally, when she faces up to the fact that she must see Boris – that doubt and debate are only hiding what is inevitable, Ex. 38b rings out triumphantly as she longs for night to fall ('Bud' jak bud'', VS 80). It is followed immediately by luridly sinister and then leeringly grotesque versions of Ex. 38b, which prepare us for the lurching entrance of Dikoj and his strict companion.

The scene is an excellent example of the flexibility and subtlety of Janáček's method. The musical material is quite simple, but highly versatile. Each bar reflects the changing dramatic situation. The short grotesque interlude between Dikoj and Kabanicha provides a perfect foil for the two highly charged scenes on either side of it. The double love-scene which concludes the act is the central climax and turning-point of the opera. It is a masterpiece of construction, and shows again Janáček's unerring sense of dramatic proportion. What is strikingly original in operatic terms is that Janáček has avoided any temptation to expand the scenes between Káťa and Boris. Their passion is brief, intense and turbulent. It seems to burn itself out in a flash. These two unhappy and wounded creatures are only permitted the briefest moment of peace and bliss. Janáček's solution is to leave his characters in silence; the orchestra develops the theme associated with their longing, punctuated by brief cries of love.

Act 3 Scene 1 is a scene of action. There is no further psychological probing to be done, and Janáček builds swiftly towards its single important event: Káťa's public confession of adultery. The music evokes the scudding storm clouds, the rain, and the swift Volga, whose theme emerges during this scene. This 'storm' music functions like a classic Hitchcock device – motorizing an increasingly hectic and catastrophic atmosphere. Indeed, the whole scene is somewhat cinematic, and the visual impression of Káťa's confession is more important than the few words she says.

It is also the only scene in which Janáček has permitted a significant amount of Ostrovsky's social detail to survive. Kudrjáš and Kuligin discuss the frescoes of hell, and laugh at the overdressed merchants' wives on the promenade. Kudrjáš and Dikoj argue about the nature of lightning. When Káťa does enter, there is a small crowd of citizens to comment on her strange behaviour. However, none of these details is brought very sharply into focus – not because Janáček could not paint vignettes if he wanted to (*The Makropulos Affair* is full of them), but because he did not want us to become interested in these minor figures. He only wished to establish a visual impression of the townspeople sheltering from the gathering storm, as a frame in which to set Káťa's confession. It is something of a paradox that the only really public scene, the only scene with definite social detail, is strikingly unreal compared to the following scene for Káťa alone. This is sharply in focus, though it could take place in limbo.

The exact time-scale of this final scene is one of those details that Janáček did not bother to tidy up. The effect, after a very brief interlude, is that it is the same day. For various reasons of logic it is preferable to suppose that two or three days have passed (see Brod's and Janáček's exchange on this point, above, pp. 67 and 68). Either way, it is not important. Janáček has typically lost interest in the mechanics of the story. He is concerned only with the last stage of his heroine's development. This is essentially Káťa's progress towards serenity – the gradual exorcism of the demons which assailed her in Act 1. Even the scene of farewell with Boris is enveloped in this process. He hardly seems to exist for himself; he comes out of the storm wind, and as he leaves his voice merges with that of the river. But his presence was necessary as the catalyst which finally allows Káťa to find peace.

The resolution, when it comes, is swift and astonishingly bold. When Káťa can at last contemplate her grave, the flowers growing over it, and the birds wheeling above, Janáček provides a startling new musical idea. A simple drumbeat accompanies the soft trilling of two clarinets. The effect is child-like and pure, and recalls the childhood happiness that Káťa described in Act 1. But whereas that was the serenity of innocence, her new peace and serenity have been achieved through knowledge and the experience of misery. This is a wholly personal achievement, reflected in music of intimate delicacy. It is a brilliant stroke by Janáček at this point, eliminating the actual death as an event. Because he allows no time for the death to take place naturalistically, he is able to follow this refined and exquisite music with the abrupt ugliness of the real world bursting onto the stage. Nothing could be a greater or more telling contrast than the squalid argument between Tichon and the Kabanicha which follows. This personal achievement of beauty and serenity, though at the cost of her life, is the primary element of optimism in *Káťa*. Among this trivial and brutish provincial community, Janáček has found that same 'spark of God' which was to lead him to the jails of the *House of the Dead.*

Notes

Works referred to in the text and notes by author or by author and title only are cited in full in the Bibliography

1 Introduction

1 Burjanek, p. 368, n. 53.
2 See P. Vrba: 'Janáčkova ruská knihovna' [Janáček's Russian library], *Slezský sborník*, lx (1962), pp. 242–9.
3 Burjanek, p. 367; Procházka, p. 18.
4 Burjanek, p. 374, n. 65.
5 M. Štědroň: 'Janáček, verismus a impresionismus', *Časopis Moravského musea: vědy společenské*, liii–liv (1968–9), pp. 145–6.
6 A detailed examination of this vexed subject can be found in A. Gozenpud: 'Janáček a Musorgskij', *Opus musicum*, xii (1980), no. 4, pp. 101–9; no. 5, supplement, pp. i–iv, vii–viii.
7 Janáček's connections with Schoenberg and Berg are usefully summarized in M. Štědroň: 'Janáček a Schönberg', *Časopis Moravského musea: vědy společenské*, xlix (1964), pp. 237–58, and 'Janáček und der Expressionismus', *Sborník prací Filosofické fakulty brněnské university*, H5 (1970), pp. 105–25.
8 Reprinted in B. Štědroň: 'Janáček a Čajkovskij', *Sborník prací Filosofické fakulty brněnské university*, ii/2–4 (1953), pp. 204–5, 208–9.
9 T. Straková: 'Janáčkova opera Osud, II' [Janáček's opera *Fate*, II], *Časopis Moravského musea: vědy společenské*, xlii (1957), p. 159.
10 It should be emphasized that this quotation shows stress patterns; vowel lengths do not always coincide with them in Czech, as they usually do in English.
11 *Manchester Guardian* (12 April 1951).
12 Leoš Janáček: *Pohled to života i díla* [A view of the life and works], ed. A. Veselý (Prague, 1924), p. 96.
13 Russian elements in Janáček's opera are discussed, and generally dismissed, by Polyakova.
14 Quoted in J. Racek: 'Leoš Janáček a Praha', *Musikologie*, iii (Prague, 1955), p. 24, n. 44.

2 Ostrovsky's play *The Thunderstorm*

1 In discussion of Ostrovsky's play the original Russian names of the characters have been retained: thus Káťa in the opera is Katerina in the

199

play, etc. See also 'Names', above, p. xiii. A number of English translations of *The Thunderstorm* are available, e.g. in *Four Russian Plays*,
trans. Joshua Cooper (Harmondsworth, 1972). Translations given here
are my own.

2 Act numbers in this chapter refer to those in Ostrovsky's play. The
different act structure of the opera is discussed in Chapter 3.

3 N. A. Dobrolyubov: 'Tyomnoye tsarstvo' [Realm of darkness],
Sovremennik, 7 (St Petersburg, 1859); English version in *idem*: *Selected
Philosophical Essays* (Moscow, 1948).

4 *Idem*: 'Luch sveta v tyomnom tsarstve' [A ray of light in the realm of
darkness], *Sovremennik*, 10 (St Petersburg, 1860); English version in
Selected Philosophical Essays.

5 For a helpful description of the various classes of Russian society at this
period see Richard Pipes: *Russia under the Old Regime* (London, 1974).

6 In 1855, as a prelude to the era of reforms, the Naval Ministry initiated a
comprehensive study of peoples engaged in seafaring or fishing in the
Russian Empire. Writers were engaged as observers, and Ostrovsky was
invited to join a 'literary expedition' to the Volga. His observations of the
way of life in the provincial towns he visited inspired his choice of setting
for several plays, including *The Thunderstorm*.

7 A. I. Revyakin: *Groza A. N. Ostrovskogo* (Moscow, 1962), p. 265; the
actress was L. P. Nikulina-Kositskaya from the Maly Theatre in
Moscow.

8 *Ibid.* pp. 328, 330.

9 Composers who wrote operas based on other plays by Ostrovsky include
Tchaikovsky, Rimsky-Korsakov, Blaramberg, Serov and Arensky.
Incidental music was composed by (among others) Tchaikovsky and
Blaramberg. For further details see articles on Ostrovsky in *The Concise
Oxford Dictionary of Opera*, ed. H. Rosenthal and J. Warrack (London,
1964, 2nd edn 1979) and in *The New Grove: Dictionary of Music and
Musicians*, ed. S. Sadie (London, 1980).

10 L. Dolgov: *A. N. Ostrovsky* (Moscow and Petrograd, 1923), pp. 152–3;
see also M. Štědroň: 'Janáček a opera Groza Vladimíra Nikitiče
Kašperova'.

3 The libretto

1 I. Prach [J. G. Pratsch]: *Sobraniye narodnykh russikikh pesen s ikh
golosami* [Collection of Russian folksongs with vocal parts] (St Petersburg, 1790, 2nd enlarged edn 1806, 3rd edn 1815), no. 32; V. M. Belyayev
(Moscow, 1955), no. 83. Janáček and the Bezručs most likely had access
to the fourth edition (1896), where the song became no. 56.

2 Quoted by Burjanek, p. 398, n. 108.

3 Most of Brod's correspondence with Janáček was published as
Korespondence Leoše Janáčka s Maxem Brodem, ed. J. Racek and A.
Rektorys, Janáčkův Archiv, 1st series, 9 (Prague, 1953). Three unpub-
lished letters have been made available by kind permission of the
Moravian Museum, Music History Division, Brno. Brod's letters are
translated here by J. B. Robinson.

4 Page numbers refer to the manuscript vocal score from which Brod was working; they are followed by references in square brackets to page numbers in the printed vocal score (Universal Edition 7103).

5 See Janáček's explanation in the next letter.

6 Emil Hertzka (1869–1932), director of Universal Edition, Vienna, which from 1917 began publishing Janáček's operas and other works.

7 Janáček had been appointed professor of the master class in composition at the Prague Conservatory in 1920.

8 Otakar Ostrčil (1879–1935), from 1920 to his death musical director at the National Theatre, where he conducted the Prague premières of *Brouček*, *Káťa*, the *Vixen* and *Makropulos*.

9 The time of day had been added to Ostrovsky's directions at the beginning of the act; in the light of the discrepancy it was altered to 'odpolední slunce' ('afternoon sun'), though not in the first edition of the Czech libretto.

10 Brod was wrong; Janáček took these lines from p. 45 of Červinka's translation, which reads 'Nu, půjdu se k Bohu pomodlit; nevyrušujte mne.' (Among his modifications Janáček omitted 'k Bohu', 'to God'). Janáček nevertheless accepted Brod's addition. See VS 73, where 'Svět nezná ted' než pletky a nesvár' ('The world today knows nothing but confusion and dissension') has been inserted after 'bylo by slušnější'. A simple 'půjdu' ('I'm going') replaces 'Půjdu se modlit' ('I'm going off to pray'). Once again these changes were not made in time to appear in the first edition of the Czech libretto.

11 Brod's page numbers here refer to Červinka's translation of the play.

12 In first edition of the Czech libretto the direction 'vítá za scenou Dikého, tlumeně' ('she welcomes Dikoj offstage, in a hushed tone') preceded her words (VS 78) 'Přišel-li si něčím...' ('If you came for something...'). In the vocal score this became 'za scenou k Dikému' ('offstage, to Dikoj'); '-li' ('if') was dropped at the same time.

13 Janáček chose neither and kept the scene as it was.

14 Janáček accepted most of this, reversing the first two sentences and then cutting to 'Ale dbej dobrých mravů!' ('But mind your manners!'), and repeating the last two words (VS 85). But there is no indication about a slow curtain. All of Kabanicha's part on VS 85 was thus inserted over the existing orchestral music.

15 This is the original opening of Kudrjáš's song at the beginning of Act 2 Scene 2; see above, p. 58.

16 Janáček accepted Brod's suggestion, see VS 91: 'Vždyt' jsem Vás varoval; zamilovat se nerozvážně!' ('But I warned you against falling in love recklessly'), replacing his previous version, which Brod quotes, with these lines. The inconsistency had arisen through Janáček's borrowing lines for his Boris–Kudrjáš discussion in Act 1 from later in the play.

17 Janáček ignored these suggestions.

18 Janáček retained the 'dull lines', but Brod's suggestion led to one of the most magical moments in this double love-scene: against the slow soaring offstage unison of Káťa and Boris, Varvara continues her more matter-of-fact conversation with Kudrjáš: 'A pak Dikoj je u ní návštěvou. Takoví hrubci a rozumějí si!' ('And then Dikoj is visiting her. Such

brutes, but they understand one another!'), VS 108. Janáček super-imposed this slightly shortened version of Brod on the existing score.
19 Janáček accepted Brod's lines, though he chose 'Mother Moscow' rather than Petersburg.
20 Janáček's previous version of this line, omitting any reference to business or town names, is given in Ex. 17. The change to the final version (not registered in the first edition of the Czech libretto) involved writing more notes over the same orchestral music. The Ostrovsky reference is to the scene between Tichon and Kuligin at the beginning of Act 5 (omitted in the opera). In his German translation Brod worked in the reference to the Chinese border, though Janáček ignored it in his version. Kyakhta (which Červinka transliterated as Ťachta, Brod in his letter as Jachta, and Janáček in his final version as Kjachta) was an important centre of Far Eastern trade until the building of Vladivostok and the Trans-Siberian Railway.

Ex. 17

Strýc mne   vy - há - ní   až   na Si - bíř!

[Uncle will send me to Siberia]

21 To fit in this line Brod had to bunch up the Czech text from VS 92, fig. 8; the Czech and German texts are in phase again on VS 93.
22 Brod replaced the 'garden gate story' in his translation with the expla-nation that it would never occur to Kabanicha that she was being hoodwinked; see also above, n. 18.
23 These include a gratuitous reference to Ivan the Terrible.
24 Janáček followed the Czech habit of stressing the first syllable; Brod, in his translation, arranges the word so that the stress falls, correctly, on the second syllable.
25 Janáček accepted Brod's suggestion (see the next letter); the lapse of time between the two scenes of Act 3 was left unspecified.
26 Janáček accepted Brod's suggestion (see the next letter), and had Boris sing a version of these words over Fekluša's existing line, despite Brod's advice in his next paragraph to omit most of her part. The page references are to the printed vocal score, whose proofs Brod was now looking at.
27 Janáček did not accept this suggestion; see VS 15–17 and the next letter. Figure numbers in this paragraph and the next are the rehearsal numbers printed in the vocal score.
28 The lower pitch, as Janáček explains in the next letter, is an alternative to the high-lying G sharp.
29 Janáček here writes out Boris's and Fekluša's voice parts from VS 24, bar 6 to the end of the page. They differ only slightly from what is now printed in the vocal score. Boris's words, from his repetition of '(Ó) hubím svoje mládí', have thus all been added to the existing score. This change came too late to be incorporated into the first edition of the Czech libretto.
30 Janáček had begun work on *The Cunning Little Vixen* earlier in the year.

5 Composition and the Brno and Prague premières: letters and reviews

1 Jiřikovský, p. 250. Václav Jiřikovský (1891–1942) was director of the Brno National Theatre 1916–19 and again 1931–41, and had got to know Janáček during the Brno revival of *Jenůfa*. Despite his claims to have interested Janáček in Ostrovsky soon after the Vienna première of *Jenůfa* (16 February 1918), there is no other evidence that Janáček considered *The Thunderstorm* as a possible opera before the autumn of 1919. It is not even clear that Janáček saw the Brno production. Červinka (see Bibliography) says that Janáček missed the production of *The Thunderstorm* in Prague (19 March 1919) and reports that Janáček's knowledge of the play came through reading his translation – which suggests that Janáček had not seen the play in Brno either.

2 František Serafínský Procházka (1861–1939), Czech poet. He wrote the texts for Janáček's choruses for women's voices and the libretto for *Mr Brouček's Excursion to the Fifteenth Century*. His correspondence with Janáček has published as *Korespondence Leoše Janáčka s F. S. Procházkou*, ed. A. Rektorys, Janáčkův Archiv, 1st series, 3 (Prague, 1949).

3 Vincenc Červinka (1877–1942), translator of *The Thunderstorm* into Czech, was at that time on a lecture tour of the USA.

4 The question of Červinka's royalties was not so easily solved. Some twenty letters were exchanged on the subject and it was only in May 1928, a few months before Janáček's death, that Universal Edition determined that Červinka should receive 15% of Janáček's royalty.

5 Kamila Stösslová, née Neumannová (1892–1935), wife of an antique-dealer in Písek. Janáček got to know her in Luhačovice, probably in the summer of 1917. Their close friendship until the end of Janáček's life is documented by 743 letters, most of them unpublished, in the Janáček Archive of the Moravian Museum, Music History Division, Brno. In them Janáček ascribes the inspiration of many of his later works, *Káťa Kabanová* among them, to Kamila.

6 According to the Janáčeks' servant, Marie Stejskalová, composition began a few days earlier, on 5 January 1920. Stejskalová's diary is quoted in R. Smetana: *Vyprávění o Leoši Janáčkovi* [Stories about Leoš Janáček] (Olomouc, 1948), p. 113.

7 While Červinka's letters to Janáček are all in the Janáček Archive, Janáček's letters to Červinka have disappeared and are known only from extracts printed by Červinka.

8 Now Gorky; Janáček attended an exhibition there during his visit to Russia in 1896.

9 Josef Svatopluk Machar (1864–1942), Czech poet, from 1919 to 1924 general inspector of the Czechoslovak Army. Janáček mentions a meeting with him in February 1918 in a letter to Gabriela Horvátová (see below, n. 24).

10 It seems unlikely that Janáček's news could be connected with the recent appointment (15 December 1920) of Otakar Ostrčil as chief conductor at the Prague National Theatre (which might mean better prospects for performances of Janáček's works there), since Janáček wrote in the same mysterious vein to Ostrčil himself on 16 December 1920.

11 Gustav Schmoranz (1858–1930), from 1900 to 1922 director of the Prague National Theatre; he produced Ostrovsky's *The Thunderstorm* there in 1919.

12 Roman Veselý (1879–1933), Czech pianist. He made the piano score of several Czech orchestral and vocal works, including Janáček's *The Excursions of Mr Brouček*. Negotiations with him over *Káťa* broke down in June 1921 and in the end the vocal score was prepared by Janáček's pupil Břetislav Bakala.

13 Otakar Nebuška (1875–1952) worked for the publishing firm Hudební Matice, set up by the Umělecká Beseda ('Artistic Society'), which in 1908 had published the first vocal score of *Jenůfa*. In 1921 Hudební Matice was negotiating for the vocal score of *Káťa Kabanová*. This was eventually published by Universal Edition, with Hudební Matice holding the Czech rights.

14 The Czech transliteration of the full Russian form of Katerina.

15 František Neumann (1874–1929), musical director from 1919 at the Brno National Theatre, where he conducted the world premières of *Káťa Kabanová*, the *Vixen*, *Šárka* and *Makropulos*, and the Brno première of *Brouček*.

16 Ostrčil's correspondence with Janáček was published as *Korespondence Leoše Janáčka s Otakarem Ostrčilem*, ed. A. Rektorys, Janáčkův Archiv, 1st series, 2 (Prague, 1948).

17 *The Excursions of Mr Brouček* received its première under Ostrčil in Prague on 23 April 1920. Difficulties with the singers and a lukewarm reception resulted in a shorter run than Janáček had expected after the success of *Jenůfa*.

18 'Katja Kabanowa' (1966), p. 52.

19 Vladimír Helfert (1886–1945), after moving to Brno University in 1922 as professor of musicology, became one of Janáček's admirers. Together with Janáček's widow he set up the Janáček Archive, and in 1939 he published the first volume of a proposed four-volume biography.

20 The Brno première took place on 23 November 1921 in what is now the Mahen Theatre (Mahenovo divadlo; Divadlo na hradbách), formerly the German Theatre, which served as the principal opera stage in Brno until 1965. The main performers are given in the List of Productions; others parts were played by Rudolf Kaulfus (Dikoj), Pavel Jeral (Tichon), Valentin Šindler (Kudrjáš), Jarmila Pustinská (Varvara), René Milan (Kuligin), Ludmila Šebestlová (Glaša), Ludmila Kvapilová (Fekluša), Václav Šindler (Passer-by), Růžena Horká (Woman).

21 Gracian Černušák (1882–1961), musicologist and critic, from 1918 Brno music critic of the *Lidové noviny*.

22 Hugo Reichenberger (1873–1938), from 1905 to 1935 at the Vienna Staatsoper (Hofoper), where in 1918 he conducted the Vienna première of *Jenůfa*.

23 All parts except three were taken at the Prague première as Ostrčil proposed: *Káťa* was sung by Kamila Ungrová, alternating with Marie Veselá, the creator of the part in Brno, who had joined the Prague National Theatre in 1922; Kuligin was sung by Jan Fifka and Fekluša by Vlasta Loukotková.

24 Gabriela Horvátová (1877–1967), mezzo-soprano/soprano at the Prague

National Theatre from 1903. She created the part of the Kostelnička in the Prague *Jenůfa* in 1916, winning Janáček's intense admiration.

25 Ostrovsky's play is set 'in the late 1850s', Janáček's opera 'in the 1860s'.

26 These doublings were not incorporated in the 1971 revision of the full score.

27 The Viennese firm Kautsky supplied sets for the National Theatre.

28 Jaromír Borecký (1869–1951), poet, and music critic of the *Národní listy* (1893–1910) and *Národní politika* (from 1919).

29 The première took place at the Prague National Theatre on 30 November 1922. Main details are given in the List of Productions; for the singers see Ostrčil's letter of 1 March 1922.

30 Boleslav Vomáčka (1887–1965), composer and critic; he wrote for *Lidové noviny* from 1921 to 1938.

31 Antonín Šilhan, in *Národní listy*, criticized Janáček's libretto, especially the combination of Kuligin and Kudrjáš, and the treatment of Fekluša. He considered the music mosaic-like and the characterization, though evocative, slow to take effect. All the reviews of the Prague 1922 production of *Káťa* are analysed in František Pala: *Opera Národního divadla v období Otakar Ostrčila* [Opera at the National Theatre during the Otakar Ostrčil era], ii (Prague, 1964), pp. 151–3.

32 Short review by Max Brod.

33 Much energy was devoted by Czech critics to approving models for the future development of the art. Smetana (with Fibich) in particular was seen as the way forward, to the detriment of Dvořák. Janáček's remark recalls Borecký's review; Borecký, however, was more an adherent of the Dvořák–Suk camp than a true-blooded Smetana propagandist.

34 Josef Bohuslav Foerster (1859–1951), one of the chief Czech composers in the first half of the century.

35 Quoted in B. Štědroň, pp. 213–14 (Czech edition); p. 160 (English edition); translated here from the Czech.

36 Štědroň suggested that Professor 'Knop' was an error for Professor Khodl, with whom Janáček was friendly in Písek.

7 Textual problems

The interludes

1 This is a slightly shortened English version of Dr Straková's article cited in the Bibliography.

2 See Charles Mackerras: 'Long-Lost Music for a Janáček Opera', *Music and Musicians*, ix (1960–1), February, pp. 16–17, 38.

3 Mackerras was wrong in assuming that the German instructions were not written by Janáček.

4 The interludes were first printed in Mackerras's revised edition of the full score (1971). (JT)

5 See Sources (p. 225). (JT)

6 All letters quoted in this article are deposited in the Janáček Archive of the Moravian Museum, Music History Division, Brno, except those of Janáček to Universal Edition, which are with Universal Edition, Vienna. (JT)

7 In a printed full score in the Janáček Archive of the Moravian Museum

(A 11.461) there is an enclosure of six sheets with Bakala's corrections (with writing on ten sides). The instruction to link both scenes of Acts 1 and 2 is among these corrections; similarly the 'attacca subito il sequente' is written in pencil in Bakala's hand in the same score on p. 70 of Act 1 and p. 34 of Act 2.

8   Among the small changes made in the new impression is the insertion of 'attacca' at the ends of Scenes 1 and 3; the extended interlude music was not included.

9   This seems to be misunderstanding. No extension was made to the conversation, only to the music after it. The few words added to Kabanicha's part over existing music (see Chapter 3, n. 14) were already printed in the score. (JT)

10   Recent practice regarding the interludes is described in Chapter 6. (JT)

11   Mackerras: 'Long-Lost Music', p. 17.

Orchestration problems and the revised edition

12   The section includes material from Charles Mackerras's unpublished preface to his edition of *Káťa Kabanová*, and from his paper to the Brno 1965 conference on Janáček's operas: 'On the problems of interpretation of Janáček's orchestration', *Operní dílo Leoše Janáčka: Sborník příspěvků z mezinárodního symposia* [The operas of Leoš Janáček: a collection of contributions to the international symposium], ed. T. Straková (Brno, 1968), pp. 102–4.

Janáček and the viola d'amore

13   This is an expanded English version of a paper delivered in Czech to the Brno Janáček Conference, autumn 1978.

14   H. Berlioz: *Instrumentationslehre*, ed. A. Dörffel (2nd edn, Leipzig 1875); Janáček's copy is in the Janáček Archive of the Moravian Museum, H 640/142.

15   For detailed survey of the use of the viola d'amore in the nineteenth century see H. Danks: *The Viola d'Amore* (Halesowen, 1976, 2nd edn 1979).

16   B. Štědroň: 'Leoš Janáček kritikem brněnské opery v letech 1890–1892' [Janáček as critic of the Brno opera in 1890–92], *Otázky divadla a filmu*, i, ed. A. Závodský (Brno, 1970), pp. 232–3.

17   J. Borecký: 'Zapomínaný nástroj' [A forgotten instrument], *Dalibor*, xxiii (1901), pp. 11–12, 17, 35, 373–5.

18   J. Racek: 'Leoš Janáček a Praha' [Janáček and Prague], *Musikologie*, iii (Prague, 1955), p. 21.

19   A. Němcová and S. Přibáňová: 'Příspěvek k dějinám opery Národního divadla v Brně 1884–1919' [Contribution to the history of opera at the National Theatre in Brno 1884–1919], *Časopis Moravského musea: vědy společenské*, xlviii (1963), p. 265.

20   Racek: 'Leoš Janáček', p. 21, n. 34.

21   Leoš Janáček: *Pohled do života i díla* [A view of the life and works], ed. A. Veselý (Prague, 1924), p. 94.

22   See T. Straková: 'Janáčkova opera Osud' [Janáček's opera *Fate*], *Časopis Moravského musea*, xli (1956), pp. 210ff.

23   Janáček Archive, A 23.464 a–c

24   Racek: 'Leoš Janáček', p. 24.

25 Janáček's use of the viola d'amore in *Káťa Kabanová* is considered in detail at the end of this chapter.

26 B. Štědroň: *Leoš Janáček: k jeho lidskému a uměleckému profilu* [Janáček's image as man and artist] (Prague, 1976), p. 142.

27 Leoš Janáček: 'Josef Zubatý', *Lidové noviny* (24 October 1925), reprinted as Leoš Janáček: *Fejetony z Lidových novin* [Feuilletons from the *Lidové noviny*], ed. J. Racek (Brno, 1958), pp. 102–3.

28 Quoted by Otakar Šourek in his preface to his revised edition of the quartet (Prague, 1949).

29 I am indebted to Dr Alena Němcová for this suggestion.

30 Marie Stejskalová's memoir of Janáček, in M. Trkanová: *U Janáčků* (2nd edn, Prague, 1964), p. 163, n. 114, gives another version of the story. On receipt of his part the violist Josef Trkan went to see Janáček and told him that it was impossible on the viola d'amore. Together they revised the part but in subsequent rehearsals they found the tone-colour differed so greatly from that of the other instruments that Janáček himself decided that the part should be played on the ordinary viola.

31 Stejskalová, however (*ibid.*), states that the Brno Theatre possessed a viola d'amore. The mention of the 'silvery tone' of the instrument in Borecký's review (see Chapter 5) is not necessarily proof that it was played in the Prague performances; Borecký, as a viola d'amore player and active propagandist for the instrument, would doubtless have known about its appearance in the score of *Káťa* and would have been anxious to draw attention to its use, whether realized or not.

8 Interpretations

(*Unless otherwise stated, notes to this chapter are by John Tyrrell*)

1 From *Leoš Janáček: Leben und Werk* (Vienna, 1925, enlarged 2nd edn 1956), pp. 45–50. The Czech translation by Alfred Fuchs (1924) includes, after the paragraph on p. 164 above ending 'ruthless inflexibility', a passage of some 650 words, which was dropped from the German version. Since Brod seems to have had second thoughts about this section it has not been reproduced here. It deals chiefly with the making of Janáček's libretto (for which see Chapter 3). Brod stresses the economy and directness of Janáček's version (which he thought might make *Káťa* more accessible than *Jenůfa*) though he regrets the inevitable omission of 'darkest Russia'. Two short passages are of documentary value and deserve quotation:

> Anyone who knows the genesis of the librettos of Janáček's earlier operas ... will know how he virtually 'gave into commission' some particular passages to friendly poets. In his most recent opera there was yet a third collaborator: one stanza of the songs inserted into the fourth scene [Act 2 Scene 2] comes from Bezruč.
> [...]
> In some places I would have wished for a more considerate, more idyllic hand. I have tried in my translation to bring to life again some of the passages describing the surroundings, in a concentrated form, without however adding to the number of notes.

2 Only the first (July–August 1896) was a study tour. Janáček accom-

panied his daughter Olga to St Petersburg in March 1902 to stay with his brother František and hastened there again with his wife in June on learning that Olga had contracted typhoid fever.

3 Two song cycles dating from his studies in Leipzig and Vienna (1879–80) are lost.

4 The motif is in fact on the oboe, with a flute decoration in semiquavers (see Ex. 10).

5 Neither the Czech text nor the original Russian specifies the type of bird in Káťa's question 'Povídám, proč lidé nelétají tak jako ptáci nelétají?' ('I mean, why don't people fly like birds?', VS 38). Brod's translation makes them swallows ('. . . so wie die kleinen *Schwalben* fliegen!').

6 E.g. Max Brod, see above p. 165; Muller regards Exx. 10–11 as a single motif.

7 This theme is in fact in a dorian B flat minor with an accompaniment of sleigh bells and arpeggios on a single flute.

8 Act 2; Muller perhaps has in mind the figuration from fig. 24 (all vocal scores) (= study score fig. 27).

9 Kabanicha is in fact thanking all the people on stage.

10 'Zdrávas královno', Act 2, figure 73 (study score fig. 88).

11 We know from his conversation with Kudrjáš in Act 1 Scene 1 that Boris is not yet of age and that he had been sent by his parents to a business school. We do not know whether Káťa is his first lover.

12 See above, p. 165.

13 See Vogel (1962), p. 340.

14 Composed 1917–22, first performed 1925.

15 This theme is developed above, Chapter 4.

16 Despite its use in the overture and several main themes.

17 This scene was a late addition; see above, p. 20.

18 Another consequence of Janáček's composite Kudrjáš–Kuligin; see Chapter 3.

19 *Translator's note*: The 'Modell' of Wörner's novel concept of 'Modellvarianten' has a double meaning in German, referring not only to the English 'model' or 'paradigm', but to 'module' in the architectural sense of a basic figure replicated to create a larger design. This second meaning has been adopted here.
For comment on Wörner's theory see Chapter 1.

20 Presumably the 'Arbeit-Motif' against which Siegfried forges his sword Nothung (Act 1 Scene 3). Wörner's similar emotional connotations are less clear; perhaps he saw a reflection of Mime's fury in Dikoj's?

21 Káťa's fear of storms is established at the end of Ostrovsky's Act 1 (Janáček omitted this). There is no mention in either Ostrovsky or Janáček of Káťa's being terrified by lightning just before her confession in Act 3 Scene 1 (Ostrovsky's Act 4).

22 On Brod's prompting, see above, p. 65 (f).

Productions of 'Káťa Kabanová'

SVATAVA PŘIBÁŇOVÁ

This table lists chronologically the first performances of all stage productions and important concert and radio performances of *Káťa Kabanová*. Revivals are generally not included, but places and dates of foreign tours are appended to the details of the original productions.

Date	Town	Theatre/ Company	Conductor	Producer	Designer/ Costume Designer	Káťa	Kabanicha	Boris
23.XI.1921	Brno	Národní divadlo	František Neumann	Vladimír Marek	Vladimír Hrška	Marie Veselá	Marie Hladíková	Karel Zavřel
30.XI.1922	Prague	Národní divadlo	Otakar Ostrčil	Robert Polák	J. M. Gottlieb	Kamila Ungrová	Marie Rejholcová	Miloslav Jeník
8.XII.1922	Cologne	Bühnen der Stadt	Otto Klemperer	Felix Dahn	Hraby	Rose Pauly	Berta Grimm-Mittelmann	Karl Schröder
24.III.1923	Bratislava	Národné divadlo	Milan Zuna	Josef Munclinger		Hana Pirková	Jelena Ježičová	V. Fujera
18.I.1924	Ostrava	Moravskoslez-ské národní divadlo	Emanuel Bastl	Jan Kühn	J. Dušek	Linda Šmidová	Sláva Mazáková	Karel Kügler
16.X.1924	Brno	Národní divadlo	František Neumann	Ota Zítek	A. Provazník	Hana Pirková	Jelena Ježičová	Antonín Pelz
13.II.1925	Plzeň	Městské divadlo	Antonín Barták	Vladimír Marek	Röschenthaler	Hana Kramperová	Viktorie Janošová	Josef Kejř
31.V.1926	Berlin	Städtische Oper	Fritz Zweig	Alex Schum	Gustav Vargo	Anny Helm	Marie Schulz-Dornburg	Josef Burgwinkel
21.I.1928	Prague	Deutsches Theater	Hans Wilhelm Steinberg	Max Semmler		Zuzana Jichová-Götzl	Paula Sommer	Max Adrian

Productions of *Káťa Kabanová* (cont.)

Date	Town	Theatre/Company	Conductor	Producer	Designer/Costume Designer	Káťa	Kabanicha	Boris
18.III.1929	Aachen	Stadttheater	Paul Pella	Walter Falk	Helmut Jürgens	Tiana Gerstung	Klara Hertzog	Ludwig Suthaus
21.XI.1931	Olomouc	Městské divadlo	Emanuel Bastl	Přemysl Pospíšil	Josef Gabriel	Marie Minářová-Strossová	Božena Stoegrová	Jaroslav Jaroš
18.V.1933	Brno	Zemské divadlo	Milan Sachs	Rudolf Walter	Antonín Klimeš	Marie Žaludová	Marie Hloušková	Gustav Talman
26.V.1934	Ljubljana	Narodno gledališče	Niko Štritof	Ciril Debevec	Vasiljev Mitrofanič Uljaniščev			
14.III.1935	Ústí nad Labem–Teplice	Stadttheater	Franz Aller	Erich von Wymetal	Manfred Miller	Edith Holland	Gerda Redlichová	Cornelius Weicher
21.IX.1935	Bratislava	Slovenské národné divadlo	Karel Nedbal	Bohuš Vilím	Ludvik Hradský	Milada Formanová	Marie Peršlová	Jaroslav Jaroš
28.III.1936	Zagreb	Narodno kazalište	Krešimir Baranović	Margareta Froman	Pavel Froman	Ančica Mitrović	Lucija Ozegović	Anatol Manoševski
16.IX.1938	Prague	Národní divadlo	Václav Talich	Ota Zítek	František Muzika	Marie Šponarová	Marta Krásová	Jindřich Blažíček
7.XII.1938	Ostrava	Moravskoslezské národní divadlo	Jaroslav Vogel	Karel Kügler	Jan Sládek	Zdeňka Spačková	Helena Zemanová	Petar Burja

Date	City	Theater	Conductor	Director	Designer			
15.II.1939	Brno	Zemské divadlo	Karel Nedbal	Branko Gavella	Antonín Klimeš	Marie Žaludová	Marie Řezníčková	Gustav Talman
4.III.1939	Plzeň	Městské divadlo	Antonín Barták	Ota Zítek	František Muzika	Marie Šponarová	Marie Veselá	Jindřich Blažíček
17.IV.1946	Brno	Národní divadlo	Bohumír Liška	Ota Zítek	Zdeněk Rossman	Emilie Zachardová	Marie Žaludová	Antonín Jurečka
17.I.1947	Prague	Velká opera 5. května	Václav Kašlík	Václav Kašlík	Josef Svoboda	Jaroslava Procházková	Marie Cyteráková	Jaromír Svoboda
25.IV.1947	Prague	Národní divadlo	Václav Talich	Hanuš Thein	František Troester	Ludmila Červinková	Marta Krásová	Beno Blachut
11.X.1947	Munich	Bayerische Staatsoper	Hans-Georg Ratjen	Max Hofmüller	Leo Dahl/ Lovis Révy	Marianne Schech	Irmgard Barth	Franz Klarwein
21.II.1948	Zurich	Stadttheater	Otto Ackermann	Oscar Fritz Schuh	Caspar Neher	Inge Borkh	Ira Malaniuk	Franz Lechleitner
25.IX.1948	Olomouc	Městské divadlo	Iša Krejčí	Václav Černý	Oldřich Šimáček	Milada Marková	Božena Stoegrová	Karel Hauser
12.I.1949	Bratislava	Slovenské národné divadlo	Milan Zuna	Bohuš Vilím	František Troester	Helena Bartošová/ Helena Lembovičová	Janka Gabčová/ Ludvika Dubovská	Štefan Hoza
30.IV.1949	Plzeň	Krajské oblastní divadlo	František Belfín	Hanuš Thein	František Troester	Blanka Vecková	Anna Kasalová	Josef Hořický
14.VIII.1949	Dresden	Staatstheater	Ernst Richter	Heinz Arnold	Karl von Appen	Elfride Trötschel	Helene Rott	Helmut Schindler
19.XI.1949	Ostrava	Státní divadlo	Rudolf Vašata	Hanuš Thein	František Troester	Ludmila Dvořáková/ Bronislava Taufrová	Helena Zemanová	František Janda

Productions of *Káťa Kabanová* (*cont.*)

Date	Town	Theatre/Company	Conductor	Producer	Designer/Costume Designer	Káťa	Kabanicha	Boris
19.XI.1949	Ústí nad Labem	Krajské krušnohorské divadlo	Josef Bartl/Václav Nosek	Rudolf Málek	Karel Rendl	Helena Lexová	Marie Jechová	Zdeněk Zouplna/Lubomír Havlák
10.IV.1951	London	Sadler's Wells Opera	Charles Mackerras/Rafael Kubelík	Dennis Arundell	John Glass and L. W. Anson/Anthony Boyes	Amy Shuard	Kate Jackson	Rowland Jones
24.III.1953	Opava	Divadlo Zdeňka Nejedlého	Ivo Jirásek	Ilja Hylas	Stanislav Kolíbal	Irena Křivánková	Božena Ministrová	Jaroslav Horal
21.IV.1953	Hagen	Städtische Bühne	Berthold Lehmann	Curt Haug	Richard Zuckmayer	Elfriede Hingst	Emma-Klara Kirchner	Hans Hassen
9.X.1953	Brno	Státní divadlo	Bohumír Liška	Oskar Linhart	Miloš Tomek	Libuše Domanínská	Marie Žaludová/Marie Řezníčková	Antonín Jurečka
15.III.1955	Schwerin	Mecklenburgisches Staatstheater	Karl Schubert	Erwin Bugge	Arvid Voigt/Ursula Witzleb	Evelyn Schildbach	Helene Kertscher-Oertel	Hermann Runge
8.VII.1956	Belgrade	Narodno pozorište	Krešimir Baranović	Mladen Sablić	Miomir Denić/Milica Babić-Jovanović	Valerija Heybalova	Melanija Bugarinović	Drago Starc

This production also played in 1957 Florence, 1958 Wiesbaden, 1959 Paris

7.XI.1956	Liberec	Severočeské divadlo	Oldřich Pipek	Oldřich Mrňák	Jarmila Konečná	Marie Rathouská	Jana Hanusová	Jan Malík
17.V.1957	Prague	Národní divadlo	Jaroslav Krombholc	Hanuš Thein	František Troester/Jan Kropáček	Ludmila Červinková/Libuše Domanínská	Marta Krásová/Zdenka Hrnčířová	Beno Blachut/Jaroslav Stříška
30.VI.1957	Berlin	Städtische Oper	Richard Kraus	Wolf Völker	Wilhelm Reinking	Elfride Trötschel	Irene Dalis	Sándor Konya
13.X.1957	Karl-Marx-Stadt	Städtisches Theater	Walter Stoschek	Carl Riha	Jost Bednar/Renate Müller	Gisela Geusch	Renate Härtel	Ludwig Pasztor
26.XI.1957	Cleveland, Ohio	Karamu House		Benno Frank				
31.V.1958	Plzeň	Divadlo J. K. Tyla	Bohumír Liška	Bohumil Zoul	František Troester	Miloslava Šeflová/Věra Vičková	Jitka Jůzková/Věra Soukupová	Zdeněk Jankovský/Oldřich Spisar
11.IX.1958	Brno	Státní divadlo	Jaroslav Vogel	Oskar Linhart	Miloš Tomek	Alena Nováková	Jarmila Palivcová	Antonín Jurečka
24.X.1958	Dessau	Landestheater	Heinz Röttger	Willy Bodenstein	Wolf Hochheim	Anita Allwardt	Magdalena Güntzel	Joachim Riecke
1959	Enschede	Opera Forum De Nederlandsche Opera	Paul Pella	Paul Pella				Harry Lance
16.VI.1959	Amsterdam		Jaroslav Krombholc	Hanuš Thein	Josef Svoboda/Marcel Pokorný	Libuše Domanínská	Mimi Aarden	Beno Blachut
28.VIII.1959 Görlitz		Gerhart-Hauptmann Theater	Alfred Schönfelder	Joachim Zschech	Hans-Joachim Löchelt/Helga Steinhoff	Gerda Briese	Ingeborg Rudolph	Richard Pfeiffer

Productions of *Káťa Kabanová* (cont.)

Date	Town	Theatre/Company	Conductor	Producer	Designer/Costume Designer	Káťa	Kabanicha	Boris
1.IX.1959	Helsinki	Suomen-kansalli-sooppera	Jussi Jalas	Yrjö Kostermaa	Paul Suominen	Anita Välkki	Maiju Huusoja	Pekka Nuotio
18.XI.1959	London	Sadler's Wells Opera	Charles Mackerras	Dennis Arundell	John Glass and L. W. Anson/Anthony Boyes	Marie Collier	Monica Sinclair/Rosina Raisbeck/Edith Coates	William McAlpine
1959	Gelsenkirchen	Städtische Bühnen	Ljubomir Romansky	Rudolf Schenke	Theo Lau/Charlotta Vocke	Maria Helm	Meta Ober	Erich Benke
1960	Antwerp	Koninklijke Vlaamse Opera						
2.VIII.1960	Bear Mountain, New York	Empire State Music Festival	Laszlo Halasz	Christopher West	Ming Cho Lee	Amy Shuard	Doris Doree	Rudolph Petrák
1.X.1960	Ostrava	Státní divadlo	Bohumil Gregor	Ilja Hylas	František Troester/Bedřiška Ustohalová	Milada Šafránková/Eva Gebauerová	Alice Spohrová	Jiří Zahradníček/Josef Lindauer
8.II.1961	Greiz	Theater der Stadt	Joachim-Dietrich Link	Wilhelm Wehner	Horst Leiteritz/Walter Jahn	Christa Schauer-Ohl	Helga-Maria Ohlf	Georg Czekalla

5.III.1961	Budapest	Magyar Állami Operaház	János Ferencsik	Ferenc Kenessey	Gábor Forray/Gisela Szeitz	Júlia Orosz/Erszébet Házy	Rózsi Delly	Alfonz Barta
16.IV.1961	Wuppertal	Wuppertaler Bühnen	Hans Drewanz	Andreas Meyer-Hannos	Siegfried Stepanek	Ingeborg Moussa	Margit Kobeck	Eugen Talley-Schmidt
27.X.1961	Olomouc	Divadlo Oldřicha Stibora	Zdeněk Košler	Emil F. Vokálek	Jiři Procházka	Agia Formán-ková/Zdeňka Talpová	Milada Marková	František Šifta
29.I.1962	Essen	Bühnen der Stadt	Paul Belker	Bohumil Herlischka	Dominik Hartmann	Käthe Graus	Trude Roesler	Helmut Meutsch
24.III.1962	České Budějovice	Jihočeské divadlo	Emil Křepelka	Oskar Linhart	Josef A. Šálek	Stanislava Součková/Eva Valentová	Marie Poštová	Karel Sekyra
31.V.1962	Darmstadt	Landestheater	Hans Zanotelli	Gerhard F. Hering	Max Bignens/Elli Büttner	Evelyn Schildbach	Dorothea von Stein	George Maran
17.II.1963	Leipzig	Opernhaus	Václav Neumann	Joachim Herz	Max Elten/Eleonore Kleiber	Maria Croonen	Katrin Wölzl	Edgar Wählte

This production also played in 1965 Gelsenkirchen

29.XI.1963	Karlsruhe	Badisches Staatstheater	Arthur Grüber	Reinhard Lehman	Hainer Hill	Ingeborg Moussa	Maria Graf	Alfred Hans Winkler
1.V.1964	New York	Juilliard School of Music	Frederic Waldman	Christopher West	Ming Cho Lee/Patton Campbell	Lorna Haywood	Bonnie Godfrey	Alexander Yancy
3.VI.1964	Prague	Národní divadlo	Jaroslav Krombholc	Hanuš Thein	Josef Svoboda/Marcel Pokorný	Libuše Domaninská/Eva Zikmundová	Jaroslava Procházková/Jaroslava Dobrá/Ivana Mixová	Beno Blachut/Viktor Koči

Productions of *Káťa Kabanová (cont.)*

Date	Town	Theatre/Company	Conductor	Producer	Designer/Costume Designer	Káťa	Kabanicha	Boris
This production also played in 1964 Edinburgh, 1968 Reggio Emilia, Bologna, Brescia, Naples, 1969 Ghent, Brussels								
20.VI.1965	Linz	Landestheater	František Jílek	Miloš Wasserbauer	František Troester	Jarmila Rudolfová	Hedwig Schubert	Herbert Doussant
20.VI.1965	Rome	Studi RAI	Armando La Rosa Parodi			Mietta Sighele	Jolanda Gardino	Luigi Infantino
14.I.1966	Basle	Stadttheater	Hans Löwlein	Walter Pohl	Annelies Corrodi	Jarmila Rudolfová	Susanne Muser	Gunnar Johnson
1.4.1966	Kassel	Staatstheater	Martin Mälzer	Wolf Völker	Artur Hamm	Hanlie van Niekerk	Carin Carlsson	János Korda
17.IV.1966	Graz	Vereinigte Bühnen	Berislav Klobučar	Mladen Sablić	Wolfram Skalicki/Hanna Wartenegg	Stefka Todorova	Erika Schubert	José Maria Perez
14.X.1966	Brunswick	Staatstheater	Heribert Esser	Friedrich Petzold	Matthias Krals/Evelyn Arm-Frank	Paula Bukovac	Margit Kobeck	Peter Gugalow
15.X.1966	Ústí nad Labem	Divadlo Zdeňka Nejedlého	František Vajnar	Norbert Snítil	Vladimír Heller/Růžena Brychtová	Karla Janečková/Jarmila Krásová	Marie Střeblová/L. Hanušová	J. Škoda/Jan Malík
8.III.1967	Kiel	Bühnen der Landeshauptstadt	Karl Heinz Strasser	Wolf Voelker	Friedhelm Strenger			

11.III.1967	Mannheim	National-theater	Horst Stein	Reinhold Schubert	Paul Walter/ Gerda Schulte	Erika Schmidt/ Eva Zikmun-dová	Eva Tamassy	Jean Cox
19.III.1967	Potsdam	Hans-Otto-Theater	Peter Gülke	Wilfried Serauky	Adolf Wenig	Ute Reinisch	Irmgard Pfeifer	Rali Ralew
25.III.1967	Hanover	Landestheater	Ernst Richter	Václav Kašlík	Walter Gondolf	Simone Mangelsdorff	Elisabeth Pack	Horst Hoffmann
22.IV.1967	Plauen	Theater der Stadt	Manfred Hänsel	Walter Blan-kenstein	Fritz Werner	Lucie König	Lisa Hübner	Joachim Riecke
14.V.1967	Opava	Slezské divadlo	Emil Křepelka	Ilja Hylas	Eva Václavková	Emilie Žáková	Irena Kellnerová/ Alena Španihelová	Karel Sekyra
23.II.1968	Paris	Opéra Comique	Jean Marie Périsson	Pierre Médecin	Annelies Corrodi	Hélène Garetti	Berthe Monmart	Ion Piso
13.IV.1968	Augsburg	Städtische Bühnen	Hans Zanotelli	Claus Thomas	Heinz-Gerhard Zircher/ Bettina Weise	Anita Salta	Elisabeth Thoma	Hans Wegman
10.V.1968	Buenos Aires	Teatro Colon	Václav Smetáček	Karel Jernek	František Troester/ Olga Filipi	Libuše Domaninská	Růžena Hořáková	Ivo Žídek
11.V.1968	Brno	Státní divadlo	František Jílek	Oskar Linhart	František Troester	Zdeňka Kareninová/ Kveta Belanová	Jarmila Palivcová/ Marie Steinerová	Vilém Přibyl/ Jiří Olejníček

This production also played in 1973 Barcelona

| 18.V.1968 | Ljubljana | Narodno gledališče | Demetrij Žebre | Hinko Leskovšek | Maks Kavčič/ Anja Dolenc | | | |

Productions of *Káťa Kabanová (cont.)*

Date	Town	Theatre/Company	Conductor	Producer	Designer/Costume Designer	Káťa	Kabanicha	Boris
28.IX.1968	Liberec	Divadlo F. X. Šaldy	Rudolf Vašata	Rudolf Málek	Vratislav Habr/Marie Bendová	Marie Kremerová	Jana Hanusová	Jan Malik
22.IV.1969	Regensburg	Stadttheater	Max Kink	Eberhard Kuhlmann	Klaus Roth/Helga Schwarz-kopf	Eva Illes	Jean Stawski	Martino Stamos
3.XII.1971	Osnabrück	Städtische Bühnen	Robert Wolf	Werner Michael Esser	Vladimir Landa/Lore Haas	Jarmila Rudolfová	Gabriella von Pécsváry/Virginia Love	Peter Pietzsch
8.V.1972	Košice	Štátne divadlo	Ladislav Holoubek	Emil F. Vokálek	Jiří Procházka/Adolf Wenig	Eva Šmalíková/Elena Gmucová	Milada Marková	Jozef Konder
14.V.1972	New York	The Bel Canto Opera at Madison Ave Baptist Church Auditorium	William Shookhoff	David Shookhoff	Ilse Kritzler	Mara Worth	Margaret Toevs	Winston Lee
27.V.1972	Stuttgart	Württemberg-ische Staats-theater	Václav Neumann	Ernst Poettgen	Leni Bauer-Ecsy	Hildegard Hillebrecht/Anja Silja	Grace Hoffmann	Josef Hopferwieser

2.VII.1972	Berlin	Komische Oper	Gert Bahner	Joachim Herz	Rudolf Heinrich/ Eleonore Kleiber	Jana Smitková	Ruth Schob-Lipka	John Moulson
28.X.1972	Wexford	Theatre Royal	Albert Rosen	David Pountney	Susan Blane/ Maria Bjørnson	Alexandra Hunt	Soňa Červená	Ivo Žídek

This production also played in 1973 York

22.III.1973	Rochester, New York	Eastman School of Music	Edwin McArthur	Leonard Treash	Thomas P. Struthers	Susan Pierson/ Susan Blum	Juliane Cross/ Laura Angus	Booker T. Wilson/ Michael Crouse
8.IV.1973	Plovdiv	Narodna opera	Václav Nosek	Georgi Prvanov	Marianna Polova	Rajna Košerska	Sonja Chamernik	Vladimir Todorov
14.IV.1973	Zurich	Opernhaus	Jaroslav Krombholc	Harry Buckwitz	Josef Svoboda/ Jan Skalický	Antigone Sgourda	Astrid Varnay	Jon Buzea
11.V.1973	Maribor	Slovensko narodno gledališče	Marko Žigon	Emil Frelih	Josef Vališ/ Vlasta Hege- dušiceva	Ada Sardova	Ada Thumova	Jernej Plahuta
20.V.1973	Weimar	Deutsches National- theater	Gerhard Pflüger	Christa Lehmann	Christian Panzer	Nelly Delibaschewa	Ingeborg Portsmann	Peter-Jürgen Schmidt
29.VI.1973	Düsseldorf	Deutsche Oper am Rhein	Peter Schneider	Bohumil Herlischka	Ruodi Barth/ Liselotte Erler	Stella Axarlis	Astrid Varnay	Werner Götz

This production also played in 1974 Duisburg

12.IX.1973	London	Sadler's Wells Opera at the Coliseum	Charles Mackerras	John Blatchley	Stefanos Lazaridis	Lorna Haywood	Sylvia Fisher	Kenneth Woollam/ William McAlpine

This production also played in 1974 Leeds, Manchester, Newcastle

Productions of *Káťa Kabanová* (cont.)

Date	Town	Theatre/Company	Conductor	Producer	Designer/Costume Designer	Káťa	Kabanicha	Boris
28.X.1973	Olomouc	Divadlo Oldřicha Stibora	Miloš Konvalinka	Jiří Glogar	Jiří Procházka/Eliška Zapletalová	Eva Kinclová	Božena Ministrová	Leo Vodička
4.XI.1973	Oldenburg	Staatstheater	Fritz Janota	Michael Rothacker	Heidrun Schmelzer	Annemarie Steffens	Johanna Gorschler	Karl Acher
31.I.1974	Frankfurt am Main	Städtische Bühnen	Peter Schrothner	Volker Schlöndorff	Ekkehard Grübler	Hildegard Behrens	Soňa Červená	Allen Cathcart

This production also played in 1975 Lisbon, 1978 Edinburgh

Date	Town	Theatre/Company	Conductor	Producer	Designer/Costume Designer	Káťa	Kabanicha	Boris
19.IV.1974	Vienna	Staatsoper	János Kulka	Joachim Herz	Rudolf Heinrich	Antigone Sgourda	Astrid Varnay	Peter Lindroos
21.VI.1974	Prague	Národní divadlo	Bohumil Gregor	Karel Jernek	Josef Svoboda/Olga Filipi	Marta Cihelníková/Gabriela Beňačková	Věra Soukupová/Naděžda Kniplová	Ivo Žídek/Miroslav Švejda

This production also played in 1975 Belgrade, Zagreb, Madrid, Moscow, 1976 Budapest

Date	Town	Theatre/Company	Conductor	Producer	Designer/Costume Designer	Káťa	Kabanicha	Boris
13.XII.1974	Freiburg im Breisgau	Städtische Bühnen	Karl Anton Rickenbacher	Johann Georg Schaarschmidt	Klaus Teepe	Ingrid Kremling	Martha Mödl	Elliot Palay
1.IV.1975	Geneva	Grand Theatre	Jaroslav Krombholc	Václav Kašlík	Josef Svoboda	Elisabeth Söderström	Naděžda Kniplová	Ivo Žídek
17.VI.1975	Bremen	Theater am Goetheplatz	Hermann Michael	Helmut Baumann	Walter Schwaab	Irja Auroora	Maria Sandulesco	Connell Byrne

Date	Place	Company	Conductor	Director	Designer			
11.XII.1975	Scheveningen, Amsterdam, Rotterdam	De Nederlandsche Opera	Bohumil Gregor	Karel Jernek	Josef Svoboda	Gabriela Beňačková	Naděžda Kniplová	René Claessen
2.I.1976	Trieste	Teatro Giuseppe Verdi	Georges Sebastian	Margherita Wallmann	Mischa Scandella	Helia T'Hezan	Djurdijevka Cakarević	Gianfranco Pastine
16.I.1976	Louisville	Kentucky Opera Association	Moritz Bomhard	Charles Janssens	Charles Janssens/Lucile Paris	Lorna Haywood	Charme Riesley	John Sandor
17.IV.1976	Bielefeld	Städtische Bühnen	Anton Marik	Federik Mirdita	Axel Schmitt-Falckenberg/Enid Strutt	Gudrun Volkert	Danielle Grima	Wolfgang Neumann
23.X.1976	Stockholm	Operan	Berislav Klobučar	Joachim Herz	Rudolf Heinrich-Günter Fischer Piscat/Eleonore Kleiber	Helena Döse	Barbro Ericson	Gösta Winbergh
17.II.1977	London	English National Opera	Charles Mackerras/David Lloyd Jones	John Blatchley	Stefanos Lazaridis	Ava June	Elizabeth Connell	Kenneth Woollam
25.III.1977	Toronto	University Opera Dept	James Craig	Constance Fisher	Brian Jackson	Heather Wilberforce/Kathy Terrell	Jill Pert	Stephen Young
9.IV.1977	Nuremberg	Städtische Bühnen	Wolfgang Gayler	Ulrich Brecht	Thomas Richter-Forgach	Elisabeth Payer	Christa Puhlmann-Richter	Günter Neubert
29.IV.1977	Trier	Theater der Stadt		Walter Pohl		Ingrid Haubold		

This production also played in 1977 Metz

Productions of *Káťa Kabanová* (cont.)

Date	Town	Theatre/Company	Conductor	Producer	Designer/Costume Designer	Káťa	Kabanicha	Boris
23.V.1977	Aachen	Stadttheater	Gabriel Chmura	Hans Hartleb	Wolfram Munz	Barbara Honn	Paula Bukovac	Udo Holdorf
27.V.1977	Meiningen	Das Meininger Theater	Wolfgang Hocke	Gunther Hofmann	Rolf-Christoph Ullmann	Karin Brandt	Ines Kurz-Margraf	Gerold Herrmann
17.IX.1977	San Francisco	San Francisco Opera	Rafael Kubelík	Günther Rennert	Günther Schneider-Siemssen/Maria-Luise Walek	Elisabeth Söderström	Beverly Wolff	William Lewis
27.XI.1977	Brno	Státní divadlo	Václav Nosek	Václav Věžník	Ladislav Vychodil/Naděžda Hanáková	Gita Abrahá-mová/Alena Žaloudková/Magdalena Blahušiaková	Jarmila Palivcová/Milada Šafránková	Jiří Olejníček/Vilém Přibyl
This production also played in 1979 Hoechst, Leverkusen, Luxembourg, Genoa								
17.XII.1977	Plzeň	Divadlo J. K. Tyla	Karel Vašata	Oldřich Kříž	Vlastimil Koutecký/Bedřich Barták	Tatána Bublíková/Helena Buldrová	Věra Vlčková	Jan Janda
24.II.1978	Bratislava	Slovenské narodné divadlo	Viktor Málek	Branislav Kriška	Ladislav Vychodil/H. Bezáková	Eva Děpoltová	Olga Hanáková	Peter Dvorský

This production also played in 1980 Wiesbaden

10.VI.1978	Hagen	Städtische Bühne	Reinhard Schwarz/ Eberhard Bäumler	Manfred Schnabel	Marco Arturo Marelli	Catherine Gayer	Danielle Grima	Donald Georg
		This production also played in 1978 Remscheid, 1979 Witten						
25.XI.1978	St Gallen	Stadttheater	Kurt Brass	Václav Věžnik	Josef A. Šálek	Ursula Volbading	Grace Hoffmann	Walter Ryals
3.XII.1978	Wroclaw	Opera	Robert Satanowski	Ryszard Peryt	Ewa Staro-wieyska	Jadwiga Gadulanka/ Elzbieta Hoffmann	Wanda Bargielowska	Ryszard Brożek/ Józef Przestrzelski
10.II.1979	Lübeck	Bühnen der Hansestadt	Eberhard Kloke	Michael Rothacker (concert performance)	Heidrun Schmelzer	Kathleen Martin	Ludmila Dvořáková	Robert Mazzarella
25.II.1979	New York	Carnegie Hall, Opera Orchestra of New York	Eve Queler			Gabriela Beňačková	Naděžda Kniplová	William Lewis
16.III.1979	Munich	Theater am Gärtner-platz	Siegfried Köhler	Kurt Horres	Herbert Wernicke	June Card	Margarethe Bence	Perry Price
4.IV.1979	Glasgow	Scottish Opera	Richard Armstrong	David Pountney	Maria Bjørnson	Josephine Barstow	Kerstin Meyer	Allen Cathcart
		This production also played in 1982 Cardiff						
23.IX.1979	Berne	Stadttheater	Ewald Körner	Václav Věžnik	Josef A. Šálek	Angelika Rode	Grace Hoffmann	Walter Ryals
18.I.1980	Ulm	Stadttheater	Friedrich Pleyer	Andreas Prohaska	Eberhard Matthies/ Renate Schmitzer	Sophia Pötscher	Martha Dewal	Reto Calli

Productions of *Káťa Kabanová* (cont.)

Date	Town	Theatre/Company	Conductor	Producer	Designer/Costume Designer	Káťa	Kabanicha	Boris
1.II.1980	Oslo	Den Norske Opera	Martin Turnovský	Dieter Bülter-Marell	Otto Werner Meyer	Else Dehli/ Mirjana Dancuo	Vessa Hanssen/ Vesla Tveten	Sten Sjøstedt/ Kare Bjorkoy
30.III.1980	Kassel	Staatstheater	James Lockhart	Václav Kašlík	Walter Perdacher	Barbara Honn	Margarete Ast	Rene Claessen
20.IV.1980	Heidelberg	Theater der Stadt	Gerhard Schäfer	Peter Osolnik	Jörg Weissenow	Maria Grosse	Stefka Popangelova	Vittorio Giam-marrusco
28.VIII.1980	Sydney	The Australian Opera	Mark Elder/ David Kram	David Pountney	Roger Butlin/ Maria Bjørnson	Marilyn Richardson/ Etela Piha	Rosina Raisbeck	Gregory Dempsey
31.X.1980	Ústí nad Labem	Divadlo Zdeňka Nejedlého	Jan Zbavitel	Norbert Snítil	Ivo Žídek/ Růžena Brychtová	Květa Koníčková	Jana Scholzeová/ Marie Stréblová	Karel Bim

Sources

Apart from Homola's fair copy of the full score (with Janáček's corrections and additions) and Bakala's vocal score, both of which served as printer's copy for the Universal Edition prints, all major musical sources for *Káťa Kabanová* are in the Janáček Archive of the Moravian Museum, Music History Division, Brno. They are usefully summarized, with their shelfmarks, by Svatava Přibáňová: 'Operní dílo Janáčkova vrcholného údobí' [The operatic works of Janáček's maturity], *Časopis Moravského muzea: vědy společenské*, lxv (1980), pp. 165–70. The original Brno orchestral parts for *Káťa*, mentioned above, p. 135, are in the Archive of the State Theatre, Brno. The Homola full score is in the Universal Edition Archive, Vienna; the Bakala vocal score is untraceable.

Except where specifically stated, all literary sources for the opera are also in the Moravian Museum. They range from Janáček's annotated copy of the play and his manuscript copy and corrected typescript of the libretto to a large number of letters, many of which have been published in the Janáčkův Archiv series of Janáček's correspondence. Other letters printed in Chapters 3 and 5 (most of them previously unpublished) are held under the following shelfmarks: B 1690, B 1691 B 1694 (Brod to Janáček); B 1159, B 426 (Červinka to Janáček); D 335 (Nebuška to Janáček); D 1124 (Neumann to Janáček); B 1009 (Janáček to Neumann); E 1142, E 1187, E 167, E 170, E 172, E 178, E 181, E 1144, E 1145, E 185, E 187, E 189, E 190, E 202, E 205, E 206 (Janáček to Stösslová); E 885, E 888, E 895 (Stösslová to Janáček); D 380 (Brno National Theatre to Janáček).

Bibliography

M. Brod: 'Katja Kabanowa', *Sternenhimmel: Musik- und Theatererlebnisse* (Prague and Munich, 1923); 2nd edn, as *Prager Sternenhimmel* (Vienna and Hamburg, 1966), pp. 52–63 (Czech trans. by B. Fučík, Prague, 1969) [brief report of the Brno première and an essay on the opera] *Leoš Janáček: život a dílo* [Life and works], trans. A. Fuchs (Prague, 1924; Ger. original, Vienna, 1925, enlarged 2nd edn, 1956) [includes revised version of essay referred to in previous entry: pp. 40–7 (Czech edn), pp. 45–50 (both German edns); Eng. trans. in Chapter 8]

J. Burjanek: 'Janáčkova Káťa Kabanová a Ostrovského Bouře' [Janáček's *Káťa Kabanová* and Ostrovsky's *The Thunderstorm*], *Musikologie*, iii (Prague, 1955), pp. 345–416

V. Červinka: 'Jak vznikla Káťa Kabanová' [The origin of *Káťa Kabanová*], *Národní politika*, 18 October 1938 [extracts in Chapter 5]

E. Chisholm: *The Operas of Leoš Janáček* (Oxford, 1971)

W. Dean: 'Janáček and "Katya Kabanova"', *The Listener*, li (1954), p. 945 [reprinted in Chapter 8]

M. Ewans: 'Káťa Kabanová', *Janáček's Tragic Operas* (London, 1977), pp. 105–36.

P. Gülke: 'Janáček: Werk- und Realisierungsprobleme: der Realismus des Komponierens bei Janáček', *Theater der Zeit DDR*, xxviii/11 (1973), pp. 26–9 [includes discussion of two monologues in *Káťa Kabanová*]

H. Hollander: *Leoš Janáček: his Life and Work*, trans P. Hamburger (London, 1963; Ger. original, Zurich, 1964)

V. Jiřikovský: 'Vzpomínky na Leoše Janáčka' [Reminiscences of Leoš Janáček], *Divadelní list Zemského divadla v Brně*, vii (1931–2), pp. 248–50 [extract in Chapter 5]

T. Kneif: 'Káťa Kabanová', *Die Bühnenwerke von Leoš Janáček* (Vienna, 1974), pp. 49–52

D. Muller: 'Les autres oeuvres dramatiques: Katia Kabanova', *Leoš Janáček* (Paris, 1930), pp. 60–6 [Eng. trans. in Chapter 8]

F. Pala: *Janáček – Káťa Kabanová* (Brno and Prague, 1938) [analysis] 'Jevištní dílo Leoše Janáčka' [The stage works of Leoš Janáček], *Musikologie*, iii (Prague, 1955), pp. 61–210, esp. 'Káťa Kabanová', pp. 135–52

L. Polyakova: 'O "ruských" operách Leoše Janáčka' [The 'Russian' operas of Leoš Janáček], *Cesty rozvoje a vzájemné vztahy ruského a československého umění* [Paths of development and reciprocal relations in the

Russian and Czechoslovak arts], Czech Academy of Sciences (Prague, 1974), pp. 247–69 [includes discussion of the supposed Russian folk elements in *Káťa Kabanová*]

J. Procházka: 'Vznik libreta a jeho zhudebnění' [The origin of the libretto and its setting], introduction to libretto of *Káťa Kabanová* Operní Libreta, i/24 (Prague, 1961) pp. 5–32; editorial note, *ibid.* pp. 33–4 [lists previous printed librettos]; cf. Procházka's earlier edition in *Divadlo* (1958), no. 4 [with editorial comments and text comparisons, pp. 20–8]

W. Siegmund-Schultze: 'Janáček: Werk- und Realisierungsprobleme: die Hoffnung auf Veränderung', *Theater der Zeit DDR*, xxviii/11 (1973), pp. 31–3 [comparison of *Káťa Kabanová* and *Wozzeck*]

B. Štědroň: *Janáček ve vzpomínkách a dopisech* [Janáček in reminiscences and letters] (Prague, 1946; Eng. trans. by G. Thomsen (Prague, 1955)

M. Štědroň: 'Janáček a opera Groza Vladimíra Nikitiče Kašperova na libreto N. A. Ostrovského (1867)' [Janáček and Kashperov's opera *The Thunderstorm* to Ostrovsky's libretto (1867)], *Svazky – vztahy – paralely* [Links – relations – parallels] (Brno, 1973), pp. 129–33

T. Straková: 'Mezihry v Káti Kabanové: k problémům interpretace Janáčkových oper' [The interludes in *Káťa Kabanová*: problems in the interpretation of Janáček's operas], *Časopis Moravského musea: vědy společenské*, xlix (1964), pp. 229–36 (Ger. trans. in *Acta janáčkiana*, i (Brno, 1968), pp. 125–30 [Eng. trans. in Chapter 7])

C. Stuart: '*Katya Kabanova* Reconsidered', *Music Review*, xii (1951), pp. 289–95

H. H. Stuckenschmidt: 'Leoš Janáček's "Katja Kabanova"', trans. by E. Mayer-Lismann, *Opera*, ii (1951), pp. 227–34 (Ger. original in *Musik der Zeit*, ed. H. Lindlar, no. 8 (1954), pp. 5–10)

J. Telcová: 'Scénografie Káti Kabanovy', *Časopis Moravského musea: vědy společenské*, li (1966), pp. 345–59 [includes illustrations of productions in Prague, 1922, 1938 and 1964, and discussion of staging of Czech and foreign productions]

J. Vogel: *Leoš Janáček: his Life and Works*, trans. G. Thomsen (London, 1962; Czech original, Prague, 1963; enlarged Eng. trans. by K. Janovický, London, 1981)

K.-H. Wörner: 'Katjas Tod: die Schlussszene der Oper Katja Kabanowa von Leoš Janáček', *Leoš Janáček a soudobá hudba: Mezinárodní hudebně vědecký kongres, Brno 1958* [Janáček and contemporary music: international musicological congress, Brno 1958] (Prague, 1963), pp. 392–8, Czech trans. pp. 399–403

'Natur, Liebe und Tod bei Janáček', *Colloquium Leoš Janáček et musica europeaea Brno 1968*, ed. R. Pečman (Brno, 1970), pp. 159–68

'Leoš Janáček', *Das Zeitalter der thematischen Prozesse in der Geschichte der Musik* (Regensburg, 1969), pp. 146–53 [Eng. trans. in Chapter 8]

Discography

BY MALCOLM WALKER

D	Dikoj	VK	Váňa Kudrjáš
B	Boris	V	Varvara
MK	Marfa Kabanová (Kabanicha)	K	Kuligin
TK	Tichon Kabanov	G	Glaša
KK	Kateřina (Káťa) Kabanová	F	Fekluša

Ⓢstereo   Ⓜmono   ④cassette recording

33⅓ rpm

1959   Kroupa D; Blachut B; Komancová MK; Vich TK; Tikalová KK; Kočí VK; Mixová V; Jedlička K; Hlobilová G; Lemariová F/Prague National Theatre Chorus and Orch/Krombholc
Suraphon Ⓢ 50781-2

1976   Jedlička D; Dvorský B; Kniplová MK; Krejčík TK; Söderström KK; Švehla VK; Márová V; Souček K; Pavlová G; Jahn F/Vienna State Opera Chorus, VPO/Mackerras
Decca Ⓢ D51D2 ④ K51K22
London Ⓢ OSA12109 ④ OSA5-12109

1946   (broadcast performance – in German) Act 1 Scene 2 (Káťa: Víš, co mi napadlo?) Trötschel KK; Grossmann V/Dresden State Opera Orch/Striegler
Acanta Ⓜ DE22315

78 rpm

c1948   (excerpts) Šíma D; Válka B; Zachardová KK; Pelc VK; Spurná V/chorus, Brno Radio SO/Bakala
Ultraphon Ⓜ H24215-7

228

Index